Martin Butler, Paul Mecheril, Lea Brenningmeyer (eds.,
Resistance

migration - power - education

Martin Butler, Paul Mecheril, Lea Brenningmeyer (eds.)
Resistance
Subjects, Representations, Contexts

[transcript]

Gefördert durch das Niedersächsische Ministerium für Wissenschaft und Kultur

 An electronic version of this book is freely available, thanks to the support of libraries working with Knowledge Unlatched. KU is a collaborative initiative designed to make high quality books Open Access for the public good. The Open Access ISBN for this book is 978-3-8394-3149-8

Bibliographic information published by the Deutsche Nationalbibliothek
The Deutsche Nationalbibliothek lists this publication in the Deutsche Nationalbibliografie; detailed bibliographic data are available in the Internet at http://dnb.d-nb.de

All rights reserved. No part of this book may be reprinted or reproduced or utilized in any form or by any electronic, mechanical, or other means, now known or hereafter invented, including photocopying and recording, or in any information storage or retrieval system, without permission in writing from the publisher.

© 2017 transcript Verlag, Bielefeld

Cover: Kordula Röckenhaus, Bielefeld
Typesetting by Mark-Sebastian Schneider, Bielefeld
Printed by Majuskel Medienproduktion GmbH, Wetzlar
Print-ISBN 978-3-8376-3149-4
PDF-ISBN 978-3-8394-3149-8

Contents

Introduction
Coming to Terms—On the Aim and Scope of this Volume
Martin Butler, Paul Mecheril & Lea Brenningmeyer | 7

Resistance
Carl von Ossietzky, Albert Leo Schlageter, and Mahatma Gandhi
Micha Brumlik | 17

More than Resistance
Striving for Universalization
Alex Demirović | 31

**Popular Culture, 'Resistance,'
'Cultural Radicalism,' and 'Self-Formation'**
Comments on the Development of a Theory
Kaspar Maase | 45

Resistance as a Way out of One-Dimensionality
The Contribution of Herbert Marcuse to a Critical Analysis
of the Present
Rainer Winter | 71

Border Crossing as Act of Resistance
The Autonomy of Migration as Theoretical Intervention
into Border Studies
Sabine Hess | 87

Reclaiming the City, Reclaiming the Rights
The Commons and the Omnipresence of Resistance
Kemal İnal & Ulaş Başar Gezgin | 101

"All Those Who Know the Term 'Gentrification' are Part of the Problem"
Self-Reflexivity in Urban Activism and Cultural Production
Jens Martin Gurr | 117

Images of Protest
On the "Woman in the Blue Bra" and Relational Testimony
Kathrin Peters | 135

Connecting Origin and Innocence
Myths of Resistance in European Memory Cultures after 1945
Stephanie Wodianka | 153

Into the Darkness: Revolutionary Critical Pedagogy for a Socialist Society
A Manifesto
Peter McLaren | 173

List of Contributors | 191

Introduction
Coming to Terms—On the Aim and Scope of this Volume

Martin Butler, Paul Mecheril & Lea Brenningmeyer

In the field of physics, resistance is commonly defined as "a force preventing a process from starting, or once started from intensifying beyond a certain threshold" (Harré 5). Though it might be odd to begin this introduction with an excursus to the sciences, it could be worth picking up on that definition, as it helps carve out the understanding of resistance that this volume takes as a starting point for its reflections. To be precise, if we conceptualize resistance in the social sphere less in analogy to a physical phenomenon, i.e., less as an obstacle, hindrance, obstruction, or barrier, whose function is to channel the 'flow' of the social and to obstruct totalization, but rather as an intervention in the struggle for the universal or a very particular social order, then, one may well argue, we are dealing with resistance as a political phenomenon. A phenomenon which, it seems, has resurfaced as a viable option of political articulation and positioning in range of different contexts and, more often than not, is informed by a distinctly normative rationale: Whenever and wherever inequality is experienced and articulated as injustice, there is resistance. This normative stance, which is proliferated, e.g., through the rhetoric and actions of social, emancipatory movements and through discourses about the universality of human rights, and which, in a very fundamental way, rests on the assumption that constellations and relations of power are contingent and changeable, can indeed be said to both characterize and, at the same time, fuel acts of resistance against the experienced and articulated injustice of unequal social relations—no matter if these relations constitute one's own situation or the situations of others and no matter if they are experienced as injustice from one's own or from others' perspectives.

If we, for the time being, allow ourselves to accept this notion of resistance as a mode of intervention based on a specifically normative rationale, through which the demand to overcome situations of disadvantaged and disregard is both legitimized and articulated, we are indeed able to spot a number of contexts in different parts of the world, in which both discourses and practices of resistance have resurged. In these different contexts, forms of resistance have taken different shapes, but are all more or less driven by either an intuitive or an explicit notion of injustice and justice: Whereas in western societies, it is indeed the (discourse on the) crisis of global capitalism, along with a general loss of trust in institutionalized politics, which is regularly held responsible for the recent emergence of new movements of protests and resistance, in regions such as Northern Africa, political uprisings have commonly been regarded as a reaction long overdue to totalitarian regimes and their infrastructures of oppression and control. The uprisings in Ukraine in 2014, Occupy Gezi in 2013, and the protests in Northern Africa known as the so-called Arab Spring starting in 2010, for instance, were considered to be (and fashioned themselves as) acts of resistance against structures of governmental dominance and control to an extent which seriously threatened and harmed the individual citizen's rights. With the disclosure of practices of surveillance through national secret services such as the NSA, by the way, or the most recent debates on the hacking of the US American election procedures by Russian activists, similar mechanisms of power have been made visible in western societies, which, in turn, are said to have enhanced tendencies towards civil disobedience and resistance.

Finally, the election of Donald Trump into the office of the American Presidency has so far not only fueled the debate on the rationale of democratic rule both in the US and in other parts of the world, but has also contributed to a more or less explicit turn towards nationalist and racist ideologies and politics across Europe—political debates and elections, e.g., in Austria, France, or the Netherlands give ample proof of this tendency. Moreover, it has also triggered movements of predominantly anti-capitalist opposition promoting social equality and/or environmental justice both in institutionalized politics and in less formal or informal ways and forms on the spot. In other words, resistance, it seems, has again become a viable option to confront a government, the formation and constitution of which has not seldom been referred to as an articulation of resistance in itself—i.e., against political corruption, against institutionalized politics which had been accused of forgetting the needs and demands of the white working class men whom Trump has so ineloquently but efficiently sided with during his campaign. Both Trump's fashioning of himself as the leader of a movement that was born out of resistance against the political establishment, and the emergence of anti-Trump movements which set out to resist this resistance at the very same time, may be indicative of a more general concern, i.e., the mistrust in the workings of capitalist democracies. This mistrust, then, which can be traced both in so-called right-wing and in left-wing rhetoric, has perhaps been the breeding ground for Trump's landslide victory, and has equally contributed to the emergence of new forms of resistance in the recent past, such as the Occupy movement, the student protests revolving around the issue of 'safe space' at US American universities, or, more recently, and in direct opposition to Trump's agenda, the 'March of Science' or the 'Women's March on Washington.'

It is this resurgence of resistance, then, which has perhaps been the central motivation for this collection of essays, which takes these developments as a starting point to explore phenomena of resistance in different historical and contemporary contexts from an interdisciplinary and transcultural perspective. To be sure, in the recent past, there has been a lot of scholarly concern with resistance in a number of volumes (cf., e.g., Byrne; Critchley; Douzinas; Dutta; Skyes; Welzer), the publication of which, just like in our case, has most probably been motivated by forms and events of political opposition in different parts of the world. The essays in this collection set out to add to this ongoing discussions and reflections, as they not only shed light on different subjects, representations, aesthetics, and contexts of resistance, but also, and perhaps more importantly, add to a theoretical discussion of terms and concepts of resistance by—albeit, at times, more implicitly—addressing the following questions: 1. What is 'resistance'? 2. On which normative grounds do forms of resistance work, how are they legitimized? 3. How is resistance represented and/or mediated, and in how far can representations be considered to be resistant? 4. Who uses the term/concept of 'resistance'? When, where, and for what purposes? In order to approach these questions, the essays collected in this volume take different routes in their exploration of resistance. They approach resistance on a theoretical level, investigate into different conceptualizations of resistance in different historical settings, and/or work on a range of different case studies taken from a variety of contexts and—through close contextualizing analyses—contribute to establishing a distinctly comparative view on the various notions of resistance in different disciplinary as well as social and/or cultural contexts.

Though not all of the contributions directly address terms and concepts of resistance on a theoretical level, we sense that they are nevertheless broadly informed by at least two different, if not opposing ideas of resistance: While one notion of resistance is based on the assumption of active agency, i.e., on the capabilities of individuals to interpret their environment and 'act upon' it deliberately through what is commonly referred to as appropriation (cf., e.g., Hall), the other one conceives of resistance as embedded in specific structures and relationships of power—in the latter sense, then, as Lawrence Grossberg puts it, "[t]he question of agency is [...] how access and investment or participation (as a structure of belonging) are distributed within particular structured terrains" ("Identity" 100; cf. also Grossberg, "Cultural Studies"). To be sure, it does not seem to be too fruitful to rule out either one of these notions of resistance when examining the question of how changes of power relations in society are set into motion—and none of the contributions actually seems to be heading into just one direction. It is perhaps far more appropriate to argue that forms of resistance that stimulate change in hegemonic regimes instead of just validating and perpetuating these regimes are neither an act of individual heroism nor are they the outcome and expression of a self-referential structural logic only. For us, then, it seems to be more productive to explore the relationships *between* these two notions of resistance as well as their relationship to other concepts and approaches, and to also reflect on the normative presuppositions inscribed into each of these perspectives, though, at times, it seems that these very presuppositions are secretly at work even if we try hard to spot and suspend them.

The present volume sets out to enhance this very endeavor, as it is supposed to be a site on which different conceptualizations of resistance are drawn upon to elucidate different historical and cultural constellations. By putting a number of different disciplinary voices into a dialogue, its goal is to disclose the specific contextual preconditions, aesthetic forms, and political/ideological implications of both past and present forms of resistance. Through their context-specific approaches to historical and current phenomena and concepts of resistance, then, the essays in this collection also—and again, more or less explicitly—

contribute to uncovering the highly ethical dimension inscribed into public and scholarly debates on resistance on the one hand and into acts of resistance (or what is designated as acts of resistance, respectively) on the other. In this way, the volume might also help draw our attention to the normative references that lie at the heart of both practices and discourses of resistance, but which are only rarely made explicit. To different degrees and in different ways, the contributions to this volume reveal that scholarly debates are not only reflecting the normative-ethical dimension of the topic of resistance, but are also affected by normative stances and motivated by political demands. In other words, scholarly discourse on resistance cannot fully escape the political and ethical aura of resistance.

As a starting point, Micha Brumlik's contribution investigates the overall question of "what can be understood as 'resistance'" and, more specifically, as 'political resistance.' By drawing on the examples of Carl von Ossietzky, Albert Leo Schlageter, and Mahatma Gandhi, he argues that the evaluation of resistance is dependent on what it is directed against. In so doing, Brumlik unfolds the normativity of the concept of 'resistance,' which is closely connected to moral, ethical, and political questions, and also investigates into its relevance for processes of subjectivization. Though resistance is commonly valued positively, the value of resistance, Brumlik explicates, depends upon which kind of 'evil' it is directed against.

Alex Demirović adds another perspective on the concept of resistance and its dependency on the 'target' it is directed against. In his contribution on "More than Resistance," he asks what resistance can turn into. Drawing on Foucault, his contribution argues that resistance is intrinsically tied to power and, thus, does itself not develop enough momentum to change what it is directed against—at least not to an extent that further resistance becomes unnecessary. By shifting the focus from forms of resistance that happened in the past to the requirements of a theory of subversion and resistance, he calls for something 'beyond resistance,' which, in a double movement, disarticulates the rejected practices of power and "strives for a new universality and universalization."

Kaspar Maase's contribution traces past and present discourses on the resistant potential of popular culture, shedding light on the theoretical and ideological presuppositions of the different concepts of resistance at work in these discourses. His journey through different conceptualizations of the status and value of popular culture takes a historical and systematic perspective, which not only illustrates that and how ideas on the relationship between popular culture and resistance are shaped by the specific sociocultural contexts in which they emerge; it also provides the ground for identifying a number of desiderata for investigating into phenomena of resistance in the field of "empirical popular culture research."

Based on and referring to Herbert Marcuse's critical theory, Rainer Winter focuses on the idea of 'one-dimensionality.' Arguing for the still prevalent importance of this approach—especially when dealing with questions of the meaning and the role of resistance—he discusses "the relationship between liberation and one-dimensionality" in Marcuse's work and points out one-dimensionality's influence on social life. Referring to Habermas, Winter suggests to maintain a dialectical perspective in order to criticize one-dimensionality and strive for social change. Referring to examples of, e.g., the Occupy movement, he discusses "how one-dimensionality can be challenged and overcome by different forms of resistance" and suggests to return to Marcuse's critical theory.

Sabine Hess also discusses the relationship between resistance and power by examining forms of borderland resistance. Starting from the observation that the 'border paradigm' is still prevalent, she illustrates how the 'autonomy of migration'-approach allows for change of perspective on borders and, consequently, provides the option of conceiving of migration *as* resistance. Showing that "the border regime can be understood as a site of constant encounter, tension, conflict, and contestation," she manages to "re-conceptualize borderlands as well as migration itself as ways of resistance," thereby turning migration from an object of scholarly discussion to a resistant practice which questions established orders of knowledge.

Kemal İnal and Ulaş Başar Gezgin focus on the agents and subjects as well as on different forms of urban resistance and set out to explore the specific contextual parameters that have contributed to their emergence. Asking who 'reclaims the cities,' in what ways, and for what particular purposes, they focus primarily on "massive popular resistances in Arab regions and in some other Western countries." Based on the argument that this form of resistance is primarily directed against capitalism, they are calling for 'the people' to organize in commons, rebuild a democratic and socially produced and productive city, and find new ways of resistance in urban environments.

Jens Martin Gurr examines urban practices of resistance, urban activism, and 'right to the city' movements in another cultural and political context and from a different perspective: Focusing on the self-reflexivity and theory-consciousness of movements against gentrification, he also problematizes the role and responsibility of scholarly research on resistance. In so doing, he distinguishes between different aims, demands, targets, constellations, and networks of, and commitments to resistance. With this critical examination of the principles of 'critical urban studies,' Gurr contextualizes his analysis of the rhetoric of the "Mission Yuppie Eradication Project" and Christoph Schäfer's activist pictorial essay *Die Stadt ist unsere Fabrik/ The City is our Factory*.

Kathrin Peters' contribution analyzes images of protest and asks "how to conceive visual testimony ... in view of the contemporary flood of digital images," particularly focusing on the "Woman in the Blue Bra"-video and its various forms of distribution, adaptation, modification, appropriation, and reception. Starting from a differentiation between center and periphery on two levels—both on the level of the camera's perspective (being informed by specific media reporting conventions and a specific postcolonial constellation) and on the level of the clip's dissemination via predominantly peripheral channels—Peters follows the journey of the footage, sheds light on the forms and functions of its repetitive use in different contexts, and, in so doing, adds to the critical discussion on the role of (social, digital, and analog) media in contexts of protest and resistance.

Stephanie Wodianka focuses on mythologization and memories of resistance in different case studies, in which she identifies "the characteristics that constitute European memory cultures of Resistance during the Second World War." Her contribution distinguishes between mythical and historical modes of remembering resistance, elucidates the development of resistance as French and Italian narratives of origin, examines "the stability and durability of the myth of Resistance," and analyzes narratives of collective resistance and collective innocence. For these analyses, Wodianka selects literary and filmographic fiction about resistance published after 1945, which represent memory cultures in France and Italy.

As a manifesto, the final contribution of this volume picks up several of the topics mentioned in the previous contributions, e.g., gentrification, capitalism, and political resistance, and calls for critical pedagogy as a revolutionary praxis and an approach to transform the world. Using the current political situation in the US as a starting point, Peter McLaren asks what he calls the final question: "Where should critical pedagogy take us and where should we take critical pedagogy?" In his response, he makes a case for a socialist society and against capitalism and state power.

***

The contributions to this volume are based on a selection of papers given at an international and interdisciplinary conference on resistance held in Oldenburg in November 2014 on the occasion of the 40th anniversary of the Carl von Ossietzky University, not least to honor its patron and namesake. Though some time has passed until the final editing of the book, practices and discourses of resistance have not ceased to be significant factors in reflecting and shaping the world. Still, or again, we seem to experience new forms of resistance in different settings and on a global scale, so this book—necessarily so—only deals with a highly random choice of cases and contexts. It has been a pleasure to put all of the perspectives gathered here into what we consider to have been a very fruitful dialogue at the conference, and we very much hope that the dialogue continues in this volume (and beyond). And, to be sure, this dialogue would not have been possible without the support of so many individuals and institutions: To be precise, we are grateful to the German Research Foundation, the Ministry of Science and Culture of Lower Saxony, and the Universitätsgesellschaft of the Carl von Ossietzky University of Oldenburg for their generous financial support. Moreover, we would like to express our gratitude to the many assistants that have supported us in the organization of the conference and the editing process: Katharina Bieloch, Britta Kölle, Birgit Manz, Laura Nini, and Katharina Sufryd. We would also like to thank the Center for Migration, Education and Cultural Studies as well as the Institute for English and American Studies at the University of Oldenburg for its organizational and infrastructural support. Moreover, we are grateful to the Kulturzentrum PFL in Oldenburg, which turned out to be an excellent venue for the 2014 conference. Last but definitely not least, we would like to thank the participants of the conference for initiating a most lively conversation as well as the contributors to this volume, who were patient enough with the editors, willingly accepting suggestions to their papers—we very much hope that you think that it was worth it. We do.

WORKS CITED

Byrne, Janet, editor. *Occupy Handbook*. Back Bay Books, 2012.
Critchley, Simon. *Infinitely Demanding: Ethics of Commitment, Politics of Resistance*. Verso, 2008.
Douzinas, Costas. *Philosophy and Resistance in the Crisis: Greece and the Future of Europe*. Politiy P, 2013.
Grossberg, Lawrence. "Identity and Cultural Studies—Is That All There Is?" *Questions of Cultural Identity*, edited by Stuart Hall and Paul Du Gay, Sage, 1996, pp. 87-107.
Grossberg, Lawrence. "Cultural Studies in/and New Worlds." *What's Going on? Cultural Studies und Popularkultur*, by Grossberg, Turia+Kant, 2000, pp. 194-230.
Hall, Stuart. "Kodieren/Dekodieren." *Cultural Studies: Grundlagentexte zur Einführung*, edited by Roger Bromley, Udo Göttlich, and Carsten Winter, zu Klampen, 1999, pp. 92-110.
Harré, Rom. "Resistance as a Concept in Physics." *Resistance and the Practice of Rationality*, edited by Martin W. Bauer, Rom Harré, and Carl Jensen, Cambridge Scholars Publishing, 2013, pp. 2-10.
Dutta, Mohan J. *Voices of Resistance: Communication and Social Change*. Purdue University P, 2012.
Sykes, Frank. *After Occupy: What Next for the World?* Trafford Publishing, 2013.
Welzer, Harald. *Selbst denken: Eine Anleitung zum Widerstand*. S. Fischer, 2013.

Resistance
Carl von Ossietzky, Albert Leo Schlageter, and Mahatma Gandhi

Micha Brumlik

1. INTRODUCTION

Carl von Ossietzky, after whom this university is named, led a life synonymous with resistance. But, he was quite unlike those who are readily cited as examples in Germany and described as the men of 20 July 1944, i.e., those who, after much hesitation and considerable pangs of conscience, finally, even though much too late, decided to eliminate Adolf Hitler in an assassination attempt. Instead, he was one of those to whom it was clear from the very beginning that Hitler's takeover had to be prevented by all possible means that were available and permissible in a democracy, however flawed it may be. It was equally clear to him that Hitler would not come to power on his own. Therefore, as the editor of the left-wing, social-democratic, and pacifist weekly, *Weltbühne* (lit. the World Stage) he repeatedly warned against the unholy alliance of nationalist and conservative circles, including the military and the militaristic cliques.

Hence, when Ossietzky exposed the secret arms build-up of the *Reichswehr*, the German Armed Forces of the Weimar Republic, in violation of the Treaty of Versailles, he was sentenced to eighteen months imprisonment by the end of 1931, and this gave him an opportunity to emerge as a sort of second Socrates. As Plato's dialogues, "Apology" and "Crito" state, although Socrates was well aware of his innocence, he was willing to accept the incorrect and unjust death sentence meted out to him out of respect for the laws of the polis. However, on his arrest, Carl von Ossietzky behaved in exactly the opposite manner and stated,

Let there be no mistake about this. And, I emphasize it for the sake of all the friends and foes, especially those who shall be monitoring my legal and physical wellbeing in the months to come: I am not going to prison on the grounds of loyalty, but because as a prisoner I would cause the most inconvenience. I do not submit to the Majesty of the Imperial Court of Justice [*Reichsgericht*], wrapped in its red velvet robes. Instead, as an inmate of a Prussian penal institution I shall continue to be a living reminder of the judgement of the highest judicial authority, which in this case appears to be politically motivated and legally skewed. (691)

After his release and reimprisonment by the National Socialists at the end of February 1933, Ossietzky, who was then critically ill, had to undergo an odyssey through the otherworld of the Nazi concentration camps: from Sonnenburg near Küstrin in Poland to Esterwegen near Oldenburg, where with other inmates he had to work on draining and dewatering the Emsland bogs until overcome by a state of complete exhaustion. The Swiss diplomat Carl Jacob Burckhardt notes coming across a "trembling, pale something, a being that seemed to be bereft of feeling, with a swollen eye and apparently his teeth knocked out" (60-61). After three years of incarceration in the concentration camps, Ossietzky was discharged in 1936 due to his friends' campaign for his release. Suffering from an advanced stage of tuberculosis, he was first transferred to the Governmental Police Hospital in Berlin and later shifted to Niederschönhausen, where he subsequently died in 1938. Two years earlier, i.e., in 1936, the concentration camp inmate had been awarded the Nobel Peace Prize retrospectively for the year 1935, an award that he was not allowed to receive due to the travel ban imposed on him. However, an article of his that appeared in 1932 in the *Weltbühne* characterizes him as a Prussian Socrates:

In the long run, the political journalist [*Publizist*] in particular cannot simply escape the connection with the totality, against which he fights and for which he struggles, without succumbing to exaltations and imbalance. If one wishes to combat the polluted spirit of a country, one has to partake in its common fate. (691)

Yes, Carl von Ossietzky indeed practiced resistance. Whether he actually did so being conscious of the threat to his person, or whether he underestimated the dangers of National Socialism, and hence, acted thoughtlessly as regards his wife's and his own fate, is still a matter of dispute in contemporary history. But, it scarcely plays a role while answering the question, what can be understood as 'resistance,' and specifically, as 'political resistance.'

Or, does it? Basically, resistance is seen as something positive, and resistant attitude or the willingness to resist as opposed to the willingness to obey or even to be subservient is regarded as a virtue particularly worthy of esteem. Moreover, despite the circumstances human beings are ready to put up sustained resistance for the sake of decisions and structures generally considered to be morally and politically correct. Resistance implies the ability to say no, and according to Klaus Heinrich (1964), it can be seen as a "problem of identity under the threat of loss to identity" (57), as a "problem of language in the state of speechlessness" (97), and as a "problem of resistance in the movements of self-destruction" (131).

Thus, it is debatable, if resistance, i.e., the ability to withstand all of the three problems, represents a position that is basically to be valued positively, or whether the value of resistance depends upon that against which it is directed. In order to clarify this, I shall remain faithful to the hitherto practiced biographical mode and discuss two cases, which can be read—*cum grano salis*—as cases of anticolonial resistance: of Albert Leo Schlageter and Mahatma Gandhi.

2. Resistance as an Expression of Existential Hardness and Clarity

Karl Radek, a Communist politician of Jewish descent, who was later denounced as a Trotskyite and murdered by the Stalinists in 1939 in the Soviet Union, had advocated in 1923 the so-called Schlageter course of action in response to the occupation of the Rhineland by the French and Belgian troops as mandated by the Treaty of Versailles. This 'Schlageter course' was a strategic proposal of the KPD, the Communist Party of Germany, through which they had hoped to attract the nationally disposed, or even the nationalist segments of the German electorate to the KPD. Thus, on 21 June 1923, Karl Radek stated in a speech at a meeting of the Comintern, which later adorned the first page of the party mouthpiece, *Rote Fahne* (Red Flag) on 26 June,

The Communist Party of Germany must openly declare to the nationalist, petty bourgeois masses that those, who in the service of the profiteers, the speculators, the owners of steel and coal try to enslave the German people and shove them into reckless adventure, have to reckon with the resistance of the German Communist workers. They will answer violence with violence. We shall combat with all means possible those who ally themselves, out of ignorance, with the mercenaries of capital. But, we believe that the vast majority of the masses with national sensibilities do not belong to the faction of the capital, but instead to the workers' faction. We wish to and indeed shall seek out and find the way to reach these masses. We shall do everything that men like Schlageter were ready to do, to seek death for the general good, not wander into oblivion, but become wanderers into a better future for the entire humanity [...]. (147)

Who was this Albert Leo Schlageter, praised with these words by the Communist, Karl Radek? Born in 1894, Schlageter was not only a soldier in the army of Imperial Germany during the First World War, but also a member of the National Socialist front organizations as well as a militant, nationalist activist, who carried out bomb attacks, was captured and subsequently sentenced to death by the French courts in May 1923. In other words, he was a man, who stood for political options that were diametrically opposed to those chosen by Ossietzky.

In fact, Schlageter's death sparked the political imagination not only of the Communist politician, but also that of one of the most significant, albeit equally controversial philosophers of the twentieth century, i.e., Martin Heidegger. However, Heidegger expressed his opinion regarding Schlageter ten years later, in May 1933, when he was already the rector of the University of Freiburg. At that time Heidegger not only stated that Schlageter had to die a "hard death" in a field of "darkness, humiliation and betrayal," but also that he needed to "achieve the greatest thing of which man is capable. Alone, drawing on his own inner strength, he had to place before his soul an image of the future awakening of the Volk to honour and greatness so that he could die believing in this future" (Farias 145).

Heidegger, who hailed from the Black Forest region and who was now the rector of a university that lay on the outskirts of the Black Forest, enjoined the value of Schlageter's courage with an ode to the Black Forest:

Whence this hardness of will to survive arduous conditions? Whence the clarity of heart to envision the greatest and the most remote? Student of Freiburg! German student! Experience and know the mountains, the forests and the valleys of the

Black Forest, when you enter the homeland of this hero on your hikes and outings: the mountains are of primitive rock, of granite, betwixt these has grown the young farmer's lad. They have been long at work hardening the will. The autumn sun of the Black Forest bathes the mountain ranges and forests in the most glorious clear light. Since yore it has nourished the clarity of the heart. (Farias 146)

In this speech, Heidegger defines the homeland (*Heimat*) in its physical, geographical and geological aspects as the mediating authority between the individual and the nation, and thus, between each individual being and a people. He ends his speech with an appeal:

Student of Freiburg, let the strength of this hero's native mountains flow into your will… let the power of the autumn sun in the native valley of this hero shine into your heart! Preserve both within you and carry them, the hardness of the will and the clarity of the heart, to your comrades at the German universities. (Farias 146-7)

Even if one were to discount the by now obscure sounding, geomantic imagery, it is evident that the character traits invoked here describe what can be characterized as heroic, i.e., "clarity" and "hardness." Both of them are characteristics belonging to Schlageter, who according to Heidegger was ready "to die for the German people and its empire with the Alemannic countryside before his eyes" (Farias 147) and as resistance against the French occupation forces.

3. Nonviolent Resistance—Gandhi

The best-known politician of an anti-colonial resistance who stood up against occupation, not in Europe but against a European power, is Mahatma Gandhi. Born in West Gujarat, Gandhi lived from 1869 to 1948, his lifespan corresponding to that of Schlageter, agitated for the civil rights of the Indians first in South Africa and later in India, and travelled as a lawyer for years and over decades between India, Great Britain, and South Africa. Finally, around 1906/1907 as a married man in his mid-thirties and a father of three sons, Gandhi decided to take a vow of celibacy not only motivated by the Hindu religion, but also to organize political resistance against the laws in Transvaal, which in many ways discriminated against the Indians living there.

The forms of passive resistance associated with Gandhi, which are even today considered to be exemplary, drew on the teachings of *Ahimsa*, i.e., non-violence, from a variety of Indian religions, i.e., the prohibition of any kind of active violence, as also on the principles of *Satyagraha* as they were developed by him. It was a theory of character traits which are, not coincidentally, reminiscent of the classical catalogue of virtues from the Christian Occident, i.e., truth, nonviolence, chastity, renunciation of possessions, as well as courage, dietetic life, renunciation of the desire to acquire the property belonging to others, insistence on the equality of all religions, rejection of the division of the Indian society into castes, and the willingness to promote regional economies. Human beings who follow this path prove themselves, according to Gandhi, to be the agents of passive resistance, which is ultimately more effective than any violent uprising. And, this held true even in extreme cases. Thus, Gandhi had suggested to the Jewish religious philosopher Martin Buber in an open letter, just before the November pogroms of 1938, that the Jews living in Germany should defend themselves against their discrimination through passive resistance. On 26 November 1938, Gandhi published an article in the weekly journal, *Harijan*, where he wrote:

Can the Jews resist this organised and shameless persecution? Is there a way to preserve their self-respect, and not to feel helpless, neglected and forlorn? I submit there is. No person who has faith in a living God need feel helpless or forlorn. Jehovah of the Jews is a God more personal than the God of the Christians, the Mussalmans or the Hindus, though as a matter of fact in essence, He is common to all and one without a second and beyond description. But as the Jews attribute personality to God and believe that He rules every action of theirs, they ought not to feel helpless. If I were a Jew and were born in Germany and earned my livelihood there, I would claim Germany as my home even as the tallest gentile German may, and challenge him to shoot me or cast me in the dungeon; I would refuse to be expelled or to submit to discriminating treatment. And for doing this, I should not wait for the fellow Jews to join me in civil resistance but would have confidence that in the end the rest are bound to follow my example. If one Jew or all the Jews were to accept the prescription here offered, he or they cannot be worse off than now. And suffering voluntarily undergone will bring them an inner strength and joy which no number of resolutions of sympathy passed in the world outside Germany can. Indeed, even if Britain, France and America were to declare hostilities against Germany, they can bring no inner joy, no inner strength. The calculated violence of

Hitler may even result in a general massacre of the Jews by way of his first answer to the declaration of such hostilities. But if the Jewish mind could be prepared for voluntary suffering, even the massacre I have imagined could be turned into a day of thanksgiving and joy that Jehovah had wrought deliverance of the race even at the hands of the tyrant. For to the godfearing, death has no terror. It is a joyful sleep to be followed by a waking that would be all the more refreshing for the long sleep. (240-41)

Martin Buber replied to this letter and the corresponding article respectfully and in detail, emphasizing above all the immense difference between the German and the Indian situation. However contemptible the colonial inequality between the British and the Indians might be in India, it could not bear comparison with the brutal repression and discrimination of the Jews in Nazi Germany. As far as is known, Gandhi did not reply to these letters, and neither did he address the National Socialist annihilation of Jews even after the Second World War.

In the meanwhile, due to in-depth historical research, questions have been raised regarding Gandhi's positions on resistance and regarding the universal character of his critical stance on colonialism. They bear not only on the beliefs expressed in *Hind Swaraj* from 1909 that machinery "represents a great sin," that the railways would "spread the bubonic plague," that hospitals were "institutions for propagating sin," and that peasants needed no "knowledge of letters" (Anderson 21). They also do not only refer to his misogynist sexual ethics, but in particular to his position vis-à-vis the Indian caste system. Although Gandhi was critical of the racial discrimination against the so-called Untouchables, he was nonetheless not ready to accept separate electoral rolls for the *Dalits*, i.e., the Untouchables.

In 1932, the government in London agreed to the proposal to allow for separate electoral rolls for the Untouchables during the elections in India, which would have increased their representation in the parliament considerably. During the internal debates within the Congress Party, Gandhi—indeed also due to party-political and tactical considerations— categorically opposed such proposals with the reasoning that no soul was more and less inferior in the logic of the Hindu doctrine of reincarnation, since its position in the structure of the society depended wholly and exclusively on its actions.

Moreover, as regards the intermixing of the castes, he stated, "Interdrinking, interdining, intermarrying, I hold, are not essential for the promotion of the spirit of democracy" (Anderson 37). Furthermore, Gandhi, the virtuoso of non-violent resistance, recommended the caste system "as the best remedy against heartless competition and social disintegration born of avarice and greed" (Anderson 38).

For Gandhi, the perpetuation of the caste hierarchy, and hence, the rejection of the separate electoral rolls for the Dalits were so vital that after the British government announced its readiness to permit such lists, he was ready to go on a fast unto death, which finally forced his political opponents to give in (cf. Anderson 41; Stein and Arnold 323). However, subsequently Gandhi travelled across India, campaigning for the social advancement of the so-called Untouchables.

The other protagonist of these contentious debates, who was Gandhi's primary opponent, if not the enemy within the party, and whose name has remained, at least in our parts of the world, far less known as regards the history of modern India, was Bhimrao Ramji Ambedkar (1891-1954). He was an Indian lawyer who actually came from an Untouchable caste, and who, despite his opposition, remained associated with Gandhi and emerged as one of the most successful and active politicians in India. What needs to be emphasized in this regard is that Ambedkar was at least equally scathing in his criticism of the subjugation of women practiced within the Indian Muslim community, and critical of child marriage as well as polygamy as he was of the caste system. Ambedkar's own form of resistance both against the caste system as well as against other forms of religious inequality resulted in his conversion to Buddhism in 1950, which attracted a great deal of attention in the public sphere.

4. Paradoxes of Resistance

If one observes the three forms of resistance that have been described so far, as also the three very different personalities, i.e., Schlageter, Gandhi, and Ambedkar, the concept of resistance seems to either simply disintegrate or reduce to a merely formal category. Hence, it all depends on which kind of evil is resisted.

If this is indeed the case, then it seems unavoidable that we return to Jesus' Sermon on the Mount, in order to formulate a consistent doctrine of resistance. Thus, we find in Matthew 5, 38-39, "You have heard that it was said, 'An eye for an eye and a tooth for a tooth.' But I say to you: Do not resist the one who is evil. But if anyone slaps you on the right cheek, turn to him the other also." Indeed, this commandment seems to circumvent all the difficulties that the concept of resistance otherwise elicits. Those who renounce resistance do not in any case run the risk of resisting an objective that in the end turns out to be morally good. Indeed, what resistance can mean in a substantive and not only in a formal sense always depends on the principles or—as one would phrase it today—'values,' to which a person or a group of persons feels committed. Nonetheless, even those who resist for the sake of a correct principle could still turn out to be morally misguided.

As is well known, it was Immanuel Kant who made an attempt to circumvent or resolve this problem by postulating a purely formal, ethical rule that refrained from stating any concrete values or maxims. The categorical imperative states in one of his formulations, "Act only on that maxim whereby you can at the same time will that it should become a universal law" (73). Thus, for instance, it would be impermissible to rob someone for the sake of aggrandizing one's property. According to the categorical imperative, if generalized, this action would destroy in terms of logic the very concept of property. But, it could still be asked, what if the theft were committed only for excitement or thrill, but not with the desire to augment one's property? And, how about lying? In one of his most contentious reflections, Kant grappled with the "supposed right to lie from philanthropy" (605). In this text, Kant attempts a thought experiment: A person, who is being pursued unjustly, flees from a murderer and seeks refuge with a local resident. After a while, the pursuers knock on the door of the house, in which they suspect the pursued has found refuge, and ask the householder, if the person they are searching for is indeed in his house. The host knows that handing over the person they are hunting down would result in her/his certain death and finds himself in the dilemma, i.e., either having to lie or to dispatch an innocent person to a certain death. In this context, Kant attempts to show that according to ethical and political laws, whatever turn the case might take, the householder can only then ethically and legally prevent punishment, if he were to reveal the truth to the murderer. In case he lied, it could still come to pass that the murderer would later see the intended victim and kill her/him. And, this action could still be attributed to the person lying from altruistic motives:

Thus one who tells a lie, however well disposed he may be, must be responsible for its consequences even before a civil court and must pay the penalty for them, however unforeseen they may have been; for truthfulness is a duty that must be regarded as the basis of all duties to be grounded on contract, the law of which is made uncertain and useless if even the least exception to it is admitted. (Kant 613)

The possible objection that still works within the Kantian sphere of argumentation, namely that such situations already indicate a state of exception in which contracts are no longer a valid basis of coexistence, could only then, if at all, hold water, when we are no longer dealing with a lawful state but with a tyranny. According to Kant, under civil conditions it would be imperative to refrain from rendering help that is based on a lie.

5. Resistance, Freedom, and Happiness

Thus, a question of further interest, and it is not a mere coincidence that it was vigorously debated in the middle of the twentieth century, concerns which moral, and not positive, laws may be broken to put an end to a political-moral state that is identified as being untenable. Bertolt Brecht addressed this problem in his play "Die Maßnahme" (The Measures Taken) as also in his poem "An die Nachgeborenen" (To Those Born Later), which was published in 1939 during his exile in Paris. The third part of the poem states,

You who will emerge from the flood/In which we have gone under/Remember/ When you speak of our failings/The dark time too/Which you have escaped./For we went, changing countries oftener than our shoes/Through the wars of the classes, despairing/When there was injustice only, and no rebellion./And yet we know:/ Hatred, even of meanness, contorts the features./Anger, even against injustice/ Makes the voice hoarse. Oh, we/ Who wanted to prepare the ground for friendliness/ Could not ourselves be friendly./But you, when the time comes at last/And man is a helper to man/Think of us/With forbearance. (Willett and Manheim 319-20)

The existentialist philosophers, most notably Simone de Beauvoir and Jean Paul Sartre, as also Albert Camus engaged as intensively with the subject of resistance as Brecht did. In Beauvoir's novel *The Blood of Others* from

1943 as well as in Sartre's play *Dirty Hands* from 1948, the moral dilemma of resistance is discussed, i.e., the readiness and the will to murder human beings, presumably in order to prevent greater injustice. As for Sartre's personal biography, he rejoined the Paris Condorcet Gymnasium as a teacher from 1942 to 1944 after his release from a German war prisoners' camp based on a medical certificate, and participated in the resistance movement as an intellectual discussant. He later looked back on this phase as a period of intensive existential experience. He reiterates in a film made in 1978,

We were never more free than during the German occupation. We had lost all our rights, beginning with the right to talk. [...] Everywhere, on billboards, in the newspapers, on the screen, we encountered the revolting and insipid picture of ourselves that our oppressors wanted us to accept. And, because of all this, we were free. (Sartre, "Republic of Silence" 498)

In fact, he went even further, when thirty years later in retrospect (cf. Biemel 21) he declared the French Resistance, i.e., the resistance against the National Socialist and Franco-Fascist dominance, the epitome of true democracy:

[T]he Resistance was a true democracy: for the soldier as for the commander, the same danger, the same forsakenness, the same total responsibility, the same absolute liberty within discipline. Thus, in darkness and in blood, a Republic was established, the strongest of Republics. Each of its citizens knew that he owed himself to all and that he could count only on himself alone. Each of them, in complete isolation, fulfilled his responsibility and his role in history. Each of them, standing against the oppressors, undertook to be himself, freely and irrevocably. And by choosing for himself in liberty, he chose the liberty of all. (Sartre, "Republic of Silence" 500)

What Sartre does here is nothing less than endorse an existentialism of action in loneliness and liberty, thus ultimately celebrating a specific form of heroism as the embodiment of liberty. In contrast, Bertolt Brecht does not care for such a celebration of heroism, as is clear from a famous passage in the *Life of Galileo*. After Galileo has denied important aspects of his conclusions on astronomy under the threat of torture, he states,

Andrea: Unhappy the land that has no heroes.
Galileo: Unhappy the land that is in need of heroes. (98)

Thus, it can be seen that a multitude of questions of profound moral, ethical, and political import are tied to the concept of resistance.

6. From Resistance to *Zivilcourage*

The moral point of view concerns itself with the problem whether the end justifies the means in the resistance against immoral circumstances, and moreover, whether human beings have to be ready to admit blame for the sake of morality. The ethical viewpoint addresses the question whether only this readiness and this willingness to admit blame, if required even in isolation for the sake of a higher good and hence to prove one's own freedom, redeems that which could be called a good and humane life. From the political perspective, it is ultimately a question about the readiness of the citizens for resistance, or in Brecht's words, for heroism to aid a country and a society to its collective wellbeing.

On the contrary, to elevate the concept of resistance or the readiness to resist to a fundamental category of a free political system based on liberty depicts above all its formality, as I have attempted to illustrate with the example of Albert Leo Schlageter. Whether resistance is meaningful, good, or even morally necessary, depends entirely on that against which it is directed. In this context, based on the theory of the 'Authoritarian Personality,' developed as early as the 1930s by Max Horkheimer et al., it can be stated with some justification that the readiness to be subservient, i.e., authoritarianism, certainly contradicts a political system based on liberty. Nonetheless, it can also be seen that these Critical Theorists do not only criticize authoritarianism but also its opposite. In Horkheimer's *Studies on Authority and Family*, the personality type of the rebel is also analyzed, who, in his blind rejection of any kind of authority, is especially prone to violence.

Fritz Bauer, the Attorney General of the State of Hessen and the initiator of the Frankfurt Auschwitz trials, suggests at a minimum a conceptual way out of the dilemma of a heroically existential, but substantively vacant concept of resistance and also out of a faith in the inner logic of liberal institutions. He does so with regard to German history and in particular to Eichmann's behavior in Jerusalem during the trials by paradoxically referring to Martin Luther:

In Jerusalem, certainly a part of the German history and perhaps even that of the German present stands accused, i.e. a certain authoritarian thinking and action vis-à-vis the state by the government officials and the citizens, a blind faith in the state and its idolatry, slavish subservience, fear of authority and arrogance towards those below, aggressiveness, herd and horde mentality, formalism and technocracy [...].

Citing a quotation from Luther's "Sermon on Good Works" *in extenso*, where the protestant reformer actually invalidates the duty to obey the authority, if "worldly power and authority would render the subject against the commandments of God" Fritz Bauer asserts:

Here allegiance to the good, and disobedience and resistance against the evil are promoted and made a virtue, which is rare to come by in these parts, i.e. the *Zivilcourage* or everyday, moral courage.

One could dispute whether Martin Luther actually called for *Zivilcourage*, but nonetheless, perhaps it is just this concept, or rather both the concept and the content of *Zivilcourage*, which can vindicate Brecht's insight from *Galileo*, i.e., only a country that is not in need of heroes is a happy one.

Thus, *Zivilcourage* is that sort of boldness that is not at all heroic, which allows one to raise one's voice in conditions that do not as yet represent the state of emergency, or even in those conditions in which it only appears as though liberty is threatened and human beings demeaned. "Happy indeed is the land that needs no heroes."

Translation, including quotations: Radhika Natarajan

Works Cited

Anderson, Perry. *The Indian Ideology*. Verso, 2013.
Beauvoir, Simone de. *The Blood of Others*. Translated by Yvonne Moyse and Roger Senhouse, Penguin, 1964.
Biemel, Walter. *Sartre*. Rowohlt, 1979.

Brecht, Bertolt. *Die Maßnahme*. 1931. Suhrkamp, 1998.
—. *Life of Galileo*. Edited by John Willett and Ralph Manheim, translated by John Willett, Methuen Drama, 2006.
Burckhardt, Carl Jacob. *Meine Danziger Mission: 1927-1939*. Callwey, 1960.
Farias, Victor. *Heidegger und der Nationalsozialismus*. Fischer, 1989.
Gandhi, Mahatma. "The Jews." *Harijan*, 26 Nov. 1938, pp. 239-42. *The Collected Works of Mahatma Gandhi*, www.gandhiserve.org/cwmg/VOL074.PDF.
Heinrich, Klaus. *Versuch über die Schwierigkeit nein zu sagen*. Stroemfeld, 1964.
Horkheimer, Max, editor. *Studien über Autorität und Familie*. Felix Alcan, 1936.
Kant, Immanuel. *Practical Philosophy*. Cambridge UP, 1996.
Ossietzky, Carl von. "Rechenschaft." *Die Weltbühne*, 10 May 1932, pp. 689-709.
Radek, Karl. "Leo Schlageter, der Wanderer ins Nichts." *Der deutsche Kommunismus: Dokumente 1915-1945*, edited by Hermann Weber, Kiepenheuer & Witsch, 1972, pp. 142-47.
Sartre, Jean-Paul. *Dirty Hands*. Gallimard French, 1948.
—. "Republic of Silence." *Republic of Silence*, edited by A. J. Liebling, Harcourt, Brace & Co, 1947, pp. 498-500.
Stein, Burton, and David Arnold. *A History of India*. Blackwell, 2010.
The Bible. English Standard Version, Crossway Bibles, 2001.
Willett, John, and Ralph Manheim, editors. *Bertolt Brecht: Poems 1913-1956*. Routledge, 1976.

More than Resistance
Striving for Universalization

Alex Demirović

1.

Social protest, dissent, non-conformism, subversion, sabotage, rebellion, revolt, disobedience, and resistance: over the last years and even decades these terms and concepts have been widely discussed within social movements, their associated critical theory and social analysis.

Subversive action should question normalizing social dispositives, delegitimize state violence, and erode social customs. It should loosen the naturally appearing relationship between signifier and signified, undermine the collectively binding meaning of discursive practices, and render the performativity of sex and everyday racism visible.

Johannes Agnoli was without a doubt one of the most important theorists of resistance and subversion in Germany. In the introduction to his 1989/1990 lecture "Subversive Theory" he gave a concise formulation of the central aspects of subversion and resistance.

Theory of overthrow: subversion as the subject of action; or as perspective of all theory 'in destitute times'—the only possibility of emancipatory thought. That is the thing itself. The thing itself develops historically as a stunning negation of both the existing 'best order' and the 'value system' of the time. (Agnoli 15)

In these few sentences, Agnoli deploys a figure of thought which can be found in the gender theory of Judith Butler, the social theory of Ernesto Laclau, the democracy theory of Jacques Rancière, as well as the ethics of Jürgen Habermas and Simon Critchley. All of these authors assume that power is located in the naturalization of meaning, the fixation of socially binding universalities, and the unquestioned monopoly of decisions, decision makers, and decision making institutions. Power causes and results from the fact that meaning—produced by the play of signifier and discourse—no longer appears as arbitrary; that universality is tied to the body and the way of life of a social group; that political institutions and decisions are presented and understood as something altogether different from what they are: the result of political struggles and negotiations. Power causes and is the cause of the coordinates of our social and political organization appearing as a foregone conclusion and natural state of affairs, rather than the totalization of a hegemonic project. In these few sentences Johannes Agnoli however—maybe unwittingly—also expresses one of the central weaknesses of the theory of subversion and resistance. Subversion undermines the established and naturalized practices, resistance turns against the practices of power, but in a singular and specific way these practices of subversion and resistance remain formal and subaltern. Again and again, subversion can or must refer itself to the established—and seen as the best possible—order. Resistance in the name of the other, the signifier and the *sans-parts* turns against the apparently inevitable and necessary crystallization of power. Subversion and resistance are not 'one-off' acts. Instead they embody a universal principle. There will always be a right to resist: a right of those who do not accept a given order, who have no part, no voice, and no visibility. Under all the thinkable forms of the social and political, there is always this irreducible space of resistance and subversion. Power, police, hegemony, and the identitary logic of fixed identities will always strive to close this space. They will make their case and claim that resistance is superfluous and dispensable, arguing that the historical calls and claims for emancipation have already been answered and honored. With liberal democracy we have reached the end of history. Radical theories of democracy turn against such an end, and yet they fail to truly go beyond liberal democracy. Everything continues to play out within its horizon. It is seen as open and pluralistic, everything is constructed and everything can be deconstructed again. Whenever as yet new and unpredictable forms of exclusion, dispossession, closure, totalization, and naturalization of the social emerge, these forms will again and again lead to renewed resistance and subversion. For this very reason a theory of subversion and resistance is about keeping a space open for the coming resistance and the coming democracy.

This should not be underestimated. Resistance against exclusion, imposed inequality, disadvantage, disfranchisement, and invisibility cannot be stopped in the name of a once achieved freedom. No tyranny is worse than that emerging from a grave: the attempt, by those in the present, to fix and regulate the life of future generations. It is a central impulse of every theory of emancipation to keep open the social space for the logical possibility of resistance. The argument for resistance is however problematic for three reasons.

Firstly, resistance is formally defined as a negation of the existing order. In this respect, the quality of the existing plays as little a role as the quality of resistance itself. We are therefore faced with the question of the criteria for resistance. What about the resistance of those who, after the establishment of a new way of life and emancipated form of communal living, want to restore the old order and traditional practices? A purely formal definition of resistance becomes even more difficult to sustain when it comes to a functional shift resistance can go through; such a shift can be that resistance becomes an affirmative action, even if many still see, fear, or suspect its critical, resistant and oppositional potential.

Secondly, the resistance of a social group is dependent on another group exercising its power and domination, organizing the social order and taking the initiative to establish the Nomos (the order of universally binding principles). The collective subject of resistance is itself the result of the power of another collective. It therefore remains subaltern, being always and only defined by that which the other group—those in power—does. Resistance does not form an own perspective, it is always only resistance; it is defined by that which it turns against.

Thirdly and finally, in the perspective of resistance, the history of humankind itself appears as a mythological fatality: a fatality in which resistance needs to assert itself from anew, again and again. Even if one were to accept or assume that those resisting were to, one day, successfully assert themselves, this would only be the forerunner to a newly constituted discriminated and oppressed subject and its new, different, as yet unknown type of resistance. After resistance is before resistance and the perspective of reconciliation appears messianic and utopian.

After these considerations, one could have the impression that resistance is external to the practice of power. But in this case we would not be dealing with resistance, but a different, positively existent, kind of power, prevented from pursuing its own goals and strategies on its own terrain. In contrast, resistance is situated within the same terrain as power. Resistance follows from power and deploys itself against power, and yet remains wholly tied to it. There therefore seems to be a dialectic between power and resistance. In a remarkable passage, Michel Foucault emphasizes the internal relation between power and resistance and points to the paradox of power and resistance: "Where there is power, there is resistance, and yet, or rather consequently, this resistance is never in a position of exteriority in relation to power" (*The History* 95). What does he mean? Is he trying to show the subalternity of resistance, or is he trying to comfort us: telling us there will never be power without resistance? That would of course be comforting and appeasing for everyone who cannot live with the infamies of power: Power will never have a final victory. One can always count on at least temporary reversals of power relations (cf. Foucault, *Discipline* 27). This reassurance however carries an ambivalence, resistance follows power and remains its subordinate. It is therefore a small comfort: There will always be resistance but power always prevails one way or another. In this respect one can, referring to Slavoj Žižek (2007) say that "resistance is surrender," that the "politics of resistance is nothing but the moralising supplement of power" (7). With his immanent-theoretical thought, Foucault suggests another question of an equally disillusioning nature: Does resistance just follow power, or conversely does power not always and also constitute itself in and as an anticipation to the resistance it will inevitably call forth? The cause of power would thereby lay in resistance, with resistance itself being written into the genesis of power. Understood this way, resistance is always and already contained in the outline of power. Resistance may drive power before it, but as long as it is not successful in leaving the field and terrain of power, it cannot be as resistant as it might imagine itself to be. In view of this circularity of power and resistance, Foucault was accused of having a functional understanding of power. Power would accordingly reproduce itself through the respective instance of resistance. That is why Foucault can also defend the idea that resistance is never located outside of power. It does not affect power from without, but is always located on the terrain of power itself. To the question whether the relationship between power and resistance is a tautological one, Foucault answered affirmatively.

Absolutely. I am not positing a substance of resistance versus a substance of power. I am just saying: as soon as there is a power relation, there is a possibility of resistance. We can never be ensnared by power: we can always modify its grip in determinate conditions and according to a precise strategy. ("Power" 123)

Objecting to Foucault's conception on the basis of a functional tautology is itself problematic, because the argument itself implies a teleological relationship between power and resistance and itself plays the game of power. Power is not just about having power over someone and breaking their resistance, but it is about having the power to prescribe the rules and terms of the fight to those who want to resist: to have power is to prompt resistance and to impose the rules of that fight. Power is therefore also powerful because it succeeds in renewing the conditions under which it exists and in transforming every moment of resistance into a moment of increased power. Resistance is reckoned with. Power which wants to reproduce itself must for that very reason deploy the techniques and rationalities of its resistant opponent: to drive on the deployment of power and to elevate itself to new levels. We are therefore not dealing with a functional tautology, but with an adequate theoretical insight. Resistance itself can induce the renewal of power and its elevation to new heights. One can only talk of a tautology of power and resistance insomuch as a real and temporary victory of power took place, which manages to subjugate any as of yet uncompliant element. One result of this power can be the self-humbling of those who become enamored in their own acts of subversion, revolt, or resistance, and thereby subordinate themselves to the function of power. But with each further step, power necessarily produces new antagonistic constellations. It is for this reason that it is in no way certain that power will assert itself; there is no absolute-zero of power and resistance; and it is wrong to think of the polar constellation of power and domination on the one side and resistance on the other. If power can determine the action of its subjects, many and asymmetrical forms of resistance still remain (cf. Lüdtke 337). The power and resistance relation is no zero sum game; they each point to alternatives beyond themselves.

2.

The relationship between power and resistance therefore needs to be de-tautologized. This means also seeing that part of resistance which is not formal, not subaltern, and which wants to go beyond resistance. Against those ideas according to which our societies are stable and integrated and deviations and delinquency are only identifiable in exceptional circumstances, in different and specific social conditions; we see resistance emerge in a variety of forms and from a variety of actors. Everyone is struggling with everyone, even the individual with itself. It is also for this reason that Foucault suggested to do away with the concept of repression: the concepts of fight, struggle, strategy, and tactic being more appropriate. In interviews he on several occasions expresses his bewilderment that the vocabulary of struggle and relation of forces is used so widely in certain political discourses in such an un-reflected way. One should, according to Foucault, take the totality of resistant practices in "tactical and strategic terms, positing that each offensive from the one side serves as leverage for a counter-offensive from the other" ("The Eye" 163). This is why the analysis of power "is a matter rather of establishing the positions occupied and modes of actions used by each of the forces at work, the possibilities of resistance and counter-attack on either side" (Foucault, "The Eye" 163-64). It is about establishing who is taking part in the struggle, what for, how, where, with which instruments, and following which rationality. From Foucault's perspective, it does not start with a struggle of external and global contradictions but with a field of powers and resistances: with a multiplicity of tactics and strategies. Power and resistance do not just face each other on opposite sides: One can turn into the other. What was once a protest can quickly become a form of exercise of power, the subaltern who up until now rejected power can in the next moment exercise power, those who are in one respect perpetrators can be victims the next moment and vice versa.

Following E. P. Thompson, and arguing very much along the lines of Foucault, the historian Alf Lüdtke argues that resistance has its big, official, statistically observable side: the protests, demonstrations, strikes, unrest, insurgencies, revolts, and acts of civil disobedience. But all these spectacular actions must be seen in a larger context: They take place on the foundation of a multitude of inconspicuous, quiet forms of resistance and are as such only the tip of the iceberg. Below the level of the calculated countermovement, numerous and ambiguous resistance movements and activities, by individuals, small or large groups, can be observed. A comprehensive analytical perspective and phenomenology is necessary to account for all of these practices: the quiet withdrawal, keeping silent, complaint and doubt, distance and non-participation, refusal and refractoriness, emigration. A large number of such quiet practices can be observed in companies, workplaces, and the military: work-to-rule, absenteeism, arriving late, prolonged breaks for smoking or to use the restroom, intentional production of defective goods, changes of work place, refusing military service, refusing military orders, attacks on bullying officers, enjoying oneself, fleeing into religion, or using art as a form of resistance to a brutal world, just not thinking about things because there is not much we can do about it anyway, or to defy the nonsense of the reigning state of affairs with rational thought; all of these can be moments of resistance. Finally, resistance can also use power to its own ends. Lüdtke, much like Foucault, sees the use individuals make of authority: Much to the distress of the military administration, housewives hang their underwear on the ramparts or use the constant meddling of the police to denounce their husbands and neighbors to the king, accusing them of alcoholism and rape (cf. Foucault, *The Punitive Society*, Lecture 7, 14 Feb. 1973). Lüdtke suggests that these micro-practices of resistance take place quietly and secretly. This may well be the case: as with the soldier Schwejk, not everything is done and justified consciously. Nonetheless, the argument of quiet unspoken resistance does not strike me as plausible: In the stairwells and kitchens, in the school yards, in the train and on the way home from the barracks, in the pub with others, people talk and discuss these things. People think and reason about to what extent dissent, resistance, and conflict is worth it; whether there are any alternatives or whether it would not just make everything worse.

Resistance seems to be deeply and widely seated in our everyday life and takes place in a multitude of local, regional, unspoken and spoken, individual and collective ways and practices. To a large extent, these practices take place way below the level of wild outbursts of protest or calculated and rationalized strategies and practices of resistant action. Foucault, who strongly emphasized this aspect of local struggles and tactics, however also clearly and emphatically emphasizes the weakness of such struggles, based only on local resistance at the workplace, in the research laboratory or within the family. He sees the danger of restricting oneself to momentary, transient struggles and to limited claims (cf. "Truth" 130). Without a global strategy, local struggles can easily find themselves in a situation in which they become isolated and far removed from that which their expansion could have made possible. The restriction to the local and the specific contradictions sets one up for failure and defeat. But strategies do not appear from nowhere. As we are dealing with a multitude of local and situative tactics, and due to the fact that the exercise of power as well as resistance can, depending on the constellation of forces, always rapidly be recoded, strategies are themselves the result of complex practices which have consolidated and universalized a multitude of opposing or marginal practices. We must also consider the resistances which form themselves in opposition to a universalizing strategy. To focus our attention on the big social contradictions and their corresponding macro-subjects, i.e., the proletariat, the women´s movement, the new social movements, is therefore misleading. It is not that such macro-subjects do not exist, but when they are presented as pre-existing subjects of a collective and rationalized resistance, the processes by which the tactics are assembled into strategies are ignored. Such collective subjectivities and their macro practices are, when they form at all, end forms: They are the result of processes in which equivalent chains and universalizations are constructed, in which those local power relationships become overdetermined, and, each in its own specific and contradictory way, become moments of a more comprehensive resistance. That such a universal resistance should emerge is fairly improbable and is a highly contingent process. It may and should not be subsumed under the name of equality or universal values, a class, a sex, a religion, or a geographic-ethnic identity. Neither should it be subsumed under the purity of the final contradiction of wage labor and capital, of men and women, of imperium and colonized, of industrialization, and a way of life closer to, and more respectful of, nature. It should not be subordinated under the purity of a unique and final contradiction in which power stands on one side, and the resistant subjects stand on the other, in unity and solidarity.

3.

Up until now, I have tried to deploy two arguments. According to the first, there is a danger that resistance should remain formal and subaltern and is trapped in a tautological relationship with power. According to the second argument, resistance goes beyond this functionality. To this end, it is necessary to take into account the localization and specificity of resistances which change power relations and power. Resistance can insert itself, both formally and functionally, in the wider reproduction of power, when it does not become the moment of a global strategy. Resistance is, in itself, not sufficient. It must want and strive for something. In that sense we are dealing with a double movement: The universality of a given and prevailing order is dissolved by a multitude of local and asymmetrical struggles. These struggles are not subservient to some pure antagonism; they are to be understood as an end form of overdetermining contradictions and as the unlikely emergence of a global strategy. It is also necessary that out of these local resistances such a will, such a desire, is developed and organized so that the resistant practices may be linked to one another and achieve a new universality. For resistance is always and already thought with the idea and finality that it will be victorious and will overcome the conditions under which it first emerged as necessary. I would like to briefly point to the fact that the tradition of critical thinking does contain attempts to be commensurate with resistance´s teleological dimension: the development of concepts including the idea that resistance is more than the development of a resistant subject which persists in a great antagonism with the powerful. It is much more a case of the rudiments and models forming a collective will, which strives for new and different order.

Resistance is an important moment, for it reacts to power and sharpens the "intolerance of both the facts of power, and those customs numbed by power" (Foucault, "Vorwort" 185; translation: Christopher Robotham). Resistance renders the fragility of power clear and visible. It opens up a dissenting relationship between individuals and the powers which organize both our individual and collective ways of life, and which render the subaltern subaltern. But the process should not restrict or limit itself through false modesty for otherwise it will be drawn in and overhauled by power. Autonomy, a collective will and a new universality must form. A form of autonomy can and may be in the first instance negative in nature. The resistant individuals collectively turn away, leave the field of power and let the antagonism be. Hardt and Negri suggest something similar when they talk of desertion and exodus:

In politics as in economics, one weapon that is constantly at the disposal of the ruled, in other words, is the threat to refuse their position of servitude and subtract themselves from the relationship. The act of refusing the relationship with the sovereign is a kind of exodus, fleeing the forces of oppression, servitude, and persecution in search of. (333)

Those who choose the exit option will be, in other spaces, subject to other and maybe stronger and abstracter power. Among those who flee, this exodus can bring forth forms of power, exploitation, or sexual oppression. It is maybe for this reason that Foucault, in his analysis of governmentality, so strongly emphasized that, under the conditions of the modern art of government, it is not the posture of "not wanting to be governed at all" ("What is Critique?" 44) which imposed itself. Within this modern art of government, he sees another question having gained preeminence. He famously expressed this question, deliberately using inverted commas, as the question of: "How not to be governed like that, by that, in the name of those principles, with such and such an objective in mind and by means of such procedures, not like that, not for that, not by them" ("What is Critique?" 44). Here Foucault is telling us that it is not about the abstract turning away from power, but the real and concrete transformation of one mode of exercising power, one form of governmentality into another. It is about the subjects of power working towards influencing and changing how they are subjected to power, and how they are governed.

It is a tragic aspect of the dialectic of power and domination that the option of turning away from power is not readily available. It is primarily the direct producers who are caught up in two types of contradiction, both directly linked with resistance and exodus: their resistance emerges on the terrain of power, reproduces power, is dependent and characterized by it. At the same time, they, in their real cooperative relations, challenge and question power, in that they aim for an overcoming of the relations under which the historically known and existing forms of domination can be overcome. They therefore stand within and without, are resistant and antagonistic. The ruling cannot just let the resistant leave. That would touch on the preservation of power itself.

Foucault's conception of resistance is again and again cited to show us that we should not expect of resistance that it should lead to the overcoming of power. It is generally read as a plea for a modest "art of not being governed quite so much" (Foucault, "What is Critique" 45). Without wanting to go too much into the details, one must keep in mind that Foucault considers this critical stance, the critical "art of not being governed quite so much," itself as a moment and form of this power technology of governmentality that is newly forming in the 18th century. It represents a specific form of resistance that is an integral moment of governmentality. Foucault is not suggesting that one should limit oneself to this critical stance, but goes well beyond that to pursue a much more extensive conception when, in his lectures on "Security, Territory, Population" of 1978, he shows that though there have already been political revolutions, there have been no revolutions against the much more deeply seated art of governing itself. This is exactly what he argues for:

I would say that the feudal type of political power undoubtedly experienced revolutions or, at any rate, came up against a series of processes that, apart from a few traces, well and truly eliminated it and chased it from the history of the West. There have been anti-feudal revolutions; there has never been an anti-pastoral revolution. The pastorate has not yet experienced the process of profound revolution that would have definitively expelled it from history. (*Security* 201)

Foucault sees it as the charge of the intellectual to restore the desirability of revolution. He explains this broadly in an interview given in 1976: to restore the desirability of revolution, from the damage it sustained through Stalinism, back to the level of desirability it had in the 19th century (cf. "Das Wissen" 114).

Although Foucault suggests to go, act and think beyond resistance, and to develop global strategies against the centuries-old practices of power, there is little in his work which helps us understand how such a collective will and universality can emerge. There is a surprising closeness between the thoughts of Gramsci and Foucault where Gramsci discusses the question of leadership and government. For this reason I would like to mention one aspect of his thought here. According to his understanding, it is necessary for resistance to develop a spirit of cleavage: the conscience and praxis not to bow to the hegemonic order and its associated ways of life, but to develop its own. Foucault argues along similar lines when he discusses the moral dissidence of groups, which fight for things such as the right to abortion, the constitution of non-family based sexual groups and laziness. What he sees here is a reversal of that articulatory praxis of the bourgeoisie of the 18th and 19th centuries, which, according to him, connected morals, capitalist production, and the state apparatus. For Foucault, such struggles are more than just the transgression of a prohibition that, for a moment, at a place and for a person, makes the law invalid and meaningless. The dissidence, as he sees it, implies the possibility to fight the power relations themselves (cf. *The Punitive Society* Lecture 6, 7 Feb. 1973). For Gramsci, the spirit of distinction contributes to helping subjects to reject and leave the actual conformity of their ways of life behind and to break out into something new: new ways of life, new organizations, and new constellations of the social collective, individuals and their every day practices. As Gramsci sees it, it is a molecular process, in which individuals break free from a variety of conformisms which play a defining role in their identities, their uneven and interrelated ways of life and practices. It is about the construction of a new collective will, a new universalism on the basis of the reorganization of the production apparatus, one without exploitation and without one hegemonic collective dominating and leading all others. This new collective will cannot, and must not, be based on the presumed and pre-given identity of the class of the direct producers. For Gramsci it is about the process of hegemony, in which one class first, in its contradiction and its struggles, emerges as a concrete collective, and in which this class then goes on to create instances of generalization and universalization based on the instances of consent and concurrence between the different social groups. Hegemony is therefore the process through which a collective will (which he calls historic bloc) forms, and in which a multitude of different emancipatory practices connect with each other.

The discussion of the concept of resistance shows that resistance, subversion, or transgression are not sufficient to change the situation that made resistance necessary in the first place, to such an extent that resistance becomes unnecessary. These practices, as necessary as they may be, bring with them the danger that, tautologically tied to power, they remain formal and subaltern to power. It requires a double movement, a double movement founded on the energy of resistance, which points beyond resistance, in which resistance firstly disarticulates the articulated moments of domination and power, and secondly strives for a new universality and universalization.

Translation, including quotations: Christopher Robotham

WORKS CITED

Agnoli, Johannes. *Die Subversive Theorie*. Edited by Barbara Görres-Agnoli, Schmetterling, 2014.

Foucault, Michel. "Das Wissen als Verbrechen." *Dits et Ecrits*, edited by Daniel Defer et al., translated by Michael Bischoff et al., vol. 3, Suhrkamp, 2003, pp. 105-14.

—. *Discipline and Punish: The Birth of the Prison*. 1976. Translated by Alan Sheridan, Vintage Books, 1991.

—. *Überwachen und Strafen: Die Geburt des Gefängnisses*. Translated by Walter Seitter, Suhrkamp, 1993.

—. "Power and Sex." *Politics, Philosophy, Culture: Interview and Other Writings 1977-1984*, edited by Lawrence D. Kritzman, translated by Alan Sheridan et al., Routledge, 1988, pp. 110-24.

—. *Security, Territory, Population: Lectures at the Collège de France, 1977-78*. Edited by Arnold I. Davidson, translated by Graham Burchell, Palgrave McMillan, 2007.

—. "The Eye of Power." *Power/Knowledge: Selected Interviews and Other Writings 1972-1977*, edited by Colin Gordon, translated by Colin Gordon et al., Pantheon, 1980, pp. 146-65.

—. *The History of Sexuality. Volume 1: An Introduction*. Translated by Robert Hurley, Pantheon Books, 1978.

—. *The Punitive Society: Lectures at the Collège de France 1972-1973*. Edited by Arnold I. Davidson, translated by Graham Burchell, Palgrave McMillan, 2015.

—. "Truth and Power." *Power/Knowledge: Selected Interviews and Other Writings 1972-1977*, edited by Colin Gordon, translated by Colin Gordon et al., Pantheon, 1980, pp. 109-33.

—. "Vorwort zu Debard, M./Hennig, J.lL., Les Juges Kaki, Paris 1977." *Dits et Ecrits*, edited by Daniel Defer et al., translated by Michael Bischoff et al., vol. 3, Suhrkamp, 2003, pp. 183-85.

—. "What Is Critique?" *The Politics of Truth*, edited by Sylvere Lotringer, translated by Lysa Hochroth and Catherine Porter, Semiotexte, 2007, pp. 41-82.

Hardt, Michael, and Antonio Negri. *Multitude: War and Democracy in the Age of Empire*. Penguin Books, 2004.

Lüdtke, Alf. "Protest—oder: Die Faszination des Spektakulären. Zur Analyse alltäglicher Widersetzlichkeit." *Sozialer Protest: Studien* zu traditioneller Resistenz und kollektiver Gewalt in Deutschland vom Vormärz bis zur Reichsgründung, edited by Heiner Volkmann and Jürgen Bergmann, VS Verlag für Sozialwissenschaften, 1984, pp. 325-41. Schriften des Zentralinstituts für sozialwissenschaftliche Forschung der Freien Universität Berlin, vol. 44.

Žižek, Slavoj. "Resistance Is Surrender." *London Review of Books*, vol. 29, no. 22, 15 Nov. 2007, p. 7, www.lrb.co.uk/v29/n22/slavoj-zizek/resistance-is-surrender. Accessed 23 Jan. 2017.

Popular Culture, 'Resistance,' 'Cultural Radicalism,' and 'Self-Formation'
Comments on the Development of a Theory

Kaspar Maase

1. PRELIMINARY COMMENTS

This article follows up on the debate over the resistance potential of popular culture. The first part traces the historical constellation of ideas in which the question arose and remains to this day. The second part attempts to systematize different dimensions of 'resistance.' The third part examines the development and criticism of this approach in the field of Cultural Studies. This leads to the fourth part, which investigates the role "cultural radicalism" (Fluck, "Die Wissenschaft" 115) has played in this discussion. The fifth part introduces the concept of self-formation. The sixth discusses the ways in which the political relevance of popular culture has been evaluated, and how the 'resistance' approach can be further developed.

'Resistance' in a specific sense, namely that established in British Cultural Studies, forms the point of reference, framing the topic of this article in three ways. Firstly, the analysis will take place within the supposed context of a clash of interests between 'the people' and 'the power bloc'; secondly, it will focus on the cultural dimension; and thirdly, it will investigate the cultural exercise of power and oppositional practices from the perspective of 'the people' with the intention of facilitating their empowerment.

The thoughts of political and academic actors as to what exactly constitutes 'resistance' are as varied and contradictory as the concerns articulated by 'the people.' Nonetheless, there is a widespread expectation that research from the perspective of 'the people' has to promote oppositional feelings, thoughts, and actions. In this situation, it seems appropriate to approach the subject (within the given context) from an inductive rather than a normative perspective. The following investigation therefore refers to texts and sources in which cultural practices are *interpreted* as critical, oppositional, empowering—or as 'resistance.' In this case, self-descriptions from the context of 'the people' and (crucially) from the perspective of Cultural Studies are equally as relevant as sources from the perspective of the 'power bloc' that attribute an oppositional quality to certain cultural practices.

What forms of expression and behavior count as resistant in a society—and thereby have resistant potential—is primarily a result of reciprocal perception, and the object of practical negotiation. No cultural form is resistant or challenges established power structures on its own, independent of any context. On the contrary, the endless cycle of rebellious disruption, alarmed reaction, commercialization, and finally the transformation of the temporarily controversial into one of many aesthetic differentiations on the market (which will be followed by a new disruption in another form) forms the standard model in popular culture research, as in the memory of the actors themselves.

A working definition of popular culture as used in the scope of this essay would comprise the commercial products and commodities that are used and assigned value by members of all social and educational strata for the purposes of entertainment. More specifically, this refers to mass arts such as film and music, computer games, dance, and popular literature. Necessarily, popular culture equally encompasses the *practices* of engaging with cultural goods and their use by the audience;[1] these fundamentally include activities that lead to the interpretation and re-interpretation of cultural goods. Put another way, popular culture is not produced or controlled by 'the people,' but rather by the culture industries;[2] yet the consumers of such culture have considerable room of action in

---

[1] | Regarding the author's position, cf. Maase "Unscharfe Begriffe" and "Populärkultur."

[2] | This term, in plural, is not meant in an evaluative way, as in critical theory (cf. Steinert), but rather in an empirical or analytical way, as in David Hesmondhalgh's *The Cultural Industries*.

their individual and collective appropriation, as in the actual attribution of *cultural* value to such goods.[3]

How they perceive this room of action and (are able to) use it in a practical sense, which interpretations they favor, and which they find inconceivable, depends, however, on the social conditions and subjectivity models that significantly limit the potential of 'the people' for perception, imagination, and action in contemporary capitalist societies. Thus, the following question forms the logical crux of the debate surrounding 'resistance': What is the nature of the room of action that actors can open up through the willful appropriation of popular culture, and what potential is generated here for action that effectively leads to a "society of equals" (Rosanvallon)?

However, it is no longer really possible for a single person to take in the highly differentiated field of popular culture, and the same is true for its corresponding field of academic study, as well as the (now worldwide) field of critical popular culture scholarship. It is only with a great deal of luck that one can avoid the danger of 'bringing owls to Athens,' and one will always deal with individual lines of enquiry disproportionately. In this context, it is understood that the present contribution is merely part of an ongoing and interminable discussion.

2. ART AS THE EXERCISE OF FREEDOM AND THE TRADITIONS OF LEFT-WING CRITICISM OF MASS CULTURE

The idea of the autonomy of art forms an important context in the debate (cf., e.g., Wolfzettel and Einfalt; Fredel; M. Müller, Bredekamp, Hinz, Verspohl, Fredel, and Apitzsch). From the last third of the 18th century, on the one hand, it addressed the creative class; they should keep their work free from non-artistic interests. On the other hand, it countered a commercial and institutional bias towards art that conformed to religious, moral, political, etc. standards, as well as the tendency to adapt or even subordinate art to the anticipated tastes of buyers. This was a reaction

---

3 | This was seminally developed by John Fiske in *Understanding Popular Culture* (esp. 23-47). A current update of this can be found in John Storey's *Cultural Theory and Popular Culture: An Introduction*.

both to the accelerated marketization of the arts and to state pressure with an anti-revolutionary thrust.

The diversity and the contradictory interpretations of the demand for autonomy cannot be fully developed here. However, one can say that at least for the bourgeois public in 19th century Germany, there was an extremely present if not dominant discourse that proclaimed the autonomy of the (inner) freedom of art, and furthermore viewed this as a model, if not the "foundation of political freedom" (Fuchs 196). Of particular relevance here is Schiller's thesis that the "aesthetic disposition of the soul" (510), because of its "rational" distance from the perceived constraints of everyday reality, "gives birth to liberty" (510). His central metaphor of the 'aesthetic game' points to the intention of creating mental and practical distance from the world of bourgeois constraints.

The educated classes were well acquainted with this tradition of thought, and it played an important role after the First World War (and especially after the successes of Italian and German fascism), when the relationship between the labor movement and commercial popular culture became the subject of public criticism, particularly in the context of concepts such as mass culture and mass art (cf. Hertel 119-26). Herbert Marcuse's reckoning with the "affirmative character" of the bourgeois humanistic understanding of culture, which "sets the realm of actual values and ends in themselves against the societal world of use and means" (63), accounts for its continuing fascination. In Walter Benjamin's model of the "scattered" reception of mass culture transmitted via media, which overcomes subjection to the aura of the original (cf. 503-05), one hears the echo of Schiller's 'ludic drive.' Adorno's desperate hope that art could succeed through negation at conveying unreified criticism of suffering under monopoly capitalism also builds upon the autonomy idea. Art would become

social by its opposition to society, and it occupies this position only as autonomous art. By crystallizing in itself as something unique to itself, rather than complying with existing social norms and qualifying as 'socially useful,' it criticizes society by merely existing, for which puritans of all stripes condemn it. (Adorno 225-26).

Initial considerations of popular culture and 'resistance' in the inter-war period were still rooted in the tradition of the Western European labor movements, which took a critical view of mass culture. This entailed two perspectives. The first understood the popular culture disseminated commercially and by the religious and political establishment as an ideological weapon against the development of proletarian class consciousness. The second interpreted these mass products as part of the mechanism of cultural inequality that kept the people away from the fruits of the true, greater culture. Particularly in German-speaking countries, this was underpinned by aesthetic standards that were oriented towards a classic art canon. From this perspective, it was simply unthinkable that pulp magazines, entertainment cinema, and *Schlager* music could have legitimate aesthetic qualities, or like art, afford their users opportunities for distanced reflection, and give free rein to the imagination (cf. Emig; Storim 151-67; Wietschorke 157-75; Maase, *Was macht Populärkultur* 88-91).

Against this background, Walter Benjamin's view of "The Work of Art in the Age of Mechanical Reproduction" presented a revolutionary new approach. He expressed a positive, at least open view of film as the paradigmatic popular art of the present age, and of its mass audience as especially sovereign. It was here that the concept of 'resistance' as a willful activity on the part of working class users first became conceivable. However, given the advance of fascism, Benjamin opted for a rather conventional idea of the "politization of art" (508), which focused on ideological messages and their intellectual producers.

This was also the line that socialist and radical intellectuals followed after the Second World War in the context of the propaganda battles of the Cold War. Their opposition to commercial mass culture united two traditional themes, the political struggle against supposedly dangerous messages and the cultural defense against taste-destroying 'non-art' or 'anti-art.' In Europe, 'national' campaigns against 'American non-culture' united opponents of pop music, jazz, and Hollywood films from across the political spectrum in a conservative anti-Americanism that was tinged with racism (cf., e.g., Poiger; Maase, *BRAVO*). In the 1960s, the left came to interpret 'American' as 'imperialistic mass culture.'

At the same time, however, a transformation that was closely connected to the protest movement in West Germany at that time got underway, changing the view of popular culture. Since the mid-1950s, rock and roll music and critical Hollywood films had already found intense resonance, initially with small groups of secondary school and university students from bourgeois families. In the 1960s, students of literature and cultural studies began to engage critically with the bourgeois understanding of culture. This was highly political, as it undermined the bourgeois claim to social superiority and leadership that was built upon a foundation of knowledge centered on traditions of high culture.

These young intellectuals took an interest in genres of popular culture that had generally been associated with audiences from social classes that were viewed as subordinate to the bourgeoisie; they did so not only as users, fans, and aficionados, but also from an analytical perspective. In the interest of elevating their own newly adopted tastes, which were conventionally understood to be illegitimate, many committed young academics looked for elements of revolt, subversion, and resistance in films, detective novels, and rock music. Alongside critical studies on popular culture (often labeled 'trivial culture' in the Federal Republic), a line of research gained a foothold in the 1960s that examined relevant material with regards to its political and aesthetic progressiveness, increasingly under the positive label 'pop(culture)' (cf., e.g., Hecken, *Pop*; Hecken, *Avant-Pop*).

3. ART AND OPPOSITION: CLASSIFICATIONS

This is the point in the present historical overview where British Cultural Studies and its concept of 'resistance' also found reception in West Germany. One can discern four principle lines of argument concerning the ways in which popular arts and practices connect their users to resistant impulses. From the German perspective, and for reasons of classification (known for being a favored preoccupation of German authors), I will add an aspect that, to my knowledge, has only been dealt with in Cultural Studies on the margins: the fictional character of art and the potential of aesthetic experience and imagination that it opens up. Of course the different dimensions are not mutually exclusive; rather, they connect and overlap in diverse ways.

A) Distancing through the Medium of Fiction

In the context of art autonomy, the aesthetic debate has, since the 19th century, repeatedly turned to the question of whether the fictional structure of artworks creates a fundamental distance from what is usually referred to as 'reality' or 'life.' This has in fact related primarily to the *position of the artist*; for our purposes, it should be asked whether the aesthetic *experience of the user* includes *practices of distancing*. Here, distance refers to a person feeling doubts about previous views that seemed to be granted, and to things losing the state of being self-evident; it refers to the emergence of alternatives in the sense that the given becomes questionable, and that different conditions might be possible and are being imagined. 'Distance' opens up spaces of thought and feeling for that which was previously unknown, for alterity and utopias, at least for the perceptions of dissatisfaction, want, and suffering that are eventually caused by oppressive systems.

Previously, one has rarely asked whether the practices of the *use of mass art* can generate comparable critical perspectives and transgressions of the status quo. However, if one looks at the forms of 'resistance' that are often attributed to the consumption of popular culture, this hypothesis appears to be extremely promising.

B) Contents, Assertions, and Messages

Socialist organizations and radical movements have, from the beginning on, engaged with their surrounding popular culture. They attacked what they perceived as the propaganda of the powerful, attempted to unmask its untruth, and promoted cultural actors from whom they expected ideological support; this was mostly in the form of non-commercial activities from the likes of songwriters, film makers, or alternative theatre groups. The diversification of the culture market led to a situation in which oppositional movements also discovered tendencies in commercial media that sought to strengthen their political goals, to the extent of the development of their own cultural-political strategies.

All political actors develop such practices; these count among the daily business of pressure groups, spreading their perspectives and demands. Such struggles for influence form the solid core of the enormously differentiated interpretation practices and conflicts that currently accompany and virtually envelope cultural production in the public sphere. Advertising texts for bestsellers are included here as much as film and literature reviews, PR campaigns convoying transmedial events (e.g., TV series, new computer games), and last but not least, time and again, attempts to scandalize undesirable messages and cultural formats on a national scale. Today, all of these interventions trigger a bewildering interplay of reactions in Social Media, thus expanding the scope of cultural, interpretive battles enormously.

Cultural research critically examines such practices, discourses, and networks. However, it is well advised to avoid getting involved in conflicts over content, meaning, and supposed effects, for example with judgments regarding what is 'really resistant' and what is not. The tendency towards this is however minimal. Since at least the 1980s, cultural scholars of all disciplines have assumed that texts and practices of popular culture do not convey any distinct and unified assertions or messages. Rather, interpretations and evaluations of popular materials are socially negotiated. In this, influential media and active audiences occupy a central position, and their interpretations accordingly turn out to be diverse, heterogeneous, and unpredictable.

C) Vigorous Self-Empowerment and Willful Appropriations

These 'semiotic wars' are usually waged in public and mostly communicated through media. We have to distinguish them from the everyday practices of interpretation, reinterpretation, parody, or reworking that users engage in; the latter practices constitute a significant part of the enjoyment of popular culture.[4] Research on subcultures at the Centre for Contemporary Cultural Studies (CCCS) illuminated the objects and practices in the fields of consumption and media, which provided material for symbolic diversions and reversals. Referring to the edited volume *Resistance Through Rituals* (Hall and Jefferson),[5] Dick Hebdige, Paul Willis, Jim Clarke, and later John Fiske and others regarded such semiotic actions as the core of 'resistance' in popular culture: they grapple with the established practices and readings of *societal hierarchization*. According to Fiske, such activities can be resistant because they arise from the clash of hegemonic opinions, norms, appeals to subjectivization, etc. with the day-to-day experiences of 'the people'; 'the people' comprises constantly shifting alliances of completely heterogeneous groups of people, insofar as they belong to the disadvantaged, marginalized, and powerless with regards to their class, gender, sexual orientation, ethnicity, education, migrant status, etc. (cf. Fiske, *Understanding* ch. 2).[6]

---

[4] | John Fiske has done extensive work on the connection between 'resistance' and 'pleasure' (cf. 49-70).
[5] | For an overview, cf. Winter 98-126.
[6] | For differentiated portrayals of Fiske's approach, cf. E. Müller 52-66 and Winter 163-281.

In his works,[7] Fiske referred to a whole series of corresponding appropriations that question, ridicule, attack, and thwart claims of hegemonic subjectivization and legitimation, as well as confront hegemonic with resistant identifications. Youths parody advertising texts by changing the words to make them obscene. TV soaps allow women to celebrate female deviance. Aborigines identify with Indians fighting in American westerns, even though and exactly when they are portrayed as savages. Wrestling shows provide a great deal of material that, in the context of an achievement-oriented society, sets them apart from the myth of sports as a fair competition; they ridicule bourgeois controlled physicality by turning it into a carnivalesque spectacle.

Such production and circulation of meanings classified as anti-hegemonic takes place among individuals, in families, among friends, peer groups, and small social circles. That is why Fiske characterizes such resistance as 'micropolitical.' In the sphere of every-day life, hierarchical order and power relations are delegitimized, playfully reversed, and perhaps changed to the benefit of subordinate parties; in Fiske's view, this produces concrete shifts in power. However, the reach and stability of such power shifts is still subject to debate, and many critics argue that they have not been conclusively proven from an empirical standpoint.

D) Questioning the Authority of High Culture

One focus of popular culture research concerns practices that are understood to challenge the bourgeois cultural order. This hegemonic discourse ascribes a special status to high culture as the most valuable formation of cultural practice, and to those who show a taste for it, a legitimate claim to intellectual and political leadership.[8] In general, this stipulates the adherence to the rules of 'civilized, cultivated' behavior in the cultural sphere, and special respect, if not deference, to the institutions, performances, and agents of recognized art. Audiences should show appreciation for the authority of the serious arts, artists, and knowledge of high culture.

---

7 | In addition to *Understanding*, cf. esp. John Fiske's *Power Plays, Power Works*.
8 | At least, many theorists of popular culture see it this way, often referring to Pierre Bourdieu's *Die feinen Unterschiede: Kritik der gesellschaftlichen Urteilskraft*.

Against this background, much attention has been paid to a specific kind of practices: actions and performances that, from the perspective of bourgeois audiences, defied the norms of appropriate behavior at cultural events and failed to show adequate respect for the 'institution of art' (cf. Bürger). This included stage performances by rock bands, as well as the audiences and fans of pop music, who appeared to lack any degree of self-control. It was precisely these fans, as Henry Jenkins has demonstrated (cf. *Fans*; *Textual*), that continually transgressed the passive position of the grateful consumer and independently developed more or less heterodox understandings of popular texts. They put these understandings into practice through the publication of fan fiction within their own networks; they disregard copyrights and trademarks, and put pressure on media companies concerning, for example, the progress of ongoing series. Such willful practices demonstrate for Jenkins and others the capacity to circulate unauthorized readings of cultural goods 'from below,' and these have been interpreted as examples of 'resistance' and self-empowerment against the might of the culture industries and against the passiveness-inducing bourgeois art regime.

E) The Reversal of Cultural Hierarchies

The attempts on the part of state and informal actors to suppress and stigmatize popular culture are a major theme in its history. The goal of such campaigns was not only to hinder such works and activities or to drive them underground; according to a long list of popular culture researchers, it was considered equally important to delegitimize or criminalize the amusements, aesthetic values, and knowledge of working people and other groups that would today be categorized as 'educationally deprived' (cf., e.g., Ross; Hausmanninger; Maase, *Was macht Populärkultur*; Maase, *Die Kinder* 244-55 and 312-24). According to this position, the campaigns against popular culture and its audience have lost their emotional fervor and generally departed from the juridical landscape in the course of the 20th century. However, battles over 'taste,' which, in the sense of Bourdieu, serve the distinction and the legitimization of the cultural capital of the 'educated class,' are still being waged with considerable energy.

From this perspective, 'resistance' could take on the form of holding on to illegitimate amusements; users eluded, outwitted, or thwarted repressive measures such as censorship, bans, and punishment in more or less fanciful ways, either individually or in groups of like-minded persons. Similarly, there were protest tactics and attempts to make cultural 'head teachers' look foolish. As new forms of pop music and their dances (which were often imported to Europe from the USA) were abhorred as a challenge and a threat to European high culture and education, any activity associated with such a genre was suspected of having a political subtext; such activity rejected the hegemonic hierarchy and insisted upon the practical value and recognition of one's own 'subordinate' taste (cf., e.g., Hall and Jefferson; Willis, *Profane*; Krüger; Maase, *BRAVO*; Maase, "Rhythmus" 145-88; Fenemore; Tamagne 99-114). Thus performances by controversial musicians, 'wild' dancing, and euphoria-inducing mass concerts could take on the character of a political demonstration demanding an end to discrimination and contempt, and calling for the equality of popular culture and its adherents with the established canon.

4. Resistance in the Historical Context: Micropolitics and Its Critics, Cultural Shifts, and Cultural Radicalism

The foundation of the model of popular culture and/as 'resistance' outlined here was developed in the 1970s and 1980s and has since been implemented in a number of empirical studies. In retrospect, some interpretations appear to be excessive, and some hopes for transfers from the every-day sphere into the transformation of social power relations seem rather naive. However, it would be unhistorical and unproductive to completely dismiss the approach. Instead, we should rather briefly recall some of the insights that have emerged in the field of cultural studies over the past five or six decades, and from which, according to this author anyway, there is no turning back.

In a nutshell, you could say that in the course of the 1960s and 1970s, debates on the left and in 'western Marxism' overcame two dogmas. The orthodox faction held that mass culture is produced by a capitalist industry; therefore, its content and effects will never seriously question the capitalist order. The dogma of the Frankfurt School said that the culture industry is part of a "context of total delusion" (Wolin 127; original: "Verblendungszusammenhang"); the entertainment tastes of the masses and the imperatives of monopoly capitalist companies interlock, and maintain the functioning of an alienated and self-destructive system. A growing academic interest in the *concrete* use of popular culture material nonetheless led inexorably away from such sweeping assumptions; the questions of *how* media texts transferred and communicated meanings and readings and what their *users* actually got from them shifted to the forefront.

Interestingly, there were few studies on production processes; questions of who creates media texts and in what way, and what interests, room for interpretation, contradictions, and inconsistencies are at play were only rarely dealt with empirically. This was certainly connected to the fact that the companies and institutions concerned placed little value on transparency and did not want any critical observation of their practices. The topic was completely absent from programs of academic research, where the primary focus lay on empirical data and theories concerning (collective) reception. In 1981, Stuart Hall provided a classic summary of the paradigm of the left that developed at that time with reference to Antonio Gramsci's theory of hegemony. Popular culture was understood as a "battlefield," a zone "where this struggle for and against the culture of the powerful is engaged," and as an "arena of consent and resistance" (Hall, "Notes" 237 and 239).

It was on this basis that the concept of 'resistance' in and against popular culture developed. The works of Dick Hebdige, Paul Willis, John Fiske, and Henry Jenkins, for example, were considered to be pioneering in this regard. Building upon the ideas of Michel de Certeau and the understanding of culture as a practice incorporated into every-day life, they combined empirical material and the model of active and experienced users in order to paint a diverse panorama of popular tactics of resistance and defiance. Fiske established that enjoyment is an underlying motive of media consumers and argued that it was often precisely these deviant, oppositional, or simply willful interpretations of popular texts that produced enjoyment for 'the people.' However, that cannot happen with any mass-cultural product, but only with cultural texts that do facilitate and stimulate the generation of unintended meanings due to their ambivalence, inconsistency, contradictions, exaggeration, subtexts, etc.

These works have contributed significantly to the fact that today the question of those practices in which the historian of every-day life Alf

Lüdtke sees 'willfulness'[9] on the part of ordinary users is now a standard element in empirical culture research. It was not long, however, before critics began to question the political quality and the power potential of resistant practices and amusements such as those described by Certeau and Fiske. This criticism of 'cultural populism' (cf. McGuigan; Babe) held that the 'resistance' approach grossly exaggerated the critical-political substance of such uses both qualitatively and quantitatively. In so doing, it was argued, the approach downplayed the real power of the culture industries and the hegemonic ideology they disseminated, as well as the limitations that the day-to-day life of subordinate people imposes on their capacity to critically decode mass media texts with their own interests in mind. In particular, the economic foundation of the ideological apparatus and its influence were omitted.

It is clear that opinions on the concept of 'resistance' and the micropolitical potential of every-day practices are significantly determined by underlying assumptions about the functioning of power and dominance in modern capitalist societies. Does one see the bastions of dominance located fundamentally in the private control of the means of production and in state authority or in the cultural structures of every-day life, lifestyles, and amusement imperceptibly oriented towards active integration into the dominance of the 'power bloc'?[10] In any case, it appears neither prudent to play these two levels against each other politically, nor to simply analyze them separately. Fiske stresses that the analysis of every-day and popular culture only encompasses *micropolitical* relations in the disputed arena between "the people" and "the power bloc," emphasizing the possible "(micro)redistribution of power" in favor of 'the people' (*Understanding* 161). Popular culture in this sense can only be "progressive," and not "revolutionary" or "radical" (Fiske, *Understanding* 161, passim). It is for this reason that "[t]he forging of productive links between the resistant tactics of the everyday and action at the strategic level [is] one of the most important and neglected tasks" (Fiske, *Understanding* 162; cf. 159-94).

---

9 | Lüdtke emphases in his findings that willful agency in every-day life decisively has to be "'by oneself' and 'for oneself'" (148), and that significantly complicates the question of the political potential of such practices. On this topic, cf. also Lindenberger.

10 | On the debates over the relationship between micropolitics and macropolitics, cf. Marchart 219-53.

This admonition refers to a weakness in the entire field of radical and post-Marxist theory. As long as there are hardly any empirical studies (and one must ask whether the relationship postulated by Fiske can be applied empirically at all), one can only draw hypothetical and speculative, and at best plausible conclusions about the transformative energy of resistant practices in the field of popular culture. That is something at least, and certainly not superfluous, but still unsatisfactory with regards to the political claims of Cultural Studies.

At this point, Winfried Fluck's considerations concerning 'cultural radicalism' following the protest movements of the 1960s and 1970s are well placed to integrate previous work into wider developments in critical theory formation, and to historicize the idea of 'resistance' as well as its criticism. The aforementioned shift from a deterministic understanding of culture as an economically shaped and controlled superstructure to the concept of culture as a battlefield in the course of the 1970s not only followed an intellectual (and generational; cf. Lindner 15-45) dynamic, but also a political one. The '1968er' movement had hoped to effect fundamental change. After the failure of these expectations, the left increasingly came to attribute the unexpected stability of the late capitalist order to its deep rooted mechanisms of cultural domination, which permeated people's innermost identities (cf. Ege, "Birmingham" 168-74). According to Winfried Fluck, this amounted to "a radical paradigm shift in the analysis of societal power structures" ("Die Wissenschaft" 115).

One can also see the remarkable resonance for Cultural Studies in this context. While here the micropolitical space for willful appropriation by subordinate groups took center stage, 'cultural radicalism' became dominant in postmodern cultural theory. A concept of power defined primarily by its economic foundations and its potential for material, physical repression was substituted with "a concept of a structural power [...] which no longer possesses a political actor, and instead manifests itself in discoursive structures and rhetorical forms of cultural consensus formation" (Fluck, "Die Wissenschaft" 116; cf. Fluck, "Resistance").

5. DECENTERING OF THE SUBJECT, SELF-FORMATION, AND THE AMBIGUITY OF THE SOCIAL SPHERE

From both a theoretical and an empirical perspective, the strength of these approaches lay in the 'decentering of the subject': in the investigation of the processes by which people in practice make themselves into recognized (capable, competent, cultivated, etc.) subjects by adopting hegemonic subject ideals, behavior norms, routines, etc. in their daily lives. The focus lay on subject forms, subject cultures, and subject formations (cf. Reckwitz, *Subjekt*) that were regulated by hegemonic discourses. This perspective confronted the basic principle of the liberal worldview, the concept of the autonomous subject which is competent and able to make *his or her own* rational decisions. The nearly mythical idea of individual choice was superseded by the apparently ineluctable potency and ultra-stability of discourse systems and cultural structures as the locations and forces of social power. Such a view had to take a critical stance against 'resistance' concepts, because the willful agency of capable and disposed persons was unthinkable within the context of cultural subjectivization theories. From this perspective, the issue could be a simple case of self-deception: it concealed from the actors the fact that they were acting out their deviant pleasures in a subject position that was inherent in the system.

Certainly there were approaches, such as Ernesto Laclau's hegemony and discourse theory (cf. Laclau; Laclau and Mouffe), Judith Butler's performatively conceived subjectivization concept (cf. *Das Unbehagen*; *Psyche*), or Andreas Reckwitz's praxeological subject theory (cf. *Das Hybride*) which explored the possibility of deviation, subversion, and change, pointing to conflicts, gaps, and contradictions within the universe of lived subjectivities. Relevant empirical studies to further solidify these themes remain rare in the field of poststructuralist thought (cf., e.g., Alkemeyer 39-40).[11] And ethnographic works such as those of Hebdige, Willis, and Jenkins that seek to show the transgressive potential of the use

---

11 | This deficit may be linked to the fact that Reckwitz and others concentrated on "the *dominant* subject forms of the modern age that have made a successful claim to cultural hegemony" (Reckwitz, *Das Hybride* 28). In subject cultures of a subordinate and precarious character, which fail or fall short according to hegemonic standards, the experience of identity formation requires further

of popular culture were quickly deemed insufficiently complex and not on the level of critical cultural studies by proponents of cultural radicalism.

Meanwhile, there have been increasing warnings that this deterministic reading, which amounts to a closed hegemonic culture system, threatens to squander the analytical potential of the subjectivization perspective.[12] Thomas Alkemeyer, for instance, has remarked: "If individuals are conceived of as determined in a strong, causal sense through conventions, a common rationality, or the structure of language, or considered to be the mere side effects of emergence processes, the question of their subjectivization is ultimately superfluous" (35). In the end, any critical analysis of today's power systems must develop an "anti-deterministic" perspective; otherwise, the study of the cultural practices of decentered subjects will not be able to really challenge exclusion and oppression. In other words: Critical analysis requires the "recognition of the uncertainty of the social sphere" (Alkemeyer 36).

According to this view, praxeological studies, in particular those that deal ethnographically with the "situational emergence of room for action in practical contexts" (Alkemeyer 47), can be extremely illuminating in terms of anti-deterministic perspectives. Situations featuring agency are never totally determined or consistently predetermined through the interplay of subjectivity forms and attempts to achieve recognition. Following Alkemeyer, Budde, and Freist, the intentions of subjectivization will consistently meet unexpected obstacles that evoke irritation and, in the practical context, prompt negotiation and reflection beyond the routines. When multiple parties are involved in collaboration, such situations are interpreted in different ways by the different parties, and these dissentient interpretations are exchanged.[13] More often than not, unforeseen dynamics of action would arise, making it possible to deviate from and even override or transform established subjectivization patterns.

---

attention; without investigating this tension, statements on the stability of subject orders can only claim a limited validity.

12 | In addition to Fluck, *Die Wissenschaft*, and Fluck, *Resistance*, also see the contributions in the volume by Alkemeyer, Budde, and Freist, *Selbst-Bildungen*.

13 | While previous subjectivization analyses focus on individuals, the self-formation approach assumes that practices of recognition by others play a crucial role in identity development (cf. Ricken 69-99).

It should be added that, in the view of this author, the formation of identity can 'fail' and lead to subjectivities which are not recognized by the hegemonic institutions; these developments cannot be fully excluded, isolated, and counteracted socially. That is to say that when the concrete practices of every-day life, careers, cooperation, etc. (including popular culture use)[14] represent the social spheres in which subjectivization occurs, then it is here that constellations of new, divergent, and resistant practices will emerge. This is precisely the area that concerns research on resistance.

6. Open Questions

It is now possible to formulate a few open questions in empirical popular culture research with respect to 'resistance.' What do recognized modes of popular culture usage in legitimate subject forms look like? What is their hegemonic effect? In which subjectivization practices are they appropriated? Most importantly, is it possible to make micropolitical power shifts empirically plausible as an impulse for change with regards to governmental subjectivity modules such as heteronormativity, willingness for exertion, self-optimization, health responsibility, etc.?

In general, popular culture is, however, (in the German context more so than in the American) rather unwieldy material for *legitimate* forms of subjectivity. How can masses of 'couch potatoes,' players of 'violent video games,' 'trash TV' viewers, 'internet addicts,' and other negative figures in public cultural discourse argumentatively and practically be transformed into acceptable subjectivities, or at least defused?[15] There is apparently a significant contradiction between widespread every-day practices such as relaxing, disengaging, daydreaming,[16] etc. on the one hand, and the demands of education, cultivation, and creativity on the other. The standards of high culture still serve as a beacon for recognized forms of subjectivity, but are difficult to integrate in the given forms of cultural

---

14 | The Germans currently spend almost 10 hours a day with media used largely for entertainment (cf. "Media Perspektiven: Basisdaten 2014" 66).

15 | On the attempt to interpret expertise in mass art as an element in self-entrepreneurial cognitive fitness, cf. Maase, "Radioten" 136-137.

16 | One author seeks to legitimize this cultural practice widely understood to be 'useless' from a utilitarian perspective (cf. Ernst).

practice. To date, theories of subjectivization show significant deficiencies in the empirical analysis of subjectivity forms with regard to those (large!) social groups and practices that count as culturally inferior. Initial insights are provided by recent ethnographies examining the experience of identity from the point of view of affected groups (cf. Wellgraf; Bachmann; Ege, *Ein Proll*; Sutter). Additional research is needed in this area.

There are no studies to date that conclusively link the concept of 'micropolitics' to the concepts of self-formation, nor is there any research that empirically operationalizes transfers into the macropolitical sphere in other theoretical contexts. After 40 years, it is therefore fitting to fundamentally re-examine the question of the 'resistance' potential of popular culture. Even the concept of popular culture as a battlefield has apparently been completely diverted by cultural radicalism. Initially, the modernization of Gramsci's theory of hegemony had nothing to do with popular culture in the sense of this paper, but rather with societal power structures and with the regulation of knowledge. A re-reading of Stuart Hall's[17] pioneering work makes it clear he was interested in the analysis of encoding/decoding and in studying popular culture as a battlefield and not purely as fiction or entertainment; he did not place the use of mass culture at the center of semiotic struggles, but rather those societal discourses that generated hegemony over 'the people' in the field of macropolitics itself.[18]

In retrospect, it must be stated that in the 1970s and 1980s many viewed the homogeneity and power of the culture industries as overwhelming. As a result, the focus was on oppositional *use*; researchers

---

17 | "Encoding and Decoding in the Television Discourse" appeared in 1973 as CCCS Stencilled Paper no. 7 at the Birmingham Centre for Contemporary Cultural Studies; a revised edition was printed under the title "Encoding/Decoding" as Chapter 10 in *Culture, Media, Language*, edited by Stuart Hall, Dorothy Hobson, Andrew Lowe, and Paul Willis.

18 | In "Notes on Deconstructing 'The Popular,'" Hall (like Raymond Williams and Richard Hoggart) dealt with "popular traditions and practices" (235), the thought and behavior patterns of ordinary people, their understanding of themselves, and their orientation to the world. There was no discussion of commercial entertainment or enjoyment. Hall was chiefly interested in the question by what statements and what discursive articulations a political actor might succeed in the arena of public debate to become accepted as speaking for 'the people.' "That is why 'popular culture' matters. Otherwise [...] I don't give a damn about it" ("Notes" 239).

neither investigated the possibility of changing *information* policy and entertainment *production* nor brought up the question of mass arts that openly ran counter to the hegemony of the power bloc. However, David Hesmondhalgh came to a different conclusion in his comprehensive study of the culture industries. Many companies are politically conservative and seek to control the circulation (i.e., mass reception) of their products accordingly; the creative class nonetheless enjoy considerable autonomy, and their texts form a diverse, contradictory, and ambiguous range of materials for reception. "These modes of thought and feeling are hardly ever directly subversive of oppressive economic and political power [... yet] they reflect and reinforce the fact that the naturalization of existing power relations is never complete" (Hesmondhalgh 384). However, according to Hesmondhalgh we have to ask whether the media pursue an equally liberal strategy concerning "the provision of information that provides an analysis of overall power relations" (384).

Hesmondhalgh addresses an important difference here, which has previously garnered little attention in the field of cultural studies: that between (simplified) information and arguments identified as political, on the one hand, and as fictional or staged entertainment on the other. In fact the whole 'resistance' debate concerned the latter. How 'the people' decode news reports and political documentaries remained a marginal theme of communication studies.

Critical popular culture research will remain fruitful for the foreseeable future, with new conceptual approaches on the horizon. From the perspective of European ethnology, one reversal of previous approaches appears to be very promising. Previously, the focus lay on the examination of rather haphazardly chosen users who dealt with popular culture in a willful manner. One possibility for the future is to apply the method of theoretical sampling and to focus on subjects who are characterized by special relevance to the issue of 'resistance': Activists who engage in movements and projects that take a critical stance towards the 'power bloc.'[19] As a research hypothesis, we might presume that such activists struggle against hegemonic interpretations of popular culture. Questions such as what amusements and mass arts they use, which of these provoke their opposition, and how they try to turn this practical conflict into a part of their continual self-formation would offer very promising insights (not

---

19 | If such studies already exist, they are not known to the present author.

least in comparison to the finding of previous research, for example on fans).

Finally, let us return to the thesis we touched upon at the beginning, that art enables its users to distance themselves from their lived reality and—in aesthetic experience and sensual perception—to challenge their lives' givenness and apparent lack of alternatives. However, art theory has previously only attributed this quality to works from the artistic canon and supposedly serious, challenging art perched at the highest level of modern aesthetic reflection; popular culture did not meet these criteria.[20] There are, by all means, serious arguments for this perspective, and they have been taken up by researchers who discussed whether popular art has a specific aesthetic structure and whether it requires special modes of reception (cf. Maase, *Die Schönheiten*; Maase, "Geschmack" 50-65). In reality, entertainment analyses for example show little interest in art's potential to challenge the status quo or in the experience of alterity. These researchers see distance, playfulness, and a lack of seriousness *in relation to aesthetic texts*, but they do not look for an altered relationship to social reality (cf., e.g., Hügel 13-32; Frizzoni and Tomkowiak; Maase, "Selbstfeier" 219-42). With regard to popular culture, the type of experience which the autonomy aesthetic presumes for their model of distancing is at best classified as a borderline case (cf., e.g., Fuhr).

However, the empirical basis for such generalizations is weak. Other studies on popular culture reception indicate that in the process of appropriation, distance and alternatives to one's own lifestyle play a significant role, and qualitative changes in subjectivization are possible (cf., e.g., Willis, *Jugend-Stile*; Geimer; Mikos). This is at least an indication that the empirical analysis of *aesthetic experiences* of mass art might reveal potential for anti-hegemonic self-formation.

In conclusion, there is, according to this author at least, cause to examine the previous debates on 'resistance,' popular culture, and the decentering of the subject with a certain soberness. The instrumentality of the micropolitical potential for change of forms of action that are meant to limit the force and hegemony of the 'power bloc' is still decidedly unclear. It appears that research approaches that focus directly on the

---

20 | Fluck concludes from the poststructuralist debate that "aesthetic experience [...] becomes the only remaining hope left for cultural transformation" ("Resistance" 22), yet popular culture is not discussed.

"analyses of macropolitical hegemonic constellations" (Marchart 244) have advantages.

Previous research on 'resistance' has certainly not led down false paths or to dead ends; on the contrary, it has established the foundations of the further development of empirical studies on micropolitics and popular culture. Issues and questions in this field are in a state of flux. Analyses of the use of mass arts by activists might open up new avenues of enquiry into every-day practices that tend towards self-formation in a predominantly hegemonically encoded popular culture landscape. In pursuing an egalitarian 'aesthetic regime' (cf. Ranciere 37-90, esp. 40-43), is its worth asking whether the potential for distancing and alterity in mass art can be discerned, and in which practices of aesthetic experience it can be appropriated for self-formation.

Translation, including quotations for which there is no official English version:
Michael Larsen

WORKS CITED

Adorno, Theodor W. *Aesthetic Theory.* Edited by Gretel Adorno and Rolf Tiedemann, translated by Robert Hullot Kentor, continuum, 1997.

Alkemeyer, Thomas, Gunilla Budde, and Dagmar Freist, editors. *Selbst- Bildungen: Soziale und kulturelle Praktiken der Subjektivierung,* transcript, 2013.

Alkemeyer, Thomas. "Subjektivierung in sozialen Praktiken: Umrisse einer praxeologischen Analytik." *Selbst-Bildungen: Soziale und kulturelle Praktiken der Subjektivierung,* edited by Thomas Alkemeyer, Gunilla Budde, and Dagmar Freist, transcript, 2013, pp. 33-68.

Babe, Robert E. *Cultural Studies and Political Economy: Toward a New Integration.* Rowman & Littlefield, 2009.

Bachmann, Götz. *Kollegialität: Eine Ethnographie der Belegschaftskultur im Kaufhaus.* Campus, 2014.

Benjamin, Walter. "Das Kunstwerk im Zeitalter der technischen Reproduzierbarkeit." *Gesammelte Schriften,* by Benjamin, vol. 1.2., Suhrkamp, 1974, pp. 471-508.

Bourdieu, Pierre. *Die feinen Unterschiede: Kritik der gesellschaftlichen Urteilskraft.* Suhrkamp, 1982.

Bürger, Peter. *Theorie der Avantgarde.* Suhrkamp, 1974
Butler, Judith. *Psyche der Macht.* Suhrkamp, 2001.
—. *Das Unbehagen der Geschlechter.* Suhrkamp, 1991.
Certeau, Michel de. *Kunst des Handelns.* Merve, 1988.
Ege, Moritz. "Birmingham—Tübingen: Cultural Studies und Empirische Kulturwissenschaft in den 1970er Jahren." *Historische Anthropologie,* vol. 22, no. 2, 2014, pp. 149-81.
—. *"Ein Proll mit Klasse": Mode, Popkultur und soziale Ungleichheiten unter jungen Männern in Berlin.* Campus, 2013.
Emig, Brigitte. *Die Veredelung des Arbeiters: Sozialdemokratie als Kulturbewegung.* Campus, 1980.
Ernst, Heiko. *Innenwelten: Warum Tagträume uns kreativer, mutiger und gelassener machen.* Klett-Cotta, 2011.
Fenemore, Mark. *Sex, Thugs and Rock'n'Roll: Teenage Rebels in Cold-War East Germany.* Berghahn, 2007.
Fiske, John. *Power Plays, Power Works.* Verso, 1993.
—. *Understanding Popular Culture.* Unwin Hyman, 1989.
Fluck, Winfried. "Die Wissenschaft vom systemischen Effekt: Von der Counter-Culture zu den Race, Class, and Gender Studies." *Der Geist der Unruhe: 1968 im Vergleich. Wissenschaft—Literatur—Medien,* edited by Rainer Rosenberg, Inge Münz-Koenen, and Petra Boden, Akademie Verlag, 2000, pp. 111-24.
—. "Resistance! Cultural Studies and the Question of Cultural Change." *REAL—Yearbook of Research in English and American Literature,* vol. 20, 2005, pp. 11-26.
Fredel, Jürgen. "Art: 'Autonomie der Kunst.'" *Historisch-Kritisches Wörterbuch des Marxismus,* vol. 1, Argument, 1994, pp. 774-79.
Frizzoni, Brigitte, and Ingrid Tomkowiak, editors. *Unterhaltung: Konzepte—Formen—Wirkungen.* Chronos, 2006.
Fuchs, Max. "Kunstfreiheit und Kunstautonomie: Facetten einer komplexen Leitformel." *Handbuch Kulturelle Bildung,* edited by Hildegard Bockhorst, Vanessa-Isabelle Reinwand, and Wolfgang Zacharias, kopaed, 2012, pp. 193-98.
Fuhr, Michael. *Populäre Musik und Ästhetik: Die historisch-philosophische Rekonstruktion einer Geringschätzung.* transcript, 2007.
Geimer, Alexander. *Filmrezeption und Filmaneignung: Eine qualitativ-rekonstruktive Studie über Praktiken der Rezeption bei Jugendlichen.* VS Verlag, 2010.

Hall, Stuart, and Tony Jefferson, editors. *Resistance through Rituals: Youth Subcultures in Post-War Britain*. Routledge, 1976.
Hall, Stuart. "Encoding/Decoding." *Culture, Media, Language*, edited by Hall et al., Hutchinson, 1980, pp. 128-38.
—. "Notes on Deconstructing 'The Popular.'" *People's History and Socialist Theory*, edited by Richard Samuel, Routledge & Kegan Paul, 1981, pp. 227-40.
Hausmanninger, Thomas. *Kritik der medienethischen Vernunft: Die ethische Diskussion über den Film in Deutschland im 20. Jahrhundert*. Fink, 1993.
Hebdige, Dick. *Subculture: The Meaning of Style*. Methuen, 1979.
Hecken, Thomas. *Avant-Pop: Von Susan Sontag über Prada und Sonic Youth bis Lady Gaga und zurück*. Posth, 2012.
—. *Pop: Geschichte eines Konzepts 1955-2009*. transcript, 2009.
Hertel, Thomas. "Von der 'Massenzivilisation' zur 'Kulturindustrie': Theodor W. Adornos Zuwendung zur 'Massenkultur'-Thematik." *Zwischen Angstmetapher und Terminus: Theorien der Massenkultur seit Nietzsche*, edited by Nobert Krenzlin, Akademie Verlag, 1992, pp. 118-48.
Hesmondhalgh, David. *The Cultural Industries*. 3rd ed., Sage, 2013.
Hügel, Hans-Otto. "Ästhetische Zweideutigkeit der Unterhaltung: Eine Skizze ihrer Theorie." *Lob des Mainstreams: Zu Begriff und Geschichte von Unterhaltung und populärer Kultur*, edited by Hügel, Halem, 2007, pp. 13-32.
Jenkins, Henry. *Fans, Bloggers, and Gamers: Exploring Participatory Culture*. New York UP, 2006.
—. *Textual Poachers*. Routledge, 1992.
Krüger, Heinz-Hermann, editor. *"Die Elvis-Tolle, die hatte ich mir unauffällig wachsen lassen": Lebensgeschichte und jugendliche Alltagskultur in den 50er Jahren*. Leske + Budrich, 1985.
Laclau, Ernesto, and Chantal Mouffe. *Hegemony and Socialist Strategy: Towards a Radical Democratic Politics*. Verso, 1985.
Laclau, Ernesto. *Politics and Ideology in Marxist Theory*. New Left, 1977.
Lindenberger, Thomas. "Eigen-Sinn, Herrschaft und kein Widerstand: Version: 1.0." *Docupedia-Zeitgeschichte*, 2 Sep. 2014, docupedia.de/zg/Eigensinn. Accessed 7 Apr. 2016.
Lindner, Rolf. *Die Stunde der Cultural Studies*. WUV, 2000, pp. 15-47.
Lüdtke, Alf. *Eigen-Sinn: Fabrikalltag, Arbeitererfahrungen und Politik vom Kaiserreich bis in den Faschismus*. Ergebnisse, 1993.

Maase, Kaspar, editor. *Die Schönheiten des Populären: Ästhetische Erfahrung der Gegenwart*. Campus, 2008.

Maase, Kaspar. *BRAVO Amerika: Erkundungen zur Jugendkultur in der Bundesrepublik der fünfziger Jahre*. Junius, 1992.

—. *Die Kinder der Massenkultur: Kontroversen um Schmutz und Schund seit dem Kaiserreich*. Campus, 2012.

—. "Geschmack und Qualität: Probleme der Wertung populärer Kultur in Alltag und Wissenschaft." *Macher—Medien—Publika: Beiträge der Europäischen Ethnologie zu Geschmack und Vergnügen*, edited by Kaspar Maase, Christoph Bareither, Brigitte Frizzoni, and Mirjam Nast, Königshausen & Neumann, 2014, pp. 50-65.

—. "Populärkultur—Unterhaltung—Vergnügung: Überlegungen zur Systematik eines Forschungsfeldes." *Unterhaltung und Vergnügung. Beiträge der Europäischen Ethnologie zur Populärkulturforschung*, edited by Christoph Bareither, Kaspar Maase, and Mirjam Nast, Königshausen & Neumann, 2013, pp. 24-36.

—. "Radioten, Glotzer, Unterschichtfernsehen? Zu den Bildungseffekten von Massenmedien." *Vom Wandel eines Ideals: Bildung, Universität und Gesellschaft in Deutschland*, edited by Nikolaus Buschmann and Ute Planert, Dietz, 2010, pp. 125-41.

—. "'Rhythmus hinter Gittern': Die Halbstarken und die innere Modernisierung der Arbeiterkultur in den fünfziger Jahren." *Das Recht der Gewöhnlichkeit: Über populäre Kultur*, by Maase, TVV, 2011, pp. 145-88.

—. "Selbstfeier und Kompensation: Zum Studium der Unterhaltung." *Unterwelten der Kultur: Themen und Theorien der volkskundlichen Kulturwissenschaft*, edited by Kaspar Maase and Bernd Jürgen Warneken, Böhlau, 2003, pp. 219-42.

—. "Unscharfe Begriffe, Unterscheidungen und Familienähnlichkeiten: Zur kulturwissenschaftlichen Theoretisierung des Populären." *Das Reine und das Vermischte—15 Jahre danach*, edited by Ines Keller and Fabian Jacobs, Waxmann, 2015, pp. 99-111.

—. *Was macht Populärkultur politisch?* VS Verlag, 2010.

Marchart, Oliver. *Cultural Studies*. UVK, 2008.

Marcuse, Herbert. "Über den affirmativen Charakter der Kultur." *Kultur und Gesellschaft I*, by Marcuse, Suhrkamp, 1965, pp. 56-101.

McGuigan, Jim. *Cultural Populism*. Routledge, 1992.

"Media Perspektiven: Basisdaten 2014." *ARD-Werbung SALES & SERVICES*, www.media-perspektiven.de/publikationen/basisdaten/. Accessed 7 Apr. 2016.

Mikos, Lothar. *"Es wird dein Leben!": Familienserien im Fernsehen und im Alltagsleben der Zuschauer*. MakS, 1993.

Müller, Michael, Horst Bredekamp, Berthold Hinz, Franz-Joachim Verspohl, Jürgen Fredel, and Ursula Apitzsch. *Autonomie der Kunst: Zur Genese und Kritik einer bürgerlichen Kategorie*. Suhrkamp, 1972.

Müller, Eggo. "'Pleasure and Resistance': John Fiskes Beitrag zur Populärkulturtheorie." *montage/av*, vol. 2, no. 1, 1993, pp. 52-66.

Poiger, Uta G. *Jazz, Rock, and Rebels: Cold War Politics and American Culture in a Divided Germany*. University of California Press, 2000.

Rancière, Jacques. *Ist Kunst widerständig?* Translated by Frank Ruda and Jan Völker, Merve, 2008.

Reckwitz, Andreas. *Das Hybride Subjekt: Eine Theorie der Subjektkulturen von der Bürgerlichen Moderne zur Postmoderne*. Velbrück Wissenschaft, 2006.

—. *Subjekt*. transcript, 2008.

Ricken, Norbert. "Anerkennung als Adressierung: Über die Bedeutung von Anerkennung für Subjektivationsprozesse." *Selbst-Bildungen*, edited by Thomas Alkemeyer, Gunilla Budde, and Dagmar Freist, transcript, 2013, pp. 69-99.

Rosanvallon, Pierre. *Die Gesellschaft der Gleichen*. Hamburger Edition, 2013.

Ross, Andrew. *No Respect: Intellectuals and Popular Culture*. Routledge, 1989.

Schiller, Friedrich. "Letters upon the Aesthetic Education of Man." *Literary and Philosophical Essays: French, German and Italian*, edited by Charles W. Elliot, vol. 32, P.F. Collier & Son, 1910, pp. 219-313.

Steinert, Heinz. *Kulturindustrie*. 3rd ed., Westfälisches Dampfboot, 2008.

Storey, John. *Cultural Theory and Popular Culture: An Introduction*. 6th ed., Pearson, 2012.

Storim, Mirjam. *Ästhetik im Umbruch: Zur Funktion der 'Rede über Kunst' um 1900 am Beispiel der Debatte um Schmutz und Schund*. Niemeyer, 2002.

Sutter, Ove. *Erzählte Prekarität: Autobiographische Verhandlungen von Arbeit und Leben im Postfordismus*. Campus, 2013.

Tamagne, Florence. "Le 'blouson noir': Codes vestimentaires, subcultures rock et sociabilités adolescentes dans la France des années 1950 et 1960." *Paraitre et apparances en Europe occidentale du Moyen-Age à nos jours*, edited by Isabelle Parésys, Presses Universitaires du Septentrion, 2008, pp. 99-114.

Wellgraf, Stefan. *Hauptschüler: Zur gesellschaftlichen Produktion von Verachtung*. transcript, 2012.

Wietschorke, Jens. "Schundkampf von links: Eine Skizze zur sozialdemokratischen Jugendschriftenkritik vor 1914." *Internationales Archiv für Sozialgeschichte der deutschen Literatur*, vol. 34, no. 2, 2009, pp. 157-75.

Willis, Paul. *Profane Culture*. Routledge and Kegan Paul, 1978.

—, with the collaboration of Simon Jones, Joyce Canaan, and Geoff Hurd. *Jugend-Stile: Zur Ästhetik der gemeinsamen Kultur*. Argument, 1991.

Winter, Rainer. *Die Kunst des Eigensinns: Cultural Studies als Kritik der Macht*. Velbrück Wissenschaft, 2001.

Wolfzettel, Friedrich, and Michael Einfalt. "Art. 'Autonomie.'" *Ästhetische Grundbegriffe*, vol. 1, Metzler, 2000, pp. 432-79.

Wolin, Richard. "Introduction to the Discussion of 'Need and Culture in Nietzsche.'" *Constellations*, vol. 8, no. 1, Mar. 2001, pp. 127-29. *Wiley Online Library*, doi: 10.1111/1467-8675.00218.

Resistance as a Way out of One-Dimensionality
The Contribution of Herbert Marcuse to a Critical Analysis of the Present

Rainer Winter

1. INTRODUCTION

Taking *One-Dimensional Man* (1964) as a starting point, I would like to show in the following what an important contribution the work of Herbert Marcuse can make to a critical theory of the present. 50 years after its first publication, this book seems more relevant than ever. It allows us to understand how domination is exerted and maintained in late capitalism that is today organized according to neoliberal principles. It also allows us to ask if there can be alternatives to this society. To date, one-dimensionality has proven itself to be a relevant basic concept of critical theory that first of all critically analyzes society as it is, by revealing the forces that sustain, legitimize, and stabilize the existing structures. However, critical theory is primarily interested in those forces that can negate and subversively circumvent the system and can contribute to emancipation. Therefore, Marcuse thought dialectically, criticizing late capitalistic society from the background of unrealized possibilities and seeking forms of resistance and escape routes. His central theme from the thirties to the end of his life was the question of how liberation can be made possible.

This questioning is, however, no longer central in more recent critical theory. For example, Jürgen Habermas scarcely mentioned Marcuse in *The Theory of Communicative Action* (1981), which was published two years after his death, although he knew his work well (cf. Habermas et al.). Instead, he develops a model of communicative understanding as a new basis of critical theory. Communicative rationality is formally defined. It follows procedures. However, there is no more space in his approach for the power of negativity, which Marcuse and also Adorno felt committed to. Saying this, however, in Habermas a decisive dimension of critical theory is lost which still has a place in social reality today. For example, transnational social movements that link the use of digital technologies with street protests show that critical resistance is possible and corporate capitalism can be challenged (cf. Juris; Winter, *Widerstand im Netz*). Besides, a form of politics is further developed in the field of aesthetics (cf. Rancière, *The Politics*) that transcends the one-dimensionality of everyday life as well.

In order to view these connections more closely and to show how important Marcuse's critical theory is for an analysis of the present and the role of resistance, I will firstly discuss the relationship between liberation and one-dimensionality in his work (2). Then I will show that one-dimensionality shapes the social life of the present (3). By discussing central aspects of Habermas's work, I will make the case for maintaining a dialectical perspective, because it gives the chance to criticize one-dimensionality and to strive for a radical transformation of society (4). Drawing on current examples from social movements and from the field of aesthetics, I will show how one-dimensionality can be challenged and overcome by different forms of resistance (5). A short conclusion follows on the relevance of Marcuse's critical theory (6).

2. The Relationship between Liberation and One-Dimensionality in the Work of Herbert Marcuse

In my view, the fascination and the uniqueness of Marcuse's work lies in the central theme of emancipation. Although Marcuse makes the structures of domination in advanced industrial society in their stability, their apparent insurmountable form, and in their power of integration quite clear, at the same time he points out that, in the face of economic productivity and social richness, a qualitative change, another world, is imaginable. According to Marcuse, human liberation is possible in late capitalism, but its system consisting of technical, political, and economic apparatuses has negated this perspective successfully and effectively until today.

Already in "The Concept of Essence" ("Zum Begriff des Wesens"), Marcuse, following Hegel, differentiated between essence, the potential of hidden possibilities, and appearance, the actual reality. "[...] At the state of human development we have reached, there are real opportunities for a fulfilment of human life in all areas which are not realized in the present form of social life processes"[1] (Marcuse, "Zum Begriff des Wesens" 71; translation: RW). Marcuse states a "tension between the potential and the existing, between what humans and things can be and what they actually are"[2] ("Zum Begriff des Wesens" 68; translation: RW). In this way, potentially liberating tendencies exist within the social process but must not be being realized. Thus, Marcuse claims that "[t]he care for the human being stands at the center of the theory; he should be liberated from real emergency and from real misery and should realize himself"[3] ("Zum Begriff des Wesens" 71; translation: RW). Here it becomes clear that dialectical thinking for Marcuse has a negating or emancipatory power. This seeks not only to understand or interpret the world, but rather to contribute to its transformation. Positivism on the contrary is content with an understanding of the 'facticity of appearances' and so perseveres with one-dimensionality.

In *One-Dimensional Man*, one-dimensionality emphatically becomes a historical concept. In advanced industrial society or in late capitalism, the emancipatory power of intrinsic negation has been lost. The proletariat, the revolutionary subject in the work of Marx, is also integrated into the repressive system of domination. This process has advanced so far that the proletariat has even become a carrier of the system. The economic, technical, and political apparatuses have successfully neutralized its

---

1 | Original: "[...] auf dem erreichten Stadium der Entwicklung der Menschheit sind reale Möglichkeiten einer Erfüllung des menschlichen Lebens in allen Bereichen vorhanden, die durch die gegenwärtige Form des gesellschaftlichen Lebensprozesses nicht verwirklicht werden."

2 | Original: "Die Spannung zwischen dem Seinkönnenden und dem Daseienden, zwischen dem, was der Mensch und die Dinge sein können, und dem, was sie faktisch sind, ist einer der zentralen Hebel der Theorie."

3 | Original: "Die Sorge um den Menschen tritt in das Zentrum der Theorie; er soll aus der wirklichen Not und dem wirklichen Elend zu sich selbst befreit werden."

inner negation. The possibility of liberation no longer seems to be given. Alternatives or potentialities that could overcome the existing system cannot be seen. The industrial and technological rationality has turned the subjects into appendages. It is marked by "pure instrumentality" and "efficacy" (Kellner, *Herbert Marcuse* 234). Society itself is no longer primarily characterized by contradictions and conflicts. Each form of resistance or opposition is apparently neutralized or integrated by a coherent and overall structure of domination.

At first glance, therefore, in the *One-Dimensional Man*, we must face an extremely pessimistic diagnosis. A world run by bureaucracy and culture industry destroys the individuality of the subject, his or her private sphere, and manipulates his or her needs. However, Douglas Kellner has suggested that we would be misunderstanding Marcuse, if we followed this interpretation of total domination (cf. *Herbert Marcuse* 234-40). Marcuse would in no way completely deny any possibility of contradiction, conflict, resistance, or revolt.

> In Marcuse's usage the adjective 'one-dimensional' describes an epistemological distinction between signifying practices that conform to pre-existing structures, norms and behaviour in thought and practice, and 'bi-dimensional' thought which appraises values, ideas and behaviour in terms of possibilities that transcend the established state of affairs. (Kellner, *Herbert Marcuse* 235)

In late capitalism, there are also values, attitudes, ideas, and behaviors that are resistant and challenge the existing order. In this context, Raymond Williams (cf. Winter, "The Perspectives") spoke of emergent perceptions, perspectives and practices that can produce an oppositional or alternative culture: "It is true that in the structure of any actual society, and especially in its class structure, there is always a social basis for elements of the cultural process that are alternative or oppositional to the dominant elements" (Williams 124). However, the one-dimensional man is bound in the dominant structure of feeling and is not interested in transforming the existing relations; he does not even consider this at all.

It is also important to put down that Marcuse describes and highlights bluntly and drastically the dominant tendencies of advanced industrial societies, its structures of domination, and as a result its one-dimensionality. Nevertheless, Marcuse has not given up hope for change however, as he makes clear in the essay, "On Changing the World," for example. On the one hand, he sees the tendency of the system to hold radical, social forces back, but on the other hand, he points to the desire of many to abolish the existing society and its structures. He feels the duty of the (socialist) intellectual is to analyze without illusion the reasons and possibilities for this. Marcuse states, "No social system is safe from change—that is an obvious truth, which should always be repeated" (qtd. in Tauber 70).

The negative social diagnosis is therefore linked to a hope for global transformation and to a call for this. Zvi Tauber has shown that this is not a contradiction in Marcuse's theory but rather is anchored in the conditions of one-dimensional existence themselves (cf. 72). At this point, we should also point out that Antonio Gramsci also argued for a connection between the pessimism of intellectual social analysis and an optimism of the will. In more recent critical theory, Alain Badiou focuses on the 'event' which is unforeseeable and more than the sum of the processes which have led to it. In a further step, I would now like to show that one-dimensionality proves to be a useful category for a critical analysis of the present as well.

3. ONE-DIMENSIONALITY AND NEO-LIBERALISM

When we consider sociological diagnoses of the present, it is often stressed that in the West, we live in pluralistic societies that are apparently characterized by social and cultural differentiation, opportunities to make choices, individualization, or a "reflexive project of the self" (Giddens, *Modernity* 180). In the process of globalization, we are confronted with processes of detraditionalization (cf. Heelas, Lash, and Morris). Traditions are seen as losing their binding character, while, at the same time, we are confronted with a multiplicity of meaning systems, from which we can or have to choose. Sir Anthony Giddens established this at the beginning of the 21st Century: "We have good reason to hope that the cosmopolitan attitude will win the day. Tolerance towards cultural diversity and democracy belong together—and democracy is spreading everywhere across the world at present" (*Entfesselte Welt* 15; translation: RW). At the same time, Ulrich Beck evoked the new "children of freedom" (*The Brave*) who would see themselves as actively engaged and would look for their own luck. Both authors accept and welcome the new possibilities of capitalism. Nevertheless, Beck—in contrast to Giddens—argues that a new critical theory from a cosmopolitan perspective is required to understand the new forms of social inequality in the global age und to develop counter-powers (cf. Beck, *Power*). But he cannot imagine a non-capitalistic world society.

A more radical analysis which is carried out principally from the two-dimensional thinking of the dialectics shows, however, that the economic organization of all parts of life presents a historically unmatchable homogenization according to the principals of the market, of competition, of efficiency, and of reproducibility.[4] This does not bar processes of heterogenization from being a part of it, for example, when the shaping of one's own life is concerned. Michael Hardt and Toni Negri rightly speak of a real subsumption of work and of all parts of life under processes of capital accumulation: "Capital has become a world. Use value and all the other references to values and processes of valorization that were conceived to be outside the capitalist mode of production have vanished" (386).

Present existence is one-dimensional because market fundamentalism acts as a type of religion, which the whole world has embraced. It did not only shape the economy but also politics, the health system, education, universities, all fields of society, as well as our thinking (cf. Freytag; Zima 53). For most, it is impossible to conceive of a society that is not organized along market capitalist lines. Possible alternatives are also forgotten or discredited. Even advanced sociology of globalization celebrates the market and its possibilities. Without doubt, contemporary sociology that has turned away from philosophy and its two-dimensional thinking is generally characterized by a "paralysis of criticism" (Marcuse, *One-Dimensional Man* xxxix).

It seems therefore advisable to use Marcuse's concept of one-dimensionality for the analysis of the present, even if Western societies have changed many of the parameters that were important for Marcuse's analysis. Examples of this are the disappearance of the (old) East-West conflict, the growing destruction of the welfare state, life's increasing uncertainty that can be seen in mass unemployment and poverty among the young and elderly. The contemporary conditions are one-dimensional because there appears to be no alternative. From this background, the importance of critical theory and a dialectical thinking bound to determinate negation becomes clear.

---

4 | Neoliberalism can be interpreted as a form of counterrevolution, as Charles Reitz and Stephan Spartan show in "The Political Economy of Predation and Counterrevolution: Recalling Marcuse on the Radical Goals of Socialism."

It can bring liberation from the social constraints of late capitalism, show forms of critical resistance and reveal emancipatory dimensions (cf. Pippin). Jürgen Habermas, however, has declared the radical potential of critical theory in its first generation as old-fashioned and has tried to eliminate it (cf. *Theory of Communicative Action. Volume 1*).

4. Liberation and Understanding

Habermas criticizes Horkheimer and Adorno for failing to clarify the principles of their own criticism in their analysis of instrumental rationality and its effects (cf. Habermas, *Theory of Communicative Action. Volume 1*; cf. Horkheimer and Adorno). In contrast, his theory of communicative action is designed from the outset as a theory of rationality that can set out its critical rules. To that end, Habermas has made a paradigm change. He no longer analyzes reason from the perspective of a theory of consciousness but on the basis of a theory of language and discourse. He is of the opinion that it is not justifiable from the view of social theory as rationality can be assigned to subjects. In contrast, the 'linguistic turn' of philosophy can show that rationality can be found in the structures of linguistic understanding. "Linguistic understanding as a mechanism of co-ordinating action is the focus of interest" (Habermaß, *Theorie* 370; translation: RW) for a theory of communicative action. This means reaching an understanding is possible if the conditions are given that make actions intersubjectively understandable.

Finally the concept of communicative action refers to the interaction of at least two subjects capable of speech and action who establish interpersonal relations [...]. The actors seek to reach an understanding about the action situation and their plans of action in order to coordinate their actions by the way of agreement. The central concept of interpretation refers in the first instance to negotiating definitions of the situation which admit of consensus. (Habermas, *Theory of Communicative Action. Volume 1* 86)

Linguistic understanding is reflexive and means validity claims must be justified. For Habermas, there is a rationality anchored in every day communicative practices that can be formally reconstructed through the reflexivity of validity claims. The actors have the capacity to act rationally and to make decisions in the context of given rules and available knowledge. In the concept of communicative rationality, understanding replaces reconciliation (Adorno) or liberation (Marcuse). For Habermas, we have surpassed thinking of the subject and its negating criticism. Instead, he has developed a formal process for reconstructing rules. However, this does not consider the content of communicative rationality under normative criteria. Therefore, it remains unclear how the communicative action of ascertained claims can lead to a critical theory (cf. Thyen 252-53).

At this point it becomes clear what we lose when critical theory focuses on understanding and the utopia of communicative rationality. It is the field of experience that plays a decisive role in the dialectics. The given state of affairs can be transcended by the subject who, in this way, can show resistance to the system. He/she is more than a cognitive and rational agent. He/she is an "embodied subject" (Farr 154-55) with feelings, phantasies and desires. For example, the "new sensibility" that Marcuse detected in the student movement of the 60s was based on a new sensual and aesthetic experience of the self, of others and of nature (*An Essay* 22). Douglas Kellner summarizes this perspective in Marcuse's *Essay on Liberation*:

> In *Essay on Liberation*, Marcuse argues that the cultural subversion contained in the new sensibility manifests in instinctual, moral and aesthetic revolt against the established society, leading to political rebellion [...]. The revolt is generated by new needs and values which represent a break with the needs and consciousness of consumer society. (Kellner, *Herbert Marcuse* 341; cf. Kellner, *Marcuse*)

So negative dialectics is a material philosophy that takes into consideration the non-identical in experience. The non-identical cannot be precisely understood through the reconstruction of rules but it can be found in experiences. Therefore, critical theory should not forgo experience that is conducted by theory or reflection (cf. Thyen 269). Marcuse's and also Adorno's works show the rationality of knowledge based on negative dialectics, which is not necessarily taken up in formally founded communicative rationality.

Therefore, the paradigm change demanded by Habermas does not seem to be required. We do not have to follow him.[5] Rather, practicing critical theory today is about integrating both paradigms. In the works of Habermas, who is a convinced social democrat, we do not find a radical criticism of late capitalistic society as we do in Marcuse. He criticizes the colonization of the lifeworld by system imperatives, but does not challenge the system itself, that is late capitalistic economy. The protests from Seattle to Occupy Wall Street have made clear that even today a radical critical resistance to capitalism exists based on the experiences of those involved.

5. Radical Criticism of Neo-liberalism

These "networks of outrage and hope" (title), as Manuel Castells calls them, are organized, like global capitalism, on the basis of digital technologies and wireless networks. They seek to effect social change and to create a different world.

By engaging in the production of mass media messages, and by developing autonomous networks of horizontal communication, citizens of the Information Age become able to invent new programs for their lives with the materials of their suffering, fears, dreams and hopes. They build their projects by sharing their experience. They subvert the practice of communication as usual by occupying the medium and creating the message. They overcome the powerlessness of their solitary despair by networking their desire. They fight the powers that be by identifying the networks that are. (Castells 9)

The question that is asked is whether a qualitative change in late capitalistic society is not only imaginable, but even realizable by these form of resistances. From this background, the networks, above all, are

---

5 | In his book *Critical Theory and Democratic Vision: Herbert Marcuse and Recent Liberation Philosophies*, Andrew Farr argues that the approach of Habermas based on the ideal of a rational discourse cannot be considered as a theory of liberation. "First, it is overly restrictive of forms of discourse or communication. Second, it is overly restrictive with respect to its understanding of the formation of subjectivity. Third, it has a narrow view of the lifeworld. As a result of these limitations Habermas's theory is one-dimensional" (151-52).

interesting that challenge the one-dimensionality of corporate capitalism and champion social justice.

At the end of the previous century, it seemed as if there were no alternatives to the one-dimensional, neo-liberal, organized society. The ideology of the free market, which was heralded incessantly in politics and the media, appeared to have finally been accepted generally. Bit by bit, but firstly in the Global South, a counter movement arose which was still unnoticed by many, until it became spectacularly visible for the first time in the protests and mobilizations against the meetings of the World Trade Organization in November 1999 in Seattle. To date, plenty of protests have come together against globalization as defined by corporations and which support democratically shaped alternatives (cf. Kahn and Kellner; cf. Juris).

Symbolically successful resistance against corporate capitalism does not only take place on the streets but primarily by means of digital technologies. Therefore, the evolving networks of activists are both locally anchored and globally interconnected. This interactive character promotes autonomy, open access and horizontal co-operation. Therefore, a protest can grow easily; it can be deliberated on and modified. In this way, resistance, participation, and direct democracy can be experienced, practiced, and lived. Now it becomes possible once more to imagine a world that is organized according to ideals of social justice and equality (cf. Smith). The late capitalistic reality, which is propagated without alternatives by politicians, scientists, and the mass media, is fundamentally challenged and opposed.

The new social movements create counter public spheres that are based on social networks 'online' and 'offline.' Therefore, movements have a viral character, which, above all, Occupy has shown. Starting from New York, this has given rise across the world to spaces for protest. These are organized horizontally and create a social bond by common experiences and practices, which can be disrupted quickly but can potentially be re-established again and again. Socially institutionalized domination meets a counter power of (digital) resistance from the new social movements. Autonomous communication networks arise in which new outlooks and concepts for life and society are developed and approved together.

We have seen that Marcuse in his analysis of one-dimensional society could not identify concrete tendencies or forces that negated this state of affairs and would remodel it in a revolutionary practice. "Confronted with the total character of the achievements of advanced industrial society, critical theory is left without the rationale for transcending this society" (Marcuse, *One-Dimensional Man* xlvi). However, he thinks this transcendence is necessary and so hopes for it. "In the face of apparently contradictory facts, the critical analysis continues to insist that the need for qualitative change is as pressing as ever before" (xlv). Marcuse therefore does not exclude the possibility for change. Throughout his life, he was searching for social and cultural forces of negation.

Thus, in his writing after *One-Dimensional Man*, for example, in *An Essay on Liberation* (1969), he closely examined and welcomed the potential for liberation in the 60s. In the students, however, he saw no revolutionary force but hoped that they could act as catalysts in their criticism and their protest. The digital activism of our time also reacts against the assimilating and integrating powers of one-dimensional capitalism. Has a real opportunity arisen here that can immanently negate and transform the established society? From the background of Marcuse's theory, skepticism is appropriate. The forces of state authority and of ideological as well as commercial incorporation are not rated highly enough. A radical social change is only then possible when this critique of corporate capitalism is taken up, shared and practiced by many. Nevertheless, this rebellious protest shows that the late capitalistic system is not monolithic and closed. Activists resist and challenge its legitimacy. They believe in a different world and show in their networks that this utopian world is more than a dream (cf. Juris 9). Finally, I will look more closely at the field of aesthetics. According to Marcuse, imagination allows, above all, transcendence of the given society and the imagining of a different world.

6. Art and Revolution

In his article, "Art in the One-dimensional Society" (1973) Marcuse writes: "[...] the survival of art may turn out to be the only weak link that today connects the present with the hope of the future" (qtd. in Reitz 166). He states that a new reality can be realized by means of art: "Not political art, not politics as art, but art as the architecture of a free society" (qtd. in Reitz 170). Marcuse continues by stating that art can convey new forms of perception and understanding that let us discern and experience social reality differently (cf. "Art" 79). Thus he also stresses here and in his last book, *The Aesthetic Dimension*, the important significance and active power of the aesthetic form, which should be materialized in society itself. Marcuse states that the quality of the aesthetic form reveals the political potential of art (cf. *The Aesthetic* ix). It transcends the existing repressive society and subverts its dominant framing of reality. It establishes its own reality principle. The fictitious world of art becomes the real reality.

> Its indictment of the established reality and its invocation of the beautiful image ('schöner Schein') of liberation are grounded precisely in the dimensions where art transcends its social determination and emancipates itself from the given universe of discourse and behaviour while preserving its overwhelming presence. Thereby art creates the realm in which the *subversion of experience* proper to art becomes possible: the world formed by art is recognized as a reality which is suppressed and distorted in the given reality. (Marcuse, *The Aesthetic* 6)

For Marcuse the aesthetic form itself carries meaning that transcends the given state of affairs. The experience of art can transform the subjectivity of recipients by liberating it from social constraints and norms. Finding its own inner voice, articulating its "inner history" (Marcuse, *The Aesthetic* 5), its "Eigensinn" (Winter, *Die Kunst*), can prepare for processes of changing culture and society (cf. Marcuse, *The Aesthetic* 32-33). "In a situation where the miserable reality can be changed only through radical political praxis, the concern with aesthetics demands justification [...] it seems that art as art expresses a truth, an experience, a necessity which, although not in the domain of radical praxis, are nevertheless essential components of revolution" (Marcuse, *The Aesthetic* 1). Marcuse states that, through its emancipatory potential, art negates the conditions of one-dimensionality. Charles Reitz comes in his comprehensive study on the development of Marcuse's aesthetics to the conclusion that

> [i]n Marcuse's estimation, the aesthetic dimension presents the emancipatory image of the social potential of the human species at the same time as it presents a depiction of factual human distress. The subject matter of genuine historical study is the highly conflicted sensuous and affective essence of humanity. The foundation of Marcuse's protest and the basis of his recommended political activity against the one-dimensional society is his theory of aesthetic negation. (226)

In the following, I will show how relevant and of current interest these considerations of Marcuse are in the works of the French philosopher Jacques Rancière on the politics of aesthetics, which are currently being intensively discussed.

For Rancière, as well, the political can also emerge from aesthetic practices. He thinks that the space is constituted through a distribution of the sensible, of the visible and sayable. Following Schiller and Kant, he sees the political meaning of art in modernity in the fact that it can produce a redistribution of the sensible by a "dissensus" (*Dissensus* 115-33). It can fabricate new objects and new forms of perception that do not occur in the everyday framings of the world. Art creates a counter-world of resistance that challenges the order of a given society and so steps into a polemic relationship with the existing world. Therefore, Rancière attributes an active force to art. It produces a dissensus when the parameters of our sensible world are unsettled and transcended. Then, this world is not only experienced differently but also structurally transformed. The aesthetic revolution consists precisely in radically changing the meaning of life.

Like Marcuse, Rancière draws on Friedrich Schiller's reflections "On the Aesthetic Education of Man": "We could reformulate this thought [of Schiller] as follows: there exists a specific sensory experience that holds the promise of both a new world of Art and a new life for individuals and the community, namely the *aesthetic*" (*Dissensus* 115). Art contains the political promise of equality and an aesthetic form of life that is dissensual to everyday experiences of the world. Through the form of art, which reveals new dimensions and perspectives, the distribution of the sensible, which according to Rancière is controlled by the police order in modernity, is challenged. At the same time, equality is created between producers and recipients in the aesthetic regime. Even the recipient is creative. As a spectator he/she is emancipated. He/she reflects on art and simultaneously articulates equality.

Rancière does not refer to Marcuse. According to his own testimony, he discovered Schiller's letter on the aesthetic education by chance in a Parisian second-hand-bookshop (cf. *La Méthode* 137). Nevertheless, his works shows why Marcuse's reflections on the political meaning of aesthetics have lost none of their relevance today. Art is another form of reality and contains a revolutionary promise (cf. Reitz; cf. Miles 126-144). "Art represents the ultimate goal of all revolutions: the freedom and happiness of the individual" (Marcuse, *The Aesthetic* 69).

7. Concluding Remarks

Throughout his life, Herbert Marcuse did not give up his belief in the revolution and in the liberation of humanity. Without illusions, he revealed the processes and mechanisms that successfully prevented emancipation. Nonetheless, he staunchly believed in radical social change. He never accepted the one-dimensionality of the present but was of the opinion, that theory, art, and social movements can testify to the multiplicity of our existence, can be resistant to the dominant order and reveal alternatives. Even when Marcuse declares in *One-Dimensional Man* that in late capitalism, domination is increasing and no alternative can be found to deny and overcome the system, he considered it his duty and purpose to champion change and liberation. This accounts for the continued fascination and the power of his critical theory that points to the future. Therefore, we should return to Marcuse's critical theory and think again about his philosophy of emancipation and connect it to the struggles of the present.

Works Cited

Badiou, Alain, with Fabien Tarby. *Philosophy and the Event*. Polity Press, 2013.
Beck, Ulrich. *Power in the Global Age: A New Global Political Economy*. Translated by Kathleen Cross, Polity Press, 2005.
—. *The Brave New World of Work*. Polity Press, 2000.
Castells, Manuel. *Networks of Outrage and Hope: Social Movements in the Internet Age*. Polity Press, 2012.
Farr, Andrew. *Critical Theory and Democratic Vision: Herbert Marcuse and Recent Liberation Philosophies*. Lexington Books, 2009.
Freytag, Tatjana. *Der unternommene Mensch: Eindimensionalitätsprozesse in der gegenwärtigen Gesellschaft*. Velbrück Wissenschaft, 2008.
Giddens, Anthony. *Entfesselte Welt: Wie die Globalisierung unser Leben verändert*. Translated by Frank Jakubzik, Suhrkamp, 2001.
—. *Modernity and Self-Identity: Self and Society in the Late Modern Age*. Polity Press, 1991.

Gramsci, Antonio. *Selections from the Prison-Notebooks*. Edited and translated by Quentin Hoare and Geoffrey Nowell Smith, Lawrence & Wishart, 1971.

Habermas, Jürgen, et al., editors. *Gespräche mit Herbert Marcuse*. Suhrkamp, 1978.

Habermas, Jürgen. *Theorie des kommunikativen Handelns: Band I: Handlungsrationalität und gesell. Rationalisierung.* Suhrkamp, 1995.

—. *The Theory of Communicative Action: Volume 1: Reason and the Rationalization of Society.* Translated by Thomas McCarthy, Beacon Press, 1985.

—. *The Theory of Communicative Action: Volume 2: Lifeworld and System: A Critique of Functionalist Reason.* Translated by Thomas McCarthy, Beacon Press, 1984.

Hardt, Michael, and Toni Negri. *Empire*. Harvard UP, 2000.

Heelas, Paul, Scott Lash, and Paul Morris, editors. *Detraditionalization*. Blackwell, 1996.

Horkheimer, Max, and Theodor W. Adorno. *Dialectic of Enlightenment*. 1947. Herder and Herder, 1972.

Juris, Jeffrey S. *Networking Futures: The Movement Against Corporate Capitalism*. Duke UP, 2008.

Kahn, Richard, and Douglas Kellner. "Internet Subcultures and Political Activism." *Cultural Studies: From Theory to Action*, edited by Pepe Leistyna, Blackwell, 2005, pp. 217-30.

Kellner, Douglas. *Herbert Marcuse and the Crisis of Marxism*. University of California Press, 1984.

—. "Marcuse and the Quest for Radical Subjectivity." *Herbert Marcuse: A Critical Reader,* edited by John Abromeit and W. Mark Cobb, Routledge, 2004, pp. 81-99.

Marcuse, Herbert. *An Essay on Liberation*. Beacon Press, 1969.

—. "Art in the One-Dimensional Society." *Radical Perspectives in the Arts*, edited by Lee Baxandall, Penguin, 1973, pp. 52-67.

—. "On Changing the World: A Reply to Karl Miller." *Monthly Review*, 19 May 1967, pp. 42-48.

—. *One-Dimensional Man: Studies in the Ideology of Advanced Industrial Society.* Edited by Douglas Keller, 2nd ed., Beacon Press, 1991.

—. *The Aesthetic Dimension: Towards a Critique of Marxist Aesthetics.* Beacon Press, 1978.

—. "Zum Begriff des Wesens." *Schriften Band 3: Aufsätze aus der Zeitschrift für Sozialforschung*, 1936, zu Klampen, 2004, pp. 45-84.

Miles, Malcom. *Herbert Marcuse: An Aesthetics of Liberation*. Pluto Press, 2012.

Pippin, Robert B., Andrew Feenberg, and Charles P. Weibel. *Marcuse: Critical Theory and the Promise of Utopia*. Macmillan Education, 1988.

Rancière, Jacques. *Dissensus: On Politics and Aesthetics*. Edited and translated by Steven Corcoran, Continuum, 2010.

—. *La Méthode de Légalité: Entretien avec Laurent Jeanpierre et Dork Zabunyan*. Bayard Editions, 2012.

—. *The Politics of Aesthetics*. Translated by Gabriel Rockhill, Continuum, 2004.

Reitz, Charles. *Art, Alienation, and the Humanities: A Critical Engagement with Herbert Marcuse*. State University of New York, 2000.

Reitz, Charles, and Stephan Spartan. "The Political Economy of Predation and Counterrevolution: Recalling Marcuse on the Radical Goals of Socialism." *Crises of Commonwealth: Marcuse, Marx, McLaren*, edited by Charles Reitz, Lexington, 2013, pp. 19-42.

Schiller, Friedrich. *On the Aesthetic Education of Man in a Series of Letters*. 1795. Ungar, 1965.

Smith, Jackie. *Social Movements for Global Democracy*. The John Hopkins UP, 2008.

Tauber, Zvi. *Befreiung und das "Absurde": Studien zur Emanzipation des Menschen bei Herbert Marcuse*. Bleicher Verlag, 1994.

Thyen, Anke. *Negative Dialektik und Erfahrung: Zur Rationalität des Nichtidentischen bei Adorno*. Suhrkamp, 1989.

Williams, Raymond. *Marxism and Literature*. Oxford UP, 1977.

Winter, Rainer. *Die Kunst des Eigensinns: Cultural Studies als Kritik der Macht*. Velbrück, 2001.

—. "The Perspectives of Radical Democracy: Raymond Williams's Work and Its Significance for a Critical Social Theory." *About Raymond Williams*, edited by Monika Seidl, Roman Horak, and Lawrence Grossberg, Routledge, 2010, pp. 45-56.

—. *Widerstand im Netz: Zur Herausbildung einer transnationalen Öffentlichkeit durch netzbasierte Kommunikation*. transcript, 2010.

Zima, Peter V. *Entfremdung: Pathologien der postmodernen Gesellschaft*. utb, 2015.

Border Crossing as Act of Resistance
The Autonomy of Migration as Theoretical Intervention into Border Studies*

Sabine Hess

In September 2015, the reality of cross-border-migration seemed to be overwhelming. Thousands of migrants and refugees tore down the fences of the European border regime and demanded the right to cross the borders towards Western European countries in unexpected numbers and with unbelievable strength. They camped on the city squares all over Europe; they jumped on ferries and trains; and whenever the official means of transportation were blocked by the police, they literally marched hundreds of kilometers to cross the next national border. This collective, unorganized uprising found international public awareness when thousands of refugees were blocked at the main station in Budapest and started the "March of Hope" at the main motorway to reach Austria and Germany by foot (cf. *bordermonitoring.eu*). The pictures of marching bodies on motorways in an attempt to cross the nearest national border and to evade police controls and registration procedures soon became iconographic images of borderland resistance. Yet, these pictures have faded away already, and have been overwritten by quite antithetical images of an intensified re-bordering in a very material sense, with newly erected fences and ditches, defended by barbed wire and dogs, e.g., along the Hungarian-Serbian or Macedonian-Greek border. Even if these re-bordering activities, especially the official closure of the so called Balkan

---

* I want to thank Fadi Saleh a lot for his English editing; Mathias Schmidt for the insights into the concept of "nonmovement" and my two colleagues Maria Schwertl and Bernd Kasparek for the collaborative work on the border regime analyses.

Route and the so called EU-Turkey Deal, managed to reduce the number of people trying to get to Europe via Turkey and Greece, they did not manage to stop the movement altogether. By means of hunger strikes and official protests, the migrants trapped on the Greek islands or in Serbia are still demanding and fighting for their right to flee and to human treatment.

These more or less spontaneous, nevertheless highly collectivized forms of action within the movements of migration have taken place on a regular basis over the last years—yet, admittedly, in fewer numbers and with less media coverage and international public attention as well as with less success. As an example, one might think of the numerous attempts by hundreds of sub-Saharan migrants to climb over the militarized fences of the Spanish enclaves Ceuta and Mellia where—for sure—many got stuck, heavily injured in the barbed wires, but hundreds have been successful entering the European Union year after year (cf. "Hunderte Flüchtlinge"; "Sendung: tagesschau 18.03.2014"). There are also the overt and more or less organized forms of borderland resistance that we could witness in the demonstrations and riots in UNHCR refugee camps, for example, in Jordan, where Syrian refugees have been protesting against this form of enforced internment (cf. "Syrian Refugee"); or in the case of the hunger and thirst strikes in the brutalized Hungarian 'prison camps,' in which all asylum seekers have to stay for one year (cf. Bayer and Speer 12-18).

Apart from these obviously collective forms of resistance, scholarly as well as media reports show an incredible richness of more individual and imperceptible acts of resistance in the social field of border crossing activities, like filing away or etching the fingertips to fool the fingerprint machines and the so called Eurodac system. Eurodac is the big database that is connected to the Dublin Regulation, which determines that refugees have to apply for asylum in the first EU-European country they enter (cf. Tsianos and Kuster). It is the Dublin Regulation that led to the new phenomenon of rising inter-European deportations, as migrants get deported back to the country of first contact if their fingerprints can be found in the Eurodac data base (cf. Schuster 404-05). Although these forms of resistance are practiced individually, they are nevertheless embedded in the social networks of transit migration and draw on the wisdom and collective knowledge of this kind of diasporic communities of border-crossing that could be conceptualized with Asef Bayat's concept of "nonmovement" (11). With this concept, Bayat refers to collectivized mass actions by non-collective actors that are not organized by an organization and that do not follow one single ideology. Instead, Bayat refers to everyday practices performed by many people at the same time. Although these practices, more often than not, are of a fragmented nature, they, in sum, may nevertheless trigger social transformations, as it was the case with the so-called Velvet Revolutions (cf. Bayat 20).

But these forms of resistance are rarely televised and publicly discussed. At times, though, they draw the public's attention, as was the case in the summer of 2015, when the marching refugees from Budapest succeeded with their demand and the Austrian and German governments opened their borders in a big humanitarian gesture. Hundreds of thousands followed their example demanding again and again the right to cross the next European border, so that, for some time in 2015, we can speak of a more or less open 'Balkan Route.' However, would we have conceived transit migration and the daily practices of border crossing as resistance during the long period prior to these events, when the border regime seemed to have the upper hand and seemed to be able to control and repress the movements of migration?

On the contrary, the everyday impression of the power of migration vis-à-vis the border regime is slightly different. In the last couple of years, the image that has dominated the European public and scholarly debate on the European border regime has been one of overloaded, sinking ships in the Mediterranean Sea and corpses lying at the quay. This image as well as the high number of migrants who have drowned in the Mediterranean Sea rather speak another 'truth'—that of a return of a solid "Wall around the West," as Peter Andreas and Timothy Snyder phrased it in their well-noticed book on the re-bordering measures and policies by the Western industrial regions of the world already in 2000. From this perspective, migrants and their border crossing endeavors also appear in a different light: The migrant appears as a mere victim at the mercy of the atrocities of the border policies and practices.

What kind of sense can we make of these two highly contrasting scenarios with regard to the topic of borderland resistance? I would like to caution against building a simple opposition—either resistance or the return of the border, especially as this would be a misconception of the new shape and function of the border in the first place. In this contribution, I would rather like to show how the border regime can be understood as a site of constant encounter, tension, conflict, and contestation due to the strength and wisdom of the movements of migration. In so doing, I would like to rethink the relationship between the movements of migration and the multiple regimes governing them, and hence to think differently about migration as such. I.e., aim at reconceptualizing migration historically and structurally as acts of "escape," as imperceptible forms of resistance by eluding and evading the condition of existence, as Dimitris Papadopoulos, Niamh Stephenson, and Vassilis Tsianos framed it (cf. *Escape Routes*). Yann Moulier Boutang referred to this dimension as "the autonomy of migration" (169). In this view, migration is a force co-constituting the border, challenging and reshaping borders by the daily acts of border crossing.

In my argument, I draw on collective/collaborative research and knowledge practices that started within the Transit Migration Research Group (2007) and are now continued within the Laboratory for Critical Migration and Border Regime Research based at Göttingen University as well as in the German-speaking, Europe-wide interdisciplinary network "kritnet" (cf. Hess and Kasparek; Heimeshoff, Hess, Kron, Schwenken, and Trzeciak).

1. THE RETURN OF THE BORDER PARADIGM

If we read the daily news on the migratory tragedies occurring in the Mediterranean Sea in an unbelievable regularity over the last years; if we study the reemergence of high fences, walls, and deep trenches as they are built along the Greek-Turkish, the Bulgarian-Turkish, and the Hungarian-Serbian land-borders, around the Spanish enclaves of Ceuta and Melilla or along the Israeli and the Sinai-borderline, we are tempted to dismiss our insights in the "power of migration" (cf. Glick Schiller) and to proclaim instead a border paradigm. Apart from these very obvious and material fence constructions, there is another myriad of technological devices established, for example, by SIVE (Sistema Integrado de Vigilancia Exterior, since 2002), EUROSUR (European Border Surveillance System, since 2013), MARSUR (Maritime Surveillance, since 2005) or whatever these kinds of digitalized, smart border technologies may be called, establishing more or less invisible networked fences. Millions of Euros are spent for this kind of research and technological development, whereas civil and military actors have been competing as well as increasingly merging. Sergio Carrera and Leonhard den Hertog from the Centre for

European Policy Studies characterized this development concerning the control of movements in the Mediterranean Sea as "the surveillance race" (16), which creates a new spatialized and digitalized border situation, which Etienne Balibar described as the "ubiquity of borders" (84).

Against the background of all these rebordering efforts, practices, and devices, we can also observe a return of the 'border' as topic and concept in migration and mobility studies alike. For example, Glick Schiller and Noel B. Salazar took up the topic in their paper "Regimes of Mobility across the Globe," speaking of the return of national borders and ethnic boundaries in the wake of the recent global economic crisis. Thereby, they follow Ronen Shamir's conceptualization of a single "global mobility regime" (200) with the following characteristics:

> Oriented to closure and to the blocking of access, premised not only on 'old' national or local grounds but on a principle of perceived universal dangerous personhoods [...]. In practice, this means that local, national, and regional boundaries are now being rebuilt and consolidated [...]. [P]rocesses of globalization are also concerned with the prevention of movement and the blocking of access. (199)

2. THE 'AUTONOMY OF MIGRATION'-APPROACH AS A CRITICAL INTERVENTION INTO BORDER STUDIES

Before I outline the 'autonomy of migration'-approach, I will briefly recall the common understanding of migration and the border. Still today or even more so today—as the European border regime has undergone severe legitimacy problems since the catastrophes of Lampedusa in 2013, when more than 600 people drowned—migration vis-à-vis the border is generally conceptualized in a functionalist and/or instrumentalist top down mode (cf. Mezzadra 794-95). This is the case with the push-and-pull model commonly applied by migration research and the public alike—today we better refer to it as push-and-closure model. The image generated by and associated with this model is the following: On the one side, there is a more or less strong and monolithic apparatus and a will to stop, to hinder, to exclude, and to suppress migration and/or to exploit it. On the other side, there are victims, either people who followed the call of capital and find themselves cheated and trapped in exploitation, as the official left-wing narrative of the so-called guest worker systems wanted to make us believe for a long time. The dominant narrative was like this: there was a labor shortage, and the German government responded to it by signing 'guest worker contracts.' Then, thousands of poor men from the European South followed the call, more or less unaware of the conditions awaiting them. In this context, the figure of the *homo exploiticus* was constructed as the other side of the *homo economicus* of classical migration theories (cf. Bojadzijev for a critical perspective on this). So either there are the 'exploited victims' or the 'real victims' in the Agambian sense of 'bare life,' driven out of their homelands, faceless masses stuck in transit. I do not want to imply here that the European border regime is not brutal and that it does not produce so much hardship and pain. However, I would like to stress what this representational regime and what this kind of conceptualization hints at, what kind of policy response and what kind of positioning (also in academic and methodological terms) it produces: It not only calls for humanitarian responses, but it establishes a hierarchical, neo-colonial matrix of the helping (and gazing) subject and the suffering (looked at) object.

This representational regime can be described as victimization and as humanitarianism, as Didier Fassin or Miriam Ticktin have called this kind of power, which calls for action to save lives and to alleviate suffering. Under the rationale of humanitarianism, we can also speak of a political economy of 'humanitarian crisis' based on the ability of the European border regime to recode incidents as emergencies (cf. Calhoun) calling for ad hoc, exceptional actions, as Didier Fassin characterizes one central dimension of humanitarianism as politics by exception (cf. 16). And indeed, if we look back, we can see that this kind of emergency policy was highly productive and one of the main driving forces in developing Frontex into a big organization with a big budget (cf. Heimershoff, Hess, Kron, Schwenken, and Trzeciak 8). The marching migrant bodies also call for humanitarian answers; but this time, their agency and political subjectivities, their demands for freedom of border crossing cannot be erased from the picture. Instead, they confront the humanitarian gesture that always rests on the good will of the powerful position to decide when to act and which lives to save—as Fassin outlines with his concept of "politics of life" (226)—with the claim to have the right to cross the border just like everybody else. This is the far-reaching political sign of the current migratory uprisings everywhere in Europe: By coming out of the shadow of irregularity and factual hiding in the transit migration hubs and marching on the streets, migrants thus do indeed reclaim a political subject position within the dominant representational and political matrix.

What is changing with regard to our understanding of the border, policy, and migration, if we conceptualize 'the migrant' not in structural terms as quintessential victim or in cultural terms as the quintessential contemporary Other, as it is still mostly the case in cultural and social science migration research? What is changing if we conceptualize migration differently, as it is provocatively expressed with the notion of the autonomy of migration?

Quite often, this notion is quite incorrectly translated and equated with autonomous migrants. But this is certainly not its intention, because 'autonomy of migration' is a structural argument based on a materialist-Marxist reading of history. It also does not intend to wipe out the sorrows and misfortunes many projects of migration are confronted with. Rather, with this notion of the 'autonomy of migration,' Yann Moulier Boutang and other proponents of this theoretical endeavor tried to reposition migration within the history of labor, capitalism, and modern forms of governance by highlighting and focusing on the unchecked capability of living labor to resist and to escape from the conditions of (re-)production (cf. also Mezzadra and Neilson). Moulier Boutang writes:

Primarily, governing means facing the challenge to dissuade society from its desire to escape and refuse by means of representative democracy. Policy has to channel the energy of flight into ever new institutions that manage to transform resistance [...]. (172; translation: SH)

In his theorization, Yann Moulier Boutang draws heavily on the theoretical traditions of operaism. *Operaismo* emerged as a political movement and as the political theory in Italy in the 1960s in opposition to mainstream Marxism. Two essential insights of operaism are of central importance to the shift of perspective proposed by the 'autonomy of migration'-approach: First, operaism reads capitalist history as being driven by labor struggles. From this perspective, industrialization and the emergence of the factory appear as reactions to workers' resistance; and second, it re-conceptualizes 'resistance' in a more empirical way by stressing silent and small forms of subversion and evasion as expressed, for instance, in slow-work or jokes and rituals on an everyday level of factory life.

In analogy, Moulier Boutang did not conceptualize capitalism as the first mover of history and society driven by some abstract parameters like sinking rates of profit. Quite on the contrary, he read capitalist developments as reactions towards mobilities, as constant attempts to regain predominance over the desire and capability of living labor to resist and escape the conditions enforced on it (cf. Moulier Boutang 172-73; cf. also Papadopoulos, Stephenson, and Tsianos). Thus, the 'autonomy of migration'-approach does not stop at the insight that migration is an active force, that it is to be understood as a form of everyday silent resistance. Rather it goes on asking how migration intervenes into the very center of our knowledge production (cf. Hess 31-32). Bernd Kasparek and Maria Schwertl recently summarized the theoretical intervention that is evoked by the notion of the autonomy of migration. They stated: "The Autonomy of Migration is less a conclusion to arrive at but a perspective that opens up new ways of interrogation and doing research. Or, to quote Moulier Boutang, autonomy of migration is not a slogan, but a method."

3. The Autonomy of Migration as Prism

If we conceive of the 'autonomy of migration'-approach as a method or a prism that allows for new perspectives, then we have to ask about what it enables us to see. Firstly, the 'autonomy of migration'-approach enables us to understand migration and mobility as social movements and thus inherently as political, social, transformative practices. Through migration, social actors escape their normalized representations; they reconfigure themselves and their conditions of existence. Following Vassilis Tsianos and Dimitris Papadopoulos, migration is thus to be conceived of as a world-making practice, an active transformation of social space:

> Migration is not the evacuation of a place and the occupation of a different one; it is the making and remaking of one's own life on the scenery of the world. World-making. You cannot measure migration in changes of position or location, but in the increase in inclusiveness and the amplitude of its intensities. Even if migration starts sometimes as a form of dislocation (forced by poverty, patriarchal exploitation, war, famine), its target is not relocation but the active transformation of social space. (169-70)

Secondly, by looking at the border and the migration regime from the perspective of the 'autonomy of migration'-approach, our conceptualization of the border and hence our understanding of the state and sovereignty changes as well. The once monolithic border apparatus decomposes and falls apart into multiple factors: into actors, practices, discourses, technologies, bodies, affects, and trajectories, whereas migration is to be understood as one of its driving forces (cf. Heimeshoof, Hess, Kron, Schwenken, and Trzeciak 13-14). This conceptualization of the border destroys clear-cut or binary models of structure versus agency, as it reconceptualizes the border as space of contestation and negotiation.

The ethnographic border regime analysis developed by the Transit Migration Research Group in the beginning of 2000 tries to translate these theoretical insights into a research methodology (cf. Transit Migration Forschungsgruppe; Tsianos and Hess). Thereby, they draw on political science as well as on the Foucauldian concept of regime, which makes it possible to include a multiplicity of actors, institutions, and other non-human and human factors without reducing all these diverse forces to a single logic or hidden agenda. Instead, the ethnographical border regime analysis starts with the empirical as well as theoretical insights that the border constitutes a site of constant encounters, tensions, and contestations, whereas migration is a co-constituent of the border. According to Giuseppe Sciortino, a regime is a "mix of rather implicit conceptual frames, generations of turf wars among bureaucracies and waves after waves of 'quick fix' to emergencies [...] the life of a regime is a result of continuous repair work through practices" (32).

Hence, the regime-approach reads the constant re-figuration of the border centrally as a reaction to the forces and movements of migration that challenge, cross, and reshape borders. Through reconceptualizing the border on the basis of the 'autonomy of migration'-approach, this perspective makes a big difference to most of the existing contemporary constructivist approaches in border studies that conceptualize the border also as result of a multiplicity of actors and practices as it is expressed in the notion of 'doing border' or 'border work' (cf., e.g., Rumford; Salter). However, most of these highly interesting constructivist approaches either completely erase migration as a constitutive force or they conceptualize the migrant again mostly as passive victim. To put border struggles at the center of the analyses instead, as Sandro Mezzadra and Brett Neilson also did in their recent book *Border as Method* (cf. 13-14), follows the 'autonomy of migration'-approach. In this view, the forces of migration produce the social and economic phenomenon of the borderland: Borderlands are the product of the collectivized excessive will to subvert and pass the border, of the networks of people on the move, and shared knowledge practices of border-crossing (cf. Fröhlich). Thereby, one central capacity and means to resist is not to be noticed, to pass and immerse oneself in the big migration hubs and the (internationalized areas of the) economies of the new transit cities; another capacity is to be flexible to take on different social roles as student, tourist, laborer, or asylum seeker along the route and to be able to tactically adapt one's own biography to the demands of the border regime. And last but not least, to seize any opportunity as soon as it comes up (cf. Hess and Kasparek).

It is this generative excess that various state agencies and policy schemes subsequently try to control, manage, and make use of by invoking the border as a stable, controllable, and manageable tool of selective or differential inclusion. In the 'long summer of migration' 2015, the border regime lost even this representational capacity, as the mass movements of migrants made clear that the will to flee is stronger than the technical and bureaucratic apparatus of the border regime. The current construction of the four meter-high fence along the Hungarian-Serbian border and the reestablishment of national border controls all over the European Union are in fact defensive-aggressive attempts to regain control.

However, the border regime transforms the legal status of the people crossing the border: It takes away the basic human right to have rights—as it is at least officially encoded in national citizenship—by putting the border crossers into the different existing categories of migration. In this sense, the border is a huge transformation regime producing new hierarchies of people by categorizing and processing the unchecked mobilities as 'migration.'

But the struggles of migrants in Germany, Hungary, Serbia, Turkey, or elsewhere for the right to flee, for the right to stay where they want to stay, and for the right to move freely within Europe—these are the new demands and fights of migration especially directed against the so-called Dublin regime—show that also people excluded from full citizenship enact citizenship rights and post-national visions of it on a daily basis (cf. Nyers and Kim; Köster-Eisenfunken, Reichhold, and Schwiertz; Hess and Lehbuhn).

To sum up, what I tried to do was to re-conceptualize borderlands as well as migration itself as ways of resistance, as products of a generative excess that cannot be fully subjectified by the forces of domination. However, if we really accept this understanding of migration following the perspective of the 'autonomy of migration'-approach, then this has radical repercussions on our general knowledge production: Migration ends to be the culturalized object of our scholarly gaze and it starts to become a method, a perspective, a prism for a situated post-national knowledge practice that itself is only thinkable as a way of resistance, as criticism of the hegemonic, objectifying mode still deeply entrenched in the postcolonial order of knowledge (cf. Hess 34-35). That is what we try to develop within the network for critical migration and border regime research "kritnet" (cf. *Movements*; *bordermonitoring.eu*).

WORKS CITED

Andreas, Peter, and Timothy Snyder. *The Wall Around the West: State Borders and Immigration Controls in North America and Europe*. Rowman & Littlefield, 2000.
Balibar, Etienne. "What is Border?" *Politics and the Other Scene*, edited by Balibar, Verso, 2002, pp. 75-86.
Bayat, Asef. *Life as Politics: How Ordinary People Change the Middle East*. Stanford UP, 2010.
Bayer, Marion, and Marc Speer. *Ungarn: Flüchtlinge zwischen Haft und Obdachlosigkeit*. bordermonitoring.eu, 2013. bordermonitoring.eu/wp-content/uploads/reports/bm.eu-2012-ungarn.de.pdf.
Bojadzijev, Manuela. *Die windige Internationale: Rassismus und Kämpfe der Migration*. Westfäl. Dampfboot, 2008.
bordermonitoring.eu: politiken, praktiken, ereignisse an den grenzen europas. bordermonitoring.eu e.V., bordermonitoring.eu/. Accessed 31 Mar. 2017.
Calhoun, Craig. "A World of Emergencies: Fear, Intervention, and the Limits of Cosmopolitan Order." *Canadian Review of Sociology/Revue Canadienne de Sociologie*, vol. 41, no. 4, 2004, pp. 373-95.
Carrera, Sergio, and Leonhard den Hertog. "Whose Mare? Rule of Law Challenges in the Field of European Border Surveillance in the

Mediterranean." *CEPS paper in Liberty and Security in Europe*, CEPS, 2015, www.ceps.eu/system/files/LSE_79.pdf.

Fassin, Didier. *Humanitarian Reason: A Moral History of the Present*. Translated by Rachel Gomme, University of California Press, 2011.

Fröhlich, Marie. "Routes of Migration: Migrationsprojekte unter Bedingungen europäisierter Regulation." *Movements of Migration Neue Positionen im Feld von Stadt, Migration und Repräsentation*, edited by Sabine Hess and Torsten Näser, Panama Verlag, 2015, pp. 150-62.

Glick Schiller, Nina. "A Global Perspective on Transnational Migration: Theorizing Migration without Methodological Nationalism." *Centre on Migration, Policy and Society Working-Paper*, no. 67, COMPAS, 2009, www.compas.ox.ac.uk/media/WP-2009-067-Schiller_Methodological_Nationalism_Migration.pdf.

Glick Schiller, Nina, and Noel B. Salazar. "Regimes of Mobility across the Globe." *Journal of Ethnic and Migration Studies*, vol. 39, no. 2, 2014, pp. 183-200.

Heimeshoff, Lisa-Marie, Sabine Hess, Stefanie Kron, Helen Schwenken, and Miriam Trzeciak, editors. *Grenzregime II: Migration—Kontrolle—Wissen: Transnationale Perspektiven*. Assoziation A, 2014.

Hess, Sabine, and Serhat Karakayali. "New Governance oder die imperiale Kunst des Regierens." *Turbulente Ränder: Neue Perspektiven auf Migration an den Grenzen Europas*, edited by Transit Migration Forschungsgruppe, transcript, 2007, pp. 39-56.

Hess, Sabine, and Bernd Kasparek, editors. *Grenzregime: Diskurse, Praktiken, Institutionen in Europa*. Assoziation A, 2010.

Hess, Sabine, and Henrik Lehbun. "Politiken der Bürgerschaft: Zur Forschungsdebatte um Migration, Stadt und Citizenship." *Sub_Urban*, vol. 2, no. 3, 2014, pp. 11-34.

Hess, Sabine. "Jenseits des Kulturalismus: Ein Plädoyer für postkulturalistische Ansätze in der kulturanthropologischen Migrationsforschung." *Spektrum Migration: Zugänge zur Vielfalt des Alltags*, edited by Matthias Klückmann and Felicia Sparacio, TVV, 2015, pp. 7-35.

"Hunderte Flüchtlinge Stürmen Spanische Enklave." ZEIT ONLINE, 28 May 2014, www.zeit.de/politik/ausland/2014-05/melilla-fluechtlinge-enklave-ansturm. Accessed 31 Mar. 2017.

Kasparek, Bernd, and Maria Schwertl. "The Ethnographic Migration and Border Regime Analysis." Mobility, Migration and Policies: Workshop and Meeting between the EPOKE research group (Aarhus University) and the Critical Migration and Border Regime Research Laboratory (University of Göttingen), 9-10 Oct. 2014, Kopenhagen. Unpublished Presentation.

Köster-Eiserfunke, Anna, Clemens Reichhold, and Helge Schwiertz. "Citizenship zwischen nationalem Status und aktivistischer Praxis. Eine Einführung." *Grenzregime II: Migration—Kontrolle—Wissen. Transnationale Perspektiven*, edited by Lisa-Marie Heimeshoff, Sabine Hess, Stefanie Kron, Helen Schwenken, and Miriam Trzeciak, Assoziation A, 2014, pp. 177-96.

Mezzadra, Sandro. "Der Blick der Autonomie." *Projekt Migration*, edited by Kölnischer Kunstverein, DuMont, 2005, pp. 794-95.

Mezzadra, Sandro, and Brett Neilson. *Border as Method, or, the Multiplication of Labor*. Duke UP, 2013.

Movements. Journal für kritische Migrations- und Grenzregimeforschung. movements-journal.org/. Accessed 31 Mar. 2017.

Moulier Boutang, Yann. "Europa, Autonomie der Migration, Biopolitik." *Empire und die biopolitische Wende: Die internationale Diskussion im Anschluss an Hardt und Negri*, edited by Marianne Pieper, Thomas Atzert, Serhat Karakayalı, and Vassilis Tsianos, Campus Verlag, 2006, pp. 169-80.

Nyers, Peter, and Kim Rygiel. "Citizenship, migrantischer Aktivismus und Politiken der Bewegung." *Grenzregime II: Migration—Kontrolle—Wissen. Transnationale Perspektiven*, edited by Lisa-Marie Heimeshoff, Sabine Hess, Stefanie Kron, Helen Schwenken, and Miriam Trzeciak, Assoziation A, 2014, pp. 197-217.

Papadopoulos, Dimitris, Niamh Stephenson, and Vassilis Tsianos. *Escape Routes: Control and Subversion in the Twenty-First Century*. Pluto Press, 2008.

Papadopoulos, Dimitris, and Vassilis Tsianos. "The Autonomy of Migration: The Animals of Undocumented Mobility. Deleuzian Encounters." 2008, translate.eipcp.net/strands/02/papadopoulostsianos-strandso1en/print. Accessed 31 Mar. 2017.

Rumford, Chris. "Introduction: Citizens and Borderwork in Europe." *Space and Polity*, vol. 12, no. 1, 2008, pp. 1–12.

Salter, Mark B. "Places Everyone! Studying the Performativity of the Border." *Political Geography*, vol. 30, 2011, pp. 66-67.

Schuster, Liza. "Dublin II and Eurodac: Examining the (Un)Intended (?) Consequences." *Gender, Place & Culture: A Journal of Feminist Geography*, vol. 18, no. 3, 2011, pp. 401-16, doi: 10.1080/0966369X.2011.566387.

Sciortino, Guiseppe. "Between Phantoms and Necessary Evils: Some Critical Points in the Study of Irregular Migrations to Western Europe." *IMIS-Beiträge: Migration and the Regulation of Social Integration*, vol. 24, 2004, pp. 17-43.

"Sendung: tagesschau 18.03.2014 20:00 Uhr." tagesschau.de, 18 Mar. 2014, www.tagesschau.de/multimedia/sendung/ts47338.html. Accessed 31 Mar. 2017.

Shamir, Ronan. "Without Borders? Notes on Globalization as a Mobility Regime." *Sociological Theory*, vol. 23, no. 2, Jun. 2005, pp. 197-217. JSTOR, www.jstor.org/stable/4148882.

"Syrian Refugee Killed in Riot at Camp Jordan." the guardian, 6 Apr. 2014, www.theguardian.com/world/2014/apr/06/damascus-opera-house-syrian-rebels-shelling. Accessed 31 Mar. 2017.

Ticktin, Miriam I. *Casualties of Care: Immigration and the Politics of Humanitarianism in France*. University of California Press, 2011.

Transit Migration Forschungsgruppe, editors. *Turbulente Ränder: Neue Perspektiven auf Migration an den Grenzen Europas*. transcript, 2007.

Tsianos, Vassilis, and Sabine Hess. "Ethnographische Grenzregimeanalyse als die Methodologie der Autonomie der Migration." *Grenzregime: Diskurse, Praktiken, Institutionen in Europa*, edited by Sabine Hess and Bernd Kasparek, Assoziation A, 2010, pp. 243-64.

Tsianos, Vassilis, and Brigitta Kuster. "Eurodac in Times of Bigness: The Power of Big Data within the Emerging European IT Agency." *Journal of Borderlands Studies*, vol. 31, no. 2, 22 Jun. 2016, pp. 235-49. Taylor Francis Online, doi: 10.1080/08865655.2016.1174606.

Reclaiming the City, Reclaiming the Rights
The Commons and the Omnipresence of Resistance

Kemal İnal & Ulaş Başar Gezgin

1. INTRODUCTION

This chapter examines the various reasons, agents, and forms of reclaiming the city in the context of what is commonly referred to as 'resistance for democracy.' Since 2011, resistance by what is called the '(urban) commons' as a new social subject/agent, mostly and especially through occupation of squares and parks in the city centers, has opened a new route against capitalism and dictatorships: Reclaiming the city means to capture the city in favor of public interests. The commons in the last years started to produce what might be called a new common sense and a shared sense of belonging to the city. Radical transitions from media activism in the virtual world into the real public sphere through a militant struggle have accelerated the process of reclaiming the cities. While the new radical approach of 'urban commons' transformed the cities into "rebel cities" (Harvey), social demands as, for example, affordable and quality housing, increasing the public spheres for the poor, putting an end to capitalist mega-projects, etc., have led to the use of multiple methods from militant fighting at squares to collective negotiations. Immense social problems (e.g., the US-American mortgage crisis, Turkish gentrification and destruction in the name of 'urban renewal,' astronomical leaps of housing prices in Beijing and Shanghai, etc.), created by neo-liberal capitalism and preventing the use of urban sites for multiple purposes such as residence, office, schools, parks, etc., turn the cities into sites of resistance. In this contribution, the contextual parameters which contributed to the emergence of massive popular resistances in Arab regions and in some other Western countries (USA, Spain, Greece, etc.), the identity of the agents or subjects of these resistances, and the forms of resistances are investigated.

2. SOCIAL MOVEMENTS IN URBAN AREAS AND REACTIONS TO THE NEO-LIBERALIZATION OF CITIES

It can be stated that, in recent years, the common denominator of the massive popular movements that emerged in Arab countries as well as in Western countries has been democracy, the venue has been the city, and the subject has been the commons. One of the inclinations of these social movements is the proposition 'cities for people, not for profit.' In other words, it is the planning, production, and administration of cities not for personal economic interests but for people's public demands. One of the most significant obstacles against these demands has been the neo-liberalization of cities. This has increasingly turned cities into the main sites of economic problems induced by capitalism, such as financial crises, land speculation, commodification, privatization, dispossession, displacement, gentrification, unemployment, housing, mortgage houses, working in precarious conditions, declines in real wages of workers, etc. These economic problems, in turn, resulted in a number of social problems, such as individual isolation, egoism, lack of solidarity, emotional impoverishment, replacement of real-life interaction with virtual forms of communication, and problems experienced by immigrants and refugees. This list may well be continued by adding problems related to environmental issues and food safety (e.g., the destruction of natural areas, pollution, traffic jams, epidemics, genetically modified food, obesity) and problems of democratic rights (e.g., low political participation, 'dirty' politics, intertwining of democracy and market values). The reaction to all of these problems appears on two different levels: First, on a theoretical level, i.e., through the formulation of the demand for a public city as a consequence of the critique of the notion of the neo-liberal city and, second, on a practical level, i.e., through popular revolts and resistances.

Regarding the first level, a new route against capitalism and dictatorship has been opened up by a number of theorists that have outlined a critical approach to capitalism within the urban context. Henri Lefebvre expressed the concept of the right to the city as a popular demand the first time in the late 1960s (cf. *Le Droit à la Ville*). He suggested that Marxist revolutionary theory should not be restricted to the site of the factory as a site of struggle and resistance, but should be expanded to include other urban social contexts. This demand was based on the idea of a city which is less alienated, with which residents are able to identify, which is arranged according to the demands of urban working class people. In the last three decades, these demands outlined in the field of urban theory have been reformulated in a number of cities through these cities' inhabitants. To be precise, as a result of these demands, the rebuilding of cities has become one of the central subjects of struggle and has been regularly articulated through massive popular demonstrations (cf. Harvey 115-19). According to Harvey, the real demand of the rebel cities is that the surplus value produced in cities should be in the control of its producers, i.e., the working class. At the same time, he considers this demand to be impossible to fulfill under capitalist conditions. Therefore, the right to the city requires, first, the optimum strategy for an anti-capitalist struggle; second, both an aim and a consistent method to overcome capitalism today; and third, the organization of the city 'as rebel.'

In the recent past, some other city theorists have repeated the claim that cities are for people and not for profit (cf. Brenner, Marcuse, and Mayer), thereby emphasizing the fact that the most important urban problem of our times is the capitalist urbanization process. Cities are increasingly being designed for profit and personal interests, but the public sections of society and their demands are not (or only rarely) considered in this process. As a consequence of this situation, public-oriented organizations located in cities stand out as the new agents of struggle. These agents try to resist various problems on the macro and micro levels, such as traffic congestion, air pollution, commodification of urban goods, and services created by capitalism by alternative urbanization practices, e.g., urban organization forums, slow city-approaches (Cittaslow),[1] urban villages, organic production, or farmer's markets. The history of these urban forms of opposition, which have become well-known in the last decades and are getting more and more common is certainly quite long.[2]

---

1 | However, anti-capitalist critiques of the slow city movement needs to be noted here, as it can be considered as a form of capitalist restoration.

2 | Harvey lists Paris (1789 French Revolution, 1830 and 1848 French Revolutions, 1871 Commune), Petrograd Soviet (1917), Seattle General Strike (1919), Barcelona of the Spanish Civil War, American urban riots (1960's), European

This urban boiling, resistance, and struggle is thus not a product of the recent past. However, while the heart of 'hot' revolutions in the past was mostly limited to the streets and squares, now it can be stated that the scope has been enlarged to cover all kinds of different urban spaces and contexts (parks and gardens, public spaces, underground stations, woods, seashores, suburbs, slums, etc.) as sites of resistance. Nevertheless, it is obvious that the most dramatic struggles have appeared in squares and streets in the last couple of years (especially from 2011 to 2013). In other words, the hearts of the cities—marked by revolutionary activities and Occupy movements that took place primarily and most intensely in city centers—started to beat in the squares (Tahrir, Puerto del Sol, Zuccoti Park/Wall Street, Syntagma, Taksim/Gezi).

The number of people who imagine the city as a 'social life venue,' i.e., as a site where one can build a democratic and humane community, is increasing. Indeed, more and more people do no longer regard the city merely as a place to reside, and they consider the option of building these democratic communities as a way to solve various urban social problems (profit-oriented local government practices, gentrification in the name of 'urban renewal,' construction of shopping malls rather than social spaces, such as parks, etc.) created by neo-liberal capitalism. The cities have thus turned into rebel cities (Harvey) by the recent protests of people who have been united by urban culture, local citizenship consciousness, rights to city, etc. For 'the poor' that were forced to leave their own life zones (slums, suburbs, outskirts, etc.), "the right to city" (Lefebvre, *Le Droit à la Ville*) became the major objection against bourgeoisie's rendering of the city as a site for the accumulation of profit in many countries of the world. While the situation portrayed by Harvey, i.e., city residents finding themselves in cities that are increasingly divided, fragmented and conflict-ridden, turns every square centimeter of urban sites into the subject of financial speculation, it closes and reproduces the loop of dispossession and deterritorialization of the urban poor majority. While urban sites, such as streets, lands, gardens, orchards, etc., are taken away from the urban poor majority which resides in them, or which are de facto owners and caretakers of them, 'the right to use the city' has been increasingly captured by official or private interest groups; and many urban sites have

---

1968, Shanghai Commune (1969), Cordoba Uprising (1969), etc., under this long history.

been turned into ultra-luxury niches³ isolated and saved from the poor with maximum security for the urban rich minority (cf. Hartmann).

In that sense, class and identity conflicts (ethnic, migrant, religious, etc.) get intermingled; and the pseudo-social housing units produced in the past, such as French *HLM*⁴ and Turkey's *Toplukonut*⁵ projects, turn into isolated zones lacking some of the municipal services and being excluded from the center and its facilities. But, in fact, they are always on the verge of chaos, which might break lose one day or another, as exemplified in suburban riots in France (2005) and elsewhere. Then, the cities can be viewed as the sites of both extreme poverty and ultra luxury, with the contrasts and conflicts between the former and the latter being

---

3 | Such cases have been observed multiple times in Turkey in the last couple of decades. Especially in Istanbul, the values of urban land have skyrocketed as a result of its transformation into a so-called global metropolis. Urban poor trying their best to survive in neighborhoods such as Sulukule, Küçükçekmece, or Tarlabaşı have been devastated by the gentrification process. Other cities such as the capital Ankara have experienced the same destructive processes. For instance, Dikmen Valley, which is quite close to the Ankara city center, has been the site of resistance as a response to gentrification in the name of 'urban renewal.' Dikmen district and its resistance have been reported on frequently by various newspapers and documented by a number of academic works. For two outstanding theses on the district and resistance, cf. Aykan and Mühürdaroğlu. For other remarkable academic works on phenomena such as 'urban renewal' and gentrification, cf. Adanalı, Doğru, Türkün, and Uzunçarşılı Baysal.

4 | *HLMs* are the social housing units with affordable rents built for poor, workers, migrants, and ethnic minorities by the central government or local government in France. There are claims that these housing units are inhibiting poors', workers' and migrants' integration to the larger society (cf. Taïeb).

5 | Turkish social housing units that were built the first time in 1974 by the CHP-MSP coalition government were designed as affordable units mostly for urban poor, just like French *HLM*. Nowadays the Housing Development Administration (Toplu Konut İdaresi, TOKİ) under the Prime Minister's Office is supposed to continue this mission; however, it now produces two new forms of property: Firstly, it produces luxury units in addition to social low-cost units, and secondly, capital transfer is claimed to take place to support the pro-government bourgeoisie by cash-cow housing auctions.

highly visible, and with people of various welfare levels living in the same city without any form of social contact.[6]

The marginalized, excluded, and criminalized urban poor populations have been developing various forms of resistance as a response to the neoliberal attacks on the cities as public sites. The demand for affordable and high-quality social housing units, increasing numbers of parks and green areas, the wish to be offered various local services, such as transportation, culture, and cleaning for free, the demand for a solution for the most pressing problems of the city, such as traffic congestion and air pollution, among other demands and wishes have been turning urban constituents (individuals, groups, communities, organizations, etc.) to commons, i.e., to subjects that reflect together, that demand together, and that take action together (cf. Walljasper). Various poor sections of the society (slum dwellers, villagers, workers, migrants, miscellaneous minority groups, etc.), whose political participation used to be merely formal or pseudo-representational can now take roles in the political scene as directly participating political subjects and, in so doing, move towards direct political action, as they realize that even their most fundamental demands are in fact inherently political. The new conjuncture that we encounter is the redefinition of the notion of citizenship: I.e., in this new era, citizenship has inseparably become identified with the objects through which it defines itself (country, city, street, park, neighborhood, household, etc.) and has turned all struggles—from those on urban sites to those on natural resources in remote areas (e.g., privatization of rivers and forests; threats to wild and semi-wild life, the disastrous consequences of capitalistic mining activities, etc.)—into matters of fighting for rights in general. This situation allows various groups of people oppressed due to, e.g., different political beliefs, ethnic identity, sexual orientation, religious beliefs, and cultural backgrounds, to meet and unite under the umbrella of a new collective subject, i.e., the commons.

The construction of new collective structures (communes, solidarity groups, online network organizations, etc.) against the so-called crazy projects driven by the ruling elites, e.g., privatizations, the closure of

---

6 | In his well-known work *Planet of Slums*, Mike Davis presents with rich empirical data how the slum areas were formed in mega cities of many of the countries of the world (Mumbai, Cairo, Istanbul, Sao Paulo, Seoul, etc.) evolve into a poverty-based way of living.

common spaces against the public, spatial control, and police surveillance, has created a new source of motivation for a different, alternative type of urbanization. However, the real problem here appears to be the following: Various intellectual and social circles, which are somehow inspired by the so-called failure of real socialism, started to mobilize their followers by promoting a more anarchist and libertarian (i.e., non-hierarchical, horizontal, leaderless) model instead of a more conventional socialist form of organization. The biggest deficit of this new organization form, fetishized mostly by middle class urban activists, is its incompatibility with the demands of the productive classes (i.e., workers and villagers). That the policies suggested by these anti-hierarchical intellectuals (such as Bookchin, Holloway, and others) could not form an effective alternative against capitalism, is one of the major factors behind the failures of the urban resistances in the struggle for social and political victory. Cities which have been subject to and subject of speculative profits (in the 2010s more frequently than in the past) continue to be the sites for class conflicts and struggles despite of all the social gains, past or present (e.g., a limited number of affordable housing units, affordable health services, education, clean environment, water services, etc.).

Although different motives were behind the emergence of the resistances against the transportation price hike in Brazil and the shopping mall planned to be built in Istanbul's Gezi Park, these resistances have easily and swiftly been able to turn into radical protests against the system as a whole. Just like in the years of 1789, 1871, and 1968, the streets, squares, and parks were heated up again in the period from 2011 to 2014; and the cities became the sites of various forms of substantial protests, organized actions, and demonstrations of the mobilized masses that moved back and forth like the unstoppable waves of social forces. The struggle for transforming the city back into a public site where social provisions are secured affordably, at a high level of quality, and in situ became one of the most significant aims of the resisting movements. The claim to the 'right to the city' articulated by those who resisted stood against the capitalists' exploitation of the cities, against their transformation of cities into sites of profit accumulation and into unliveable spaces both from an ecological and a social point of view. This claim provided evidence to the fact that the commons involved in the process of reclaiming the city pursue a distinctly political ideal. What remained open was the question of how to name and position this ideal.

3. THE NOTION OF THE COMMONS AND URBAN RESISTANCE

The reclaiming of the city by the commons produced a new common sense that was based on a shared sense of belonging to the city. To be organized as/in commons in cities and to work against neoliberal dominant forces meant to be a direct and true democracy on the local level. The aim was to make public spaces social again in order to create a 'social city.' For this, as mentioned above, multiple methods of struggle were used by the commons.[7] During the revolts in urban areas, many agents involved in this process of reclaiming the city introduced themselves as forces organized on behalf of different groups in society: the working class (highly organized, classical commons), the peasant class (with an emergent class consciousness in the fight for natural environment and products, especially in countries such as Brazil and Mexico, as well as Turkey, where constructions of power plants and dams are strongly resisted), armed or peaceful local-indigenous movements (e.g., the Zapatistas, the Brazilian landless movement, democratic participation and armed defense in Rojava, etc.), the underclass (i.e., the homeless, street children, people in need of care and social support), the youth (i.e., students, young workers, unemployed youth, etc.), the so-called precariat (i.e., flexible and precarious workers without contracts or zero-hour contracts), public employees, the intellectual working class, and others (LGBTI, ecological movements, anti-nuclear groups, social forums, coalitions, and so on). In addition to these groups, middle-class urbanites who want to maintain their quality of life, radical autonomist anarchists, alternative groups, occupiers, cultural activists, housing activists, artists, and small shopkeepers were included in the revolts that set out to reclaim urban spaces during the last years.

The new structures for reclaiming the city produced by the commons were alternative youth and culture centers for free culture, transportation as well as education services (ideologically framed by slogans such as 'education is nor for sale' or 'another world is possible'). Revolting people demanded low-cost housing, i.e., affordable housing, local clearing systems (through what has become known as 'anti-shopping act'), organic production spaces or gardens in cities, farmers' markets selling organic products (i.e., no intermediate dealers), self-determined projects (i.e.,

---

7 | For the detailed information on the multiple methods of struggle used by the commons around the world, cf. Walljasper.

no corporations), and Cittaslow (i.e., the clean, silent, and slow city). These demands created new forms of struggles in cities, especially those organized through the internet or social media,[8] which eventually brought forth what may be called networked resistance that, in turn, led to the occupation of public spaces (peacefully or by using violence), as seen in the movements of the Arab Spring, Occupy Wall Street, Indignados, Syntagma, Gezi revolts, and so on. The commons used social forums, coalitions, councils, alliances, movements, networks, NGOs, autonomous groups, initiatives, park and neighborhood forums as new grassroots social organizations in order to create direct democratic cultures and structures. Alternative political structures, such as autonomous groups, communalist living, and democratized habitats, were also regarded as a step towards a more direct democracy.

4. MOTIVES AND REASONS BEHIND RECLAMING THE CITY

The main question is that about the motives for reclaiming the cities. First, this process of reclaiming was induced by a dramatic aggravation of economic problems such as poverty, unemployment, and insufficient incomes. Second, it gained momentum as a reaction to the severe humiliation of marginal, ethnic, sexual, and migrant identities and their exclusion from the city centers. To be precise, expulsions and forced evacuations from the city centers preceding or accompanying the so-called urban renewal and gentrification processes were used as a social mass destruction weapon.[9] Third, reclaiming the city could also be

---

8 | For a discussion of the contributory or facilitating role of the social media use for the urban struggles, cf. Gezgin, "Istanbul Mobil'ized"; "Sosyal Medya Psikolojisi ve Toplumsal Hareketler"; "Sosyal Medya Psikolojisi ve Şanlı Gezi Direnişi"; "Apolitik Olanın Politikleşmesi"; "The 2013 Gezi Park Protest and #resistgezi"; Gezgin, İnal, and Hill, *The Gezi Revolt*.

9 | This destructive process is dealt with in a Turkish protest song called "The Shanty and the Skypscraper" ("Gecekonduyla Gökdelen") by Grup Yorum (2008), which depicts a conversation between a skyscraper and a shanty town and thus can be read as a rendering of the urban struggles: "Skyscraper: 'You spread all over the city / Stretching your arms / You shanty, you shanty / Go back to where you came from / You have ruinous walls / You disturb my vision / You have muddy

regarded as a response to the political domination over labor. Fourth, it reacted to the environmental massacre that destroyed green fields to build business and shopping centers. One can add many other issues to this list of issues that the reclaiming-movement responded to: inefficient and short-termist mega-projects (e.g., facilities built for mega-events in cities of unfortunate residents, as in the cases of the FIFA World Cup and the Olympics), the dominant perception of the city (i.e., cities produced/consumed as a form of commodity), spatial segregation (the fragmentation of cities into separate parts financially, culturally, and ethnically), urban renewal (e.g., gentrification, displacement, imposition of mega projects to neighborhoods, the closure of institutions providing local public services) (cf. Brenner, Marcuse, and Mayer).

These issues produced many socio-economic problems for the urban poor (as already indicated in the previous sections: an increasing number of squatters as a result of dispossession and deterritorialization, social isolation, new forms of poverty, cultural exclusion, communication on social media only, etc. Moreover, the destruction of public spaces, such as streets / You pollute the city' / Shanty: 'We laid your bricks / We mixed your mortars / The skyscraper, that bulk of concrete / We were here before you came into being / I won't move a single step / Stand out of my sunlight / Don't make shadows / That's all I want' / Skyscraper: 'You came when I was not here / Such a good deed you did / You seized the vacant lot / And squatted at midnight / These are all illegal deeds / The bulldozer arrives at your door / Take your belongings and leave / You stayed for long, that's enough' / Shanty: 'Even wolves didn't come here / These lands were totally vacant / Gendarmerie, police swarmed / When we squatted / When you occupied the sky / Which law allowed you? / Mine is the right of living / By which right were you built?' / Skyscraper: 'You all will be demolished / I will take your place / I will be shopping malls / And residence areas / Here is the heart of fashion / There is the finance center / You shanty, I want / Gleaming limousines' / Shanty: 'I hope your dirty profit greed would vanish / All the money and assets are yours / Each and every brick of the neighborhood / Is the honor of the squatters / You are the monument of exploitation / You are the symbol of ostentation / You are the statue of mammon / What kind of a creature you are, skyscraper' / Skyscraper: 'When the world is being globalized / You are still in the Stone Age / We say 'urban renewal' / You will be demolished all together' / Shanty: 'The stones in the bosom / Of the barefoot children / Will turn you upside down / They will rebuild the life'" (translation: IK/UBG).

parks, public buildings, streets, and forests, was planned and executed by the short-term goal of accumulating profit.

The rights to reclaim the cities according to the World Social Forum in Porto Allegre in 2005 (Universal Convention of City Rights) include the rights to work, cheap housing, health insurance and social security, an adequate standard of living, access to all public services, education, culture and leisure time, clean and cheaper water supply, free and quality education, a healthy and safe environment, freedom to travel and public transportation, democratic participation in decision-making, the right to self-expression, and land rights (cf. Brown and Kristiansen). These demands have completely or partially been expressed by many other organizations such as Taksim Solidarity in Istanbul (Turkey), Not in Our Name—Challenging the Brand Hamburg (Germany), My Poznanciacy (Poland), the alliance for the right to the city (USA), etc. The organizations reclaimed the cities either by revolutionary or armed forms or in democratic and peaceful ways that paved the way for the emancipatory social practices with which the commons tried to reconstruct the urban arena as an area of public space. The creation of new local autonomous structures as neighborhood and youth centers, alternative feminist collectives, independent media infrastructures, self-governance projects (cf. Brenner, Marcuse, and Mayer), etc., produced a shared conception of the city for urban dwellers.

5. GEZI PARK REVOLT IN TURKEY

The Gezi revolt in Turkey in June 2013 first appeared as a reaction to the government's plans to redesign Gezi Park, but, within a few days, took the form of a much more substantial political revolt against the government and neoliberal capitalism as a consequence of multiple acts of oppression and repression by the incumbent government in the recent years. The first demand of the Gezi commons was to stop the construction of a big mall in the area of the park. But they also had other demands, such as stopping the construction of mega-projects in Istanbul (the third airport, the third bridge over the Bosphorus, a huge canal project in addition to the Bosphorus, etc.).[10]

What happened in Gezi?[11] Mass protests all over Turkey, which lasted for two weeks, led to the rise of ecological and then political sensitivities. The protesters were organized and reorganized by/in Taksim Solidarity,[12] which consisted of more than 120 NGOs, initiatives, trade unions, political parties, foundations, associations, and so on. Taksim Solidarity released a number of declarations as demands made by the commons and the people. This organization was an umbrella organization in a new form, as it did not endorse any form of hierarchy among the commons, while most of the constituents (such as political parties, trade unions, or movements) were hierarchical within themselves. Taksim Solidarity continuously challenged the government by declaring to reclaim the city in favor of the people. But during the Gezi revolt, brutal police violence led to the deaths of many young people. The national and international media witnessed tortures, mass arrests, and lawsuits during the police violence that ran in tandem with the withdrawal of commons from the squares and streets to the park forums and neighborhood assemblies.

The reasons for the emergence of the Gezi protests are manifold. Firstly, and perhaps most significantly, they can be regarded as a critical reaction to the land speculation in Istanbul. Of course, one can add many others to the list of reasons why these protests appeared. They also criticized privatization, corruption and bribery, prohibition regulations by the government for daily life based on a pseudo-religious ideology (bans and restrictions on alcohol, cigarettes, students houses, billboards, clothing, and so on), environmental massacres, media and social media

---

10 | For three book-length editions on the analysis and discussion of the Gezi revolt from the perspectives of the participants from various social, political, and economic positions, cf. Gezgin, İnal, and Hill, "The Gezi Revolt"; İnal, "Gezi, İsyan, Özgürlük"; and Sancar, "Sıcak Haziran."

11 | Gezgin's "Dünyayı Sarsan 40 Gün: Gezi Direnişi'nin Psikolojisi ve Sosyolojisi," which partially consists of field notes from Gezi Park, can support the response to this question.

12 | Among these are socialist or leftist groups, movements, and political parties, LGBTI (alternative sexual identities), apolitical and soccer fan groups, anti-capitalist groups, laborers, street children and the homeless, artists and intellectuals, the youth and their parents.

bans, police violence, vote rigging claims in elections, the president Erdogan's (former prime minister) exclusionist and polarizing discourses and practices, threats on secular ways of life, the decline of the welfare state, etc. As the famous Gezi slogan says: "This is just the beginning," because all the reasons leading to the social explosion in Gezi Park and elsewhere continue to press Istanbulites and other citizens hard. That means that debates on Gezi discussions will probably be endless, and would eventually converge with the long-term influences of the revolts in 1968 in Western Europe, especially French 1968, among others. Any discussion about Gezi protests will thus be incomplete.[13]

6. Conclusion

Reclaiming the city all over the world in the context of urban settings has been a response to the commodification of the city as a financially profitable space. Capitalism is mainly responsible for various negative socio-economic developments, such as economic exploitation of urban space, the decline of the welfare state, heavy air pollution, speculation on urban land, privatization of public spaces, alienated forms of living, environmental massacres, and so on. Understood as a life of struggle, urban life turns urban citizens into the commons who are involved in different forms of urban resistance against capitalism to create a socially produced city by its 'real owners,' namely the people. This means that one now has to look at the cities from an alternative perspective. Capitalism is powerful, but it perhaps lacks the people as a resource that backs the public grounds in order to organize as commons in fast and efficient ways, reminiscent of Bertolt Brecht's poem "General Your Tank is a Powerful Vehicle."

Defending the cities in favor of public interest can push us ahead of capitalist profits. This defense, however, should be based on strengthening democracy not on the formal level, but in people's minds and interests in the first place. It must be our duty to rebuild our cities in new democratic ways as exemplified in direct grassroots movements' non-governmental

---

13 | For a collection of discussions about Gezi Park protests and beyond and especially about what would happen after Gezi as well as its status as a historical turning point, cf. Çakır and Aktükün (2015).

paths. To achieve this, we have three steps for a solution: The first is to raise the awareness of the people by means of identifying the problems in new ways (e.g., by providing a structural explanation with regard to capitalism and its consequences). The second is to realize the potential in the organization and practice of the commons as a new social subject/agent on the road to democracy. The third one is to identify new forms of revolt, ranging from a direct form of democracy to the occupation of urban spaces (i.e., squares, parks, streets, and other sites, where hegemonic power might be contested).

This contribution aimed to elaborate on the conceptualization of the commons and the recent urban movements with regard to the notion of the 'right to the city' coined by Lefebvre and further developed by David Harvey. However, the real developers of these ideas are and will be the people which are supposed to make history, rather than take history, i.e., accept it as an excuse for their dispossession and deterritorialization from the materialist dialectical point of view. That means this chapter can never be over. It will be rewritten and extended multiple times to pay homage to updated experiences of urban struggles. Fair enough, right? The city is dynamic, thus any modest attempt to elaborate on urban struggles would have to be dynamic as well. Thus, 'the conclusion' is a nominal misnomer. There will be no end to struggles. That is why we can be hopeful. Another welcoming note for the commons...

WORKS CITED

Adanalı, Yaşar Adnan. "AKP Döneminde Şehirler, Kentsel Dönüşüm ve Mimari: Mekansallaşan İktidar, İktisat ve İtirazlar." *Marka, Takva, Tuğra: AKP Döneminde Kültür ve Politika*, edited by Kemal İnal, Nuray Sancar, and Ulaş Başar Gezgin, Evrensel Kültür Basım Yayın, 2015, pp. 119-24.

Aykan, Begüm. Frame Alignment Strategies in the Right to Sheltering Movement: The Case of Dikmen Valley. MA thesis, METU, Ankara, 2011.

Brecht, Bertolt. "General Your Tank is a Powerful Vehicle." *Bertolt Brecht Poems 1913-1956*, edited by John Willett and Ralph Mannheim, Routledge, 1987, p. 289.

Brenner, Neil, Peter Marcuse, and Margital Mayer. *Cities for People, Not for Profit: Critical Urban Theory and the Right to the City*. Routledge, 2012.
Brown, Alison, and Annali Kristiansen. *Urban Policies and the Right to the City: Rights, Responsibilities and Citizenship*. UN Habitat, 2009. unesdoc.unesco.org/images/0017/001780/178090e.pdf.
Çakır, Gencer, and Özgür Aktükün Başpınar, editors. *Gezi Tartışmaları: İsyanın Dünü, Bugünü ve Yarını*. Ütopya Yayınevi, 2015.
Davis, Mike. *Planet of Slums*. Verso, 2006.
Doğru, Havva Ezgi. "Kapitalist Modernitenin Kentsel Aklı: Toplu Konut İdaresi (TOKİ)." *Marka, Takva, Tuğra: AKP Döneminde Kültür ve Politika*, edited by Kemal İnal et al., Evrensel Kültür Basım Yayın, 2015, pp. 149-53.
Gezgin, Ulaş Başar. "Apolitik Olanın Politikleşmesi ve Politik Olanın Dijitalleşmesi." Akademik Bilişim Konferansı, 5-7 Feb. 2014, Mersin Üniversitesi. www.slideshare.net/dr_gezgin/apolitik-olanin-politikles mesimersinulasbasargezgin.
—. "Dünyayı Sarsan 40 Gün: Gezi Direnişi'nin Psikolojisi ve Sosyolojisi." 26 Jun. 2013. www.slideshare.net/dr_gezgin/gez-drennn-pskolojs-ve -sosyolojs-direnisin-psikolojisivesosyolojisidunyayidegistiren40gun.
—. "Istanbul Mobil'ized: Mobile Phones' Contribution to Political Participation and Activism in 2013 Istanbul Gezi Park Protests and Onwards." *Alternatif Eğitim* (under review).
—. "Sosyal Medya Psikolojisi ve Şanlı Gezi Direnişi." *Direnişin @hali*, edited by Savaş Çoban, Yeşil Düşünce Derneği ve AB, 2014, pp. 40-48.
—. "Sosyal Medya Psikolojisi ve Toplumsal Hareketler." Türk-Alman Medya Semineri: Sosyal Medya ve Sosyal Hareketler (Invited speaker for the seminar organized by the German Consulate, Istanbul). 7-8 Nov. 2013, Antalya. www.slideshare.net/dr_gezgin/sosyal-medya-psikolojisi-ve-toplumsal-hareketler.
—. "The 2013 Gezi Park Protest and #resistgezi." *Civic Media Reader*, 2015, civicmediaproject.org/.
Gezgin, Ulaş Başar, Kemal İnal, and Dave Hill, editors. *The Gezi Revolt: People's Revolutionary Resistance against Neoliberal Capitalism in Turkey*. The Institute for Education Policy Studies, 2014.
Grup Yorum. "Gecekonduyla Gökdelen." *YouTube*, uploaded by halklarinsesiyiz, 18 Apr. 2014, www.youtube.com/watch?v=imaPbU 8ssHM.

Hartmann, Kathrin. *Küresel Çarkın Dışında Kalanlar: Tüketim Toplumundaki Yeni Fakirlik*. Translated by Etem Levent Bakaç, Ayrıntı, 2014.

Harvey, David. *Rebel Cities: From the Right to the City to the Urban Revolution*. Verso, 2012.

İnal, Kemal, editor. *Gezi, İsyan, Özgürlük: Sokağın Şenlikli Muhalefeti*. Ayrıntı, 2014.

Lefebvre, Henri. *Le Droit à la Ville*. Anthropos, 1968.

Mühürdaroğlu, Anıl. De-regulatory Urban Redevelopment Policies in Gecekondu Areas in Turkey: The Case of Dikmen Valley, MA thesis, METU, Ankara, 2005.

Sancar, Nuray, editor. *Sıcak Haziran: Sonraki Direnişe Mektup*. Evrensel Basım-Yayın, 2014.

Taïeb, Eric. *Immigrés: l'effet Générations. Rejet, Assimilation, Intégration d'hier à aujourd'hui*. Les Editions Ouvrières, 1998.

Türkün, Asuman. "Kentsel Dönüşümün Toplumsal Maliyeti: Yeni Konut Alanlarında Bıçak Sırtı Yaşamlar." *Marka, Takva, Tuğra. AKP Döneminde Kültür ve Politika*, edited by Kemal İnal et al., Evrensel Kültür Basım Yayın, 2015, pp. 139-48.

Uzunçarşılı Baysal, Cihan. "Kötücül Siluet." *Marka, Takva, Tuğra. AKP Döneminde Kültür ve Politika*, edited by Kemal İnal, Nuray Sancar, and Ulaş Başar Gezgin, Evrensel Kültür Basım Yayın, 2015, pp. 125-38.

Walljasper, Jay. *All That We Share: A Field Guide to the Commons*. The New Press, 2010.

"All Those Who Know the Term 'Gentrification' Are Part of the Problem"[1]
Self-Reflexivity in Urban Activism and Cultural Production

Jens Martin Gurr

> *The City is our Factory*—under this banner we might actually be able to finally escape the narcissist trap of the Left, which brands itself or the subculture as the real motor of gentrification and consequently sinks into a protestant discourse of guilt-ethics and self-accusation. [...] If we want to develop a post-crisis urbanisation model, if we want to replace the neoliberal model, we not only need to make the city greener or more social, but more accessible and designable by its inhabitants. Insofar it is no coincidence that artists play a major role in these struggles. (Schäfer, *Die Stadt* 300-1)

There have recently been numerous publications conceptually engaging with what appears to be a surge of anti-gentrification activities and 'right to the city' (*sensu* Lefebvre) movements in the 'neoliberal city' and especially in the wake of the fiscal crisis beginning in 2008. However, while much of the scholarly interest has been concerned with theorizing *about* or *for* such movements, there have been far fewer studies focusing on how these movements themselves conceptually frame their activities. Studying what might broadly speaking be subsumed under 'right to the city' activism, it is worth distinguishing between different aims: Is activism directed against gentrification, against concrete building projects or the privatization of public space, against 'neoliberal' urban

---

[1] | User comment on Kettcar's "Schrilles buntes Hamburg" video on YouTube; original: "Alle, die das Wort 'Gentrifizierung' kennen, sind Teil des Problems."

growth policies, foreclosure, the housing crisis, or homelessness, or does it more generally advocate the 'right to the city'? Since urban activism has frequently come to crystallize around anti-gentrification movements, the implicit or explicit understanding of gentrification is frequently related to the forms of activism chosen: The emphasis may here be on a demand or consumption-side understanding ('yuppies want to move to the inner city') or the supply or production side ('real estate owners can make more money if they upgrade their property'; for this 'rent gap theory,' cf. especially Smith, "Toward a Theory of Gentrification" and *The New Urban Frontier*). Accordingly, the implications for activism will be markedly different: 'Yuppies' are a far more identifiable target than economic structures and frequently invisible—often corporate—investors. Depending on the concrete target and aim of a specific movement, the types of coalitions will also frequently differ and may involve various constellations of tenants, artists, small shop owners, professionals, or leftist groups, and may be organized in local, regional, national, or even transnational networks. Moreover, we may heuristically distinguish between three forms of commitment: (1) community activism (whether explicitly theory-conscious or not), (2) activist or politically committed scholarship, (3) activist cultural production. As for the degree of explicit engagement with urban theory, we might differentiate between activism and cultural production that (1) appear to make no use of notions borrowed from 'critical urban studies,' (2) that implicitly use such notions or appear to be indebted to them, (3) that affirmatively deploy theoretical concepts, (4) that reflexively and critically make use of such concepts, occasionally with the more or less explicit aim to contribute new facets to theoretical discussions.

This contribution largely addresses the two latter forms as arguably the more common types: Given the demographics of many activist groups and the frequently academic background of many leading members (cf. Liss 257), it is hardly surprising that anti-gentrification and 'right to the city' movements in the US, Britain, Germany, and elsewhere frequently appear to be highly theory-conscious and deploy notions borrowed from Lefebvre, Castells, Harvey, Soja, and other key thinkers in 'critical urban studies.'[2]

---

2 | For the city as a location central to the formation of social movements and for a discussion of literature on 'urban social movements' (Lefebvre, Castells, Harvey, etc.), cf. Miller and Nicholls.

In a 2008 essay in the *New Left Review*, David Harvey captures the essence of what I take 'critical urban studies' to mean here:

The question of what kind of city we want cannot be divorced from that of what kind of social ties, relationship to nature, lifestyles, technologies and aesthetic values we desire. The right to the city is far more than the individual liberty to access urban resources: it is a right to change ourselves by changing the city. [...] The freedom to make and remake our cities and ourselves is, I want to argue, one of the most precious yet most neglected of our human rights. [...] At this point in history, this has to be a global struggle, predominantly with finance capital, for that is the scale at which urbanization processes now work. [...] Lefebvre was right to insist that the revolution has to be urban, in the broadest sense of that term, or nothing at all. (23-40)

We can thus conceive of 'critical urban studies' as a broadly coherent tradition of leftist inquiry into the relations between the city and capitalism, questions of marginalization, power structures, and sociospatial developments, which seeks to point out strategies for alternative urban communities, taking its cues from leading exponents such as Henri Lefebvre, David Harvey, Manuel Castells, or Peter Marcuse. In a recent essay, Neil Brenner has conveniently identified four key principles of the tradition of 'critical urban studies': (1) it is interested in theory as such (not just as a tool for practice), (2) it is reflexive and situationally specific in the sense that it is aware of its local and historical positionality, (3) it is critical of merely descriptive (or even boosterist) urban studies that "promote the maintenance and reproduction of extant urban formations" (19), (4) it is interested in the distance "between the actual and the possible," between what is and what might be—the "ultimate goal being a different city as an expression of a different, just, democratic and sustainable society" (19 et passim; cf. also Brenner, Marcuse, and Mayer 5 et passim and further contributions in their volume). One can observe that many such movements generally seeking to foster a more equitable, sustainable, or democratic society, crystallize around fairly concrete issues such as activities against gentrification, specific building projects, the privatization of public space, 'neoliberal' urban growth policies, or protests drawing attention to housing issues in the city.

It is also to be observed, however, that most scholarly work in 'critical urban studies' and on urban activism tends to theorize *for* and *about* these movements, an observation one may find somewhat surprising in the context of a movement so centrally concerned with questions of agency, voice, participation, and self-directedness. Take as a representative example the recent rather ambitious collection of essays entitled *Cities for People, not for Profit*, which brings together a number of the major figures in critical urban studies. The editors state as one of their main goals "to contribute intellectual resources that may be useful for those institutions, movements, and actors that aim to roll back the contemporary hypercommodification of urban life, and on this basis to promote alternative, radically democratic, socially just, and sustainable forms of urbanism" (Brenner, Marcuse, and Mayer 2). In fact, in the entire volume, Jon Liss' essay on the nation-wide Right to the City (RTTC) Alliance in the US, largely a report of the organizational efforts and strategies of this group to move beyond traditional Alinsky-style community organizing, is the only one by an activist rather than by a scholar. This essay is also clearly the odd one out in the volume for being large devoid of theorizing. Addressing the issue of voice and agency, Liss states that the "leadership of NWCOs [New Working Class Organizations] is primarily university-educated, 'middle class', and oppressed nationality" and also comments on conflicts between university-educated middle-class activists and members of the class they are supposedly struggling for (257).

The heuristic categories introduced above and the efficacy—or lack thereof—of specific constellations of actors can be illustrated by means of the "Mission Yuppie Eradication Project" (MYEP) in San Francisco (1998-2000), which, because of the aggressive rhetoric of its posters, gained substantial press coverage (cf. Solnit and Schwartzenberg 124-28; Keating). In the years 1998-2000, when, in the wake of the 'dot-com boom,' gentrification became an increasingly pressing issue in San Francisco, protest crystallized in the city's Mission District, traditionally a working-class neighborhood. In this period, a number of pithily phrased posters called for vandalism against 'yuppie' vehicles and restaurants:

MISSION YUPPIE ERADICATION PROJECT. Over the past several years the Mission has been colonized by pigs with money. Yuppie scumbags have crawled out of their haunts on Union Street and [in] the suburbs to take our neighborhood away from us. [...] They come to party, and end up moving in to what used to be affordable rental housing. They help landlords drive up rents, pushing working and poor people out of their homes. [...] This yuppie takeover can be turned back. [...]

VANDALIZE YUPPIE CARS: BMWs—Porsches—Jaguars—SPORT-UTILITY VEHICLES [sic]. Break the Glass—Scratch the Paint—Slash Their Tires and Upholstery—Trash Them All. If yuppie scum know their precious cars aren't safe on the streets of this neighborhood, they'll go away and they won't come back—and the trendoid restaurants, bars and shops that cater to them will go out of business. [...] TAKE ACTION NOW. ("Mission Yuppie Eradication Project")

Unsurprisingly, the aggressive rhetoric of the poster is based on a demand-side understanding of gentrification and identifies "yuppie scumbags" as the targets of activism. While this poster does not make explicit use of any theoretical notion (and, though providing a by-the-book description of the process, appears deliberately to avoid the term 'gentrification'), a later poster from 1999 alludes to a key moment of urban protest and thus suggests familiarity with a tradition of theoretically informed activism. Translating a widely known Situationist graffiti from May 1968, "bientôt des ruines pittoresques," it calls for the destruction of what appear to have been iconic 'yuppie' bars and restaurants:

Soon to be picturesque ruins: During the next major urban riots, we must attack and destroy the following yuppie bars and restaurants in the Mission: [...] Beauty Bar [...] Tokyo A Go-Go, [...] the corporate-types inside make it look like a scene from a bad '80s movie starring Rob Lowe and Demi Moore [...] Blowfish Sushi [...], a nest of cell phone yuppies and upper middle class privilege [...] Circadia, a Starbucks [...] where virtual humans surf the Internet all day while slurping 7$ coffee drinks. [...] There are other places to be targeted—use your imagination. Be creative. Take action. Don't get caught. ("Mission Yuppie Eradication Project")

In a 2007 essay, "A Critique of the Mission Yuppie Eradication Project," Kevin Keating, who identifies himself as having been the MYEP's leading activist—partly, it seems, its *only* activist—engages with what he regards as the achievements and limitations of his professedly radical and revolutionary commitment. He comments on the high visibility gained by the aggressive rhetoric of the posters and regards the lack of a dedicated network as the key weakness of his stand-alone initiative. His highly self-conscious assessment needs to be quoted at some length:

In a de-politicized culture rampaging market forces can't be confronted effectively with conventional political language. So a logical first step in an effort to foment resistance was to cover the walls of the Mission with a thousand photocopied posters calling for working people to resist the bourgeois invasion by vandalizing yuppie cars. [...] The posters communicated an extremist message in clear, simple language, avoiding Marxist or anarchist buzz-words. I described the process of gentrification without using the word 'gentrification.' As the posters hit the walls working people started fighting back. [...] And I used the global news media attention focused on the gentrification of the Mission as a soapbox for a larger anti-capitalist perspective. [...] The posters succeeded on the basic level that anti-capitalist agitprop efforts should aim at; they helped define a contemporary social problem in clear class conflict terms, and tried to move the fight away from the atomization and powerlessness of the democratic process toward some kind of large-scale direct action. Exactly what form that large-scale direct action would take wasn't clear to me [...] In the face of many decades of failure of a work-within-the-system perspective, and its inability to deliver the goods in both small ways and large, the field is wide open for a wholly different kind of autonomous direct action response, outside of and against the conventional, legitimate decision-making structures of democratic capitalism. [...] My focus was too narrow. I concentrated solely on the Mission District. My anti-gentrification effort happened at the high point of my love affair with the neighborhood I live in, and my passion blinded me to opportunities I might have otherwise taken advantage of. I should have exploited media coverage that came my way to get out more of a city-wide message against rent and landlords and the larger issue of housing as a commodity. Under the best circumstances a subversive effort can have a 'bleed-through' effect. What starts in one collective conflict between wage slaves and capital can spread or cross-pollinate into other everyday life situations, even ones that don't appear to be related to the initial issue. (Keating)

In keeping with these insights, Keating points to the 'dot-com bust' and the recession rather than to any activism to account for the fact that, at the time of his writing (2007), the Mission District was still largely working class and that gentrification had significantly slowed down (for an account of the MYEP, including an interview with Keating, cf. also Solnit and Schwartzenberg 124-28).

A particularly illuminating example of explicit engagement with 'critical urban studies' in urban activism and particularly in what might be termed 'activist cultural production' commenting *on* this phenomenon is to be found in the work of Christoph Schäfer, especially in his *Die Stadt ist unsere Fabrik/The City is Our Factory* an activist pictorial essay on the history of the urban, detailing especially the 'right to the city' movement in Hamburg. How are theoretical concepts in urban studies appropriated and strategically deployed in these representations? To what extent are urban activism and activist cultural production self-reflexive and aware of their own ambivalence and potential for commodification? I will argue that some of the most theoretically informed exponents of these movements are keenly aware of this ambivalence and time and again ironically portray theory-inflected urban activism as to some extent the pursuit of an internationally connected urban elite failing to address the concerns of those groups most severely hit by gentrification and exclusion.

With the caveat that a discussion in print with only few illustrations is bound to fall short of fully doing justice to the primarily visual format of a large-format pictorial essay, I turn to this case study of activist cultural production of the highly theory-conscious and reflexive type.

Christoph Schäfer is a central figure in Hamburg's 'Recht auf Stadt' ('right to the city') movement, a network of some 25 initiatives working towards affordable housing, the preservation of public space and of urban green spaces, more participation, and a more democratic city. He has been called an "embedded artist" of the movement (moderator in Schäfer, "The City"), and his 2010 book *Die Stadt ist unsere Fabrik/The City is Our Factory*, a pictorial essay in some 160 drawings, is "a rhizomatic history of the urban" (publisher's blurb) from the first cities thousands of years ago to Hamburg in 2009. In the form of exploratory and annotated drawings and in some 15 pages of more discursive text densely printed in five columns per page,[3] it discusses issues such as the origin and development of urban settlements, the production of space, urban anthropology, the connections between social and spatial developments, urban imaginaries and identities, changing forms of work, participation, and bottom-up community organizing, gentrification, squatting, and the struggle against the privatization and commercialization of public space, city branding and marketing, the creative class discourse, or the role of art and artists in urban development.[4] Throughout, the book displays an acute

---

3 | Like the entire book, these texts are in both English and German.

4 | The five chapters are titled as follows: "Lefebvre 4 Kids" (3), "Appropriated Space" (69), "1979: The City is Our Factory" (115), "Black Holes" (151), "Hamburg: Surrounding the 'Expanding City' with Projects" (165), "The Evening I Would Like to Have on Film" (272).

theory-consciousness and familiarity with central concepts of 'critical urban studies' in the sense outlined above. Here, as well as in interviews (cf. "Maschinen"), Schäfer very adeptly employs, cites, and alludes to Benjamin, Heidegger's reading of Hölderlin, Lefebvre, Foucault, Deleuze and Guattari, David Harvey, or Siqueiros and the aesthetics and politics of Mexican *muralismo*, as well as innumerable further directly apposite as well as arcanely related notions and concepts. I can here only discuss a small selection of issues and their negotiation and will do so focusing on those which (1) are most prominent in 'right to the city' movements generally and (2) best illustrate the poetics and politics of Schäfer's approach.

The more explicitly political sections dealing with the recent Hamburg initiatives revolve around the intersecting concerns of city branding and imagineering, the attempt at tailoring the city to the needs of the 'creative class,' and the privatization and commercialization of public space: "Unnoticed at first, something essential began to change in the cities when we started walking around with cardboard cups full of hot milk and coffee. Entire neighbourhoods soon gave you the feeling that you were purchasing a stay permit with your latte" (Schäfer, *Die Stadt* 142).

An impressive sequence of drawings explores the connection between neoliberal urban policies and the loss of urban memory emblematized in the collapse of the Cologne City Archive. On 3 March 2009, the Cologne City Archive, containing millions of documents dating all the way back to the High Middle Ages, collapsed into an open building excavation some 25 meters deep, resulting in the damage and partial loss of invaluable historical documents. The collapse appears to have been the result of criminal negligence and insufficient construction site security in privatized construction work on a new underground line: "Cologne, March 2009: Suddenly the earth opened up and the entire history of the city disappeared down a hole" (152).

Fig. 1: Schäfer's representation of the Cologne City Archive disaster: "an almost biblical omen."

In an interview, Schäfer commented on the collapse as "an almost biblical omen for the end of the neoliberal city model" ("Biblisches Warnzeichen" 106; translation: JMG).

In a related vein, Schäfer attacks the way in which the City of Hamburg uncritically deployed Richard Florida's widely debated, reductionist 'creative class' policies (cf. Florida) in its urban development strategies in order to target this 'economically desirable' segment of the population. In addition to overstating the contribution of specific forms of culture to an attractive economic milieu, which has led to a socially exclusionist latte-macchiatoization of parts of the city, the concomitant instrumentalization of art and artists, as well as the gentrification associated with these processes have also met with significant resistance from artists refusing to be commodified as mere location factors conducive to the 'bohemian index' of a city.[5] The connection is captured as follows: "In 2004, Senator of Science Dräger hands out books by Richard Florida in the Hamburg

---

5 | Cf. also the much-publicized protest of artists in Hamburg against such endeavours: "Kunst als Protest" from 2009.

city senate. Florida holds lectures. Roland Berger develops 'Hamburg, City of Talent'. Artists leave city" (174).

Arguably the central issue in this most topical and specific chapter "Hamburg: Surrounding the 'Expanding City' with Projects" (165-271) is that of gentrification, in response to which numerous projects and initiatives have been launched.

Fig. 2: The "degentrification kit": how to make a neighborhood unattractive to investors.

In addition to the more conventional flyers, protests, public lectures, performances, or squatting, one of the more humorous ideas is the "degentrification kit," a set of items and ideas to "ruin the image of the neighbourhood" so as to scare away investors: "add foreign names to your door bell [...] dry ugly clothing outdoors [the illustration suggests the type of ribbed undershirt popularly known as a 'wifebeater'] [...] [use] broken windows effect foil[6] [...] hang Lidl bag out of your window [...] add satellite

---

6 | There is a certain irony here in the reference to Wilson and Kelling's notorious "Broken Windows" essay in that the 'broken windows theory' is usually vehemently attacked by 'critical urban theory'-inflected urban activism and scholarship.

dish (or 2, or 3!)" (183).[7] The caveat "But watch it—don't get too creative [where the creatives are working, rents go up]" (183) is characteristic of the constant awareness of the 'anti-gentrifier's dilemma,' the insight that even (and especially) resistant cultural production can be commodified.[8]

It is not least the ongoing light-hearted reflections on this ambivalence of activist art and the self-mockery in the awareness of a privileged form of theory Sudoku—insights which in no way trivialize the sincerity of the commitment—that makes Schäfer's work so compelling. This is especially prominent in the final chapter entitled "The Evening I Would Like to Have on Film." The book here represents the gathering of a group of—apparently privileged—activist friends engaging in clever 'urban studies talk' in a place none other than the McDonald's in Hamburg Central Station:

> The evening I'd like to have as a movie began like this: We had arranged to meet with the Utopia Salon & Spa Group at the McDonald's in the central station. We drank lattes and gazed at the tracks. Only 3 people showed up. The conversation revolved around arcades, urbanity, rambling, the promises of a by-gone age as encapsulated in architecture. After a while we left and went on talking as we walked. The evening was dry and warm. It was August 21, 2009. (274)[9]

---

7 | The phrases appear in the drawing, hence in no particular order; the order is mine.

8 | More generally, the 'anti-gentrifier's dilemma' refers to the problem that an awareness of one's own privileged position and even activism against gentrification may not be enough to avoid supporting the process by one's mere presence as someone able to pay higher rents. A pithy literary representation of the issue is to be found in Kiran Desai's *The Inheritance of Loss*: "One evening, Biju was sent to deliver hot-and-sour soups and egg foo yong to three Indian girls, students, new additions to the neighborhood in an apartment just opened under reviewed city laws to raised rents. Banners reading 'Antigentrification Day' had been hauled up over the street by the longtime residents for a festival earlier in the afternoon [...] One day the Indian girls hoped to be gentry, but right now, despite being unwelcome in the neighborhood, they were in the student stage of vehemently siding with the poor people who wished them gone" (49).

9 | Cf. also 284: "We stopped at a cellar restaurant. A place I had never been before. We got hold of a corner sofa and on went the conversation: Lefebvre and the urban revolution, David Harvey and the urban roots of the fiscal crisis, how

The corresponding drawing is highly allusive: three figures at a table perched above the platforms and underneath the steel arches of the station architecture reminiscent of the arches of the 19th-century Paris arcades memorialized in Benjamin's *Passagenwerk*.[10]

Fig. 3: Schäfer's allusive and self-reflexive mockery of privileged 'critical urban studies' talk in a Benjaminean setting.

The ambivalence of subversion and the awareness of the anti-gentrifier's dilemma directly tie in with the questions raised in my initial discussion of voice, agency, privilege, and the question of who, given the potential for commodification, ultimately benefits from such activism:

It was our most radical gestures that could best be made use of.—To increase the value of real estate, to construct new neighbourhood identities. As soon as there was an illegal club somewhere, a cappuccino bar would open next door,

---

a post-crisis urbanisation model might look, the invention of the Bohemian and its totalisation today, the 3D printer and Fab Lab ... Hours later we left the pub, poisoned with alcohol and nicotine" (284).

10 | In the Bergermann interview, he explicitly speaks of this as "a Benjaminean situation" (122; translation: JMG).

followed by a new media agency [...] we were management consultants. [...] [W]e had acquired precisely the skills that image capitalism needs—visually literate, consumption-competent truffle pigs. (132, 134)

This is remarkably close to Mayer's thoughts in her recent essay on some of the key issues in 'right to the city' activism:

Even though these coalitions do frequently succeed in preventing, or at least modifying crass neoliberal urban development projects, their struggles often end up saving some oases and protected spaces only for the *comparatively privileged protagonists*, spaces which increasingly become *instrumentalized in creative city branding efforts* in the competitive entrepreneurial urban policy game. The chapter thus raises the questions whether the 'right to the city' movements in the global North need not relate more directly to the struggles of groups that have been excluded from the model of the neoliberal city. (Mayer 64; my italics)

What Mayer here notes about the need to "relate" different types of urban struggles to each other is precisely what Mark Purcell has termed a "well-known problem for left politics [...] [the need] to combine local struggles into something larger without reducing each struggle to a homogenous unity" (562). Here, according to Purcell, "[t]he right to the city [*sensu* Lefebvre] can be useful in establishing relations of equivalence among groups in a broad counterhegemonic urban alliance" (571-72).

This need for a broad range of highly diverse urban social movements to march under *one* banner and the 'right to the city' as a claim with such an integrative potential are also a central and recurring subject in Schäfer's account of urban activism in Hamburg:

Right to the City: appropriation, social questions, counter-projects, international, tenant battles, poverty, solidarity, segregation, self-organized spaces[11] [...] *Unlikely alliance* [...] And there we are [...] a group of left activists, from different ethnical and religious backgrounds [...]. To come together and fight we use the term *Right to the City*. (Schäfer, *Die Stadt* 190)

---

11 | The terms and concepts appear in a drawing, hence in no particular order; the order is mine.

In search of 'success factors' for urban activism and activist cultural production, in addition to such organizational issues of community organizing, Schäfer in an interview also comments on the political implications of artistic form and the choice of media and genres:

> U.B.: Your book is not poly-perspectivist, but functions in a rather linear way from beginning to end, beginning with the history of the city of 'Ur' and ending in the urban present.
> C.S.: Strictly pseudo-linear. [...] I like techniques that compress things. It looks linear, fixed, pigeon-holed, but the brevity also opens up associative possibilities of jumping back and forth. Thus, even if universalism has rightly been criticized, such a schematic representation allows me to relate developments on different continents to each other—and thus also to relativize genealogies such as Eurocentrism. My book claims, first of all, to define fundamentally what a city is, what the urban revolution might be and what it aims at. At the same time, the book works against such linearity; there are constant prolepses and analepses. (Schäfer, "Maschinen" 119-20; translation: JMG)

Emphasizing the processuality and openness of drawing, he here speaks about drawing as an activity in which exploratory doodling, the deliberate putting-to-paper of an idea and the making of a product until the last moment do not have to be mutually exclusive: "A drawing can potentially escape goal-directedness and instrumentalization until the last second" (Schäfer, "Maschinen" 116). This understanding is developed further in response to a critical question about de-collectivization and his potential appropriation of drawings originally from and for a political context for his own artistic and economic self-promotion: "I was able to give talks in 'right to the city' contexts with these drawings, using them to illustrate Lefebvre's terms in a different way, thus using them for our exchange. There is no pure form that is entirely free of a potential commodification" (122).

Given this constant exploration of artistic strategies of subversion, the considerable publicity and success achieved by the Hamburg movement, and finally Schäfer's own prominent role in it as an activist, participant observer, and embedded artist, a comment on the intersection of activism and cultural production in an earlier section of the book might well be read as an oblique remark on his own successful negotiation of these issues:

"Some succeeded in connecting their sub-cultural and art practices with the struggles against gentrification" (*Die Stadt* 130).

A few tentative conclusions may be drawn based on the above observations: Strategically speaking, it seems that a success factor in urban activism is to achieve what Purcell calls "networks of equivalence [...] counterhegemonic combinations of differentiated but equivalent popular struggles" (562) and what Christoph Schäfer refers to as "unlikely alliances: *Letting disparities co-exist and emphasizing difference even while acting together*" (*Die Stadt* 236).

As far as aesthetic strategies in activist cultural production are concerned, they frequently appear to be the result of a keen awareness of 'the anti-gentrifier's dilemma.' But the more theory-conscious and self-reflexive artists and activists also appear to be aware that their own brand of urban activism is occasionally an activity of the privileged rather than of those most directly affected by gentrification and social exclusion. It seems that one of the recurring strategies in response to these dilemmas is a highly self-conscious, extremely reflexive, media-conscious form of experimentalism in cultural production, frequently with fairly explicit claims as to the emancipatory potential of this formally experimental form of presentation. In Schäfer's case, his highly self-conscious formal strategies of undercutting commodification appear to work: The drawings have been used in lectures at MIT and elsewhere and thus furnish material for academic discussions, but they also work as posters, flyers, food for thought in community workshops, etc. Thus, without claiming that Schäfer's work was pivotal in this, the Hamburg 'right to the city' initiative has had a number of very remarkable successes; and as long as activist cultural production can thus be tapped into at various levels—and the kind of deliberately open-ended, exploratory process of drawing seems to lend itself to that—, it does have the potential to be instrumental in the kind of urban resistance movement we are concerned with here.[12]

---

12 | This essay is a revised version of parts of my earlier essay "Critical Urban Studies and/in 'Right to the City' Movements: The Politics of Form in Activist Cultural Production," which is to appear in *Resistance and the City: Challenging Urban Space*, edited by Pascal Fischer and Christoph Ehland, Brill/Rodopi, forthcoming.

Images

Fig. 1: Schäfer's representation of the Cologne City Archive disaster: "an almost biblical omen."

Fig. 2: The "degentrification kit": how to make a neighborhood unattractive to investors.

Fig. 3: Schäfer's allusive and self-reflexive mockery of privileged 'critical urban studies' talk in a Benjaminean setting.

Works Cited

Brenner, Neil. "What is Critical Urban Theory?" *Cities for People, not for Profit: Critical Urban Theory and the Right to the City*, edited by Neil Brenner, Peter Marcuse, and Margit Mayer, Routledge, 2012, pp. 11-23.

Brenner, Neil, Peter Marcuse, and Margit Mayer, editors. *Cities for People, not for Profit: Critical Urban Theory and the Right to the City*. Routledge, 2012.

Desai, Kiran. *The Inheritance of Loss*. Penguin, 2006.

Florida, Richard. *Cities and the Creative Class*. Routledge, 2005.

Gurr, Jens Martin. "Critical Urban Studies and/in 'Right to the City' Movements: The Politics of Form in Activist Cultural Production." *Resistance and the City: Challenging Urban Space*, edited by Pascal Fischer and Christoph Ehland, Rodopi/Brill, forthcoming.

Harvey, David. "The Right to the City." *New Left Review*, vol. 53, 2008, pp. 23-40.

Keating, Kevin. "A Critique of San Francisco's Mission Yuppie Eradication Project." *Infoshop*, 2007, www.infoshop.org/myep/mission-yuppie-eradication-project.

Kettcar. "Schrilles Buntes Hamburg." *YouTube*, uploaded by Grand Hotel van Cleef, 18 Jan. 2012, www.youtube.com/watch?v=rdL4sRBZ-Hk. Accessed 5 Jul. 2013.

"Kunst als Protest: Lasst den Scheiß!: Hamburg nur noch als 'Marke,' der wir Aura, Ambiente und Freizeitwert verpassen sollen? Das machen wir nicht mit: Ein Künstler-Manifest gegen die Hamburger Kulturpolitik." *Zeit Online*, 5 Nov. 2009, www.zeit.de/2009/46/Kuenstlermanifest. Accessed 1 Jul. 2013.

Lefebvre, Henri. *Le Droit à la Ville*. Anthropos, 1968.

Liss, John. "The Right to the City: From Theory to Grassroots Alliance." *Cities for People, not for Profit: Critical Urban Theory and the Right to the City*, edited by Neil Brenner, Peter Marcuse, and Margit Mayer, Routledge, 2012, pp. 250-63.

Mayer, Margit. "The 'Right to the City' in Urban Social Movements." *Cities for People, not for Profit: Critical Urban Theory and the Right to the City*, edited by Neil Brenner, Peter Marcuse, and Margit Mayer, Routledge, 2012, pp. 63-85.

Miller, Byron, and Walter Nicholls. "Social Movements in Urban Society: The City as a Space of Politicization." *Cities, Spatialities, and Politicization*, special issue of *Urban Geography*, vol. 34, no. 4, 2013, pp. 452-73.

"Mission Yuppie Eradication Project." *FoundSF*, foundsf.org/index.php?title=Mission_Yuppie_Eradication_Project. Accessed 1 Jul. 2013.

Purcell, Mark. "To Inhabit Well: Counterhegemonic Movements and the Right to the City." *Cities, Spatialities, and Politicization*, special issue of *Urban Geography*, vol. 34, no. 4, 2013, pp. 560-74.

Schäfer, Christoph. *Die Stadt ist unsere Fabrik/The City is our Factory*. Spector Books, 2010.

—. "Ein Biblisches Warnzeichen." *Der Spiegel*, vol. 21, 22 Jun. 2010, p. 106.

—. "Maschinen aus Möglichkeiten: *Die Stadt ist unsere Fabrik*—Christoph Schäfer im Gespräch mit Ulrike Bergermann." *Zeitschrift für Medienwissenschaft*, vol. 3, 2010, pp. 115-23.

—. "The City Is Our Factory: Politics of Desire and the Production of Urban Spaces between Grande Latte and Park Fiction." Lecture at MIT, 28 Sep. 2009. *MIT Video*, video.mit.edu/watch/christoph-schaefer-factory-city-4585/. Accessed 1 Jul. 2013.

Smith, Neil. *The New Urban Frontier: Gentrification and the Revanchist City*. Routledge, 1996.

—. "Toward a Theory of Gentrification: A Back to the City Movement by Capital, not People." *Journal of the American Planning Association*, vol. 45, no. 4, 1979, pp. 538-48.

Solnit, Rebecca, and Susan Schwartzenberg. *Hollow City: The Siege of San Francisco and the Crisis of American Urbanism*. Verso, 2000.

Wilson, James Q., and George L. Kelling. "Broken Windows: The Police and Neighborhood Safety." *Atlantic Monthly*, March 1982, pp. 29–38.

Images of Protest
On the "Woman in the Blue Bra" and Relational Testimony

Kathrin Peters

In an incident during the protests in Cairo in December 2011, a woman is beaten up in broad daylight by Egyptian soldiers. Uniformed, helmeted men, about ten of them altogether, beat the woman, who is already lying on the ground, with sticks. In the course of the blows and kicks, being pulled and dragged about, her black abaya slides up and falls open. Underneath she is wearing jeans, trainers, and a blue bra. At this point, one of the men kicks her bared chest hard, as if her very nakedness has to be beaten and punished. Her torso flops lifelessly to and fro. Finally, one of the men covers the supine woman with the black fabric and leaves the scene, just as the camera pans up to show a crowd running away in the light of the setting sun. At the top, the recording bears the green logo of the Russian state broadcaster Russia Today.

Fig. 1: Screenshot of the CNN report, Dec. 2011.

The video spread very quickly on the internet, and can still be viewed on various websites.[1] But what exactly does the clip show? Or, put another way, who sees what in it? For whose argumentation was it used? Where, in what context, and under what conditions does one come across a video in such a series of manifestations—some of them in fact transcending into other media? In my contribution, I wish to explore these questions with the example of the video, which quickly became known as "The Woman in the Blue Bra." This venture touches on the differentiation of center and periphery in two ways. Firstly, Cairo's Tahrir Square is seen through a center/periphery lens defined by media reporting conventions and postcolonial relationships. The peripheral attribution stems directly from an Occident/Orient distinction that is transported and perpetuated not least by ideas of gender progress and backwardness. Secondly, the video was disseminated under conditions that redefine the periphery question. Compared to the traditional institutions, the news and photo agencies with their geographical, architectural, and technical centers, this footage was circulated through peripheral channels. Just ninety seconds long, it joined the mass of authorless or unauthorized video clips circulating in social media to be linked, copied, and appropriated in blogs, sharing platforms, and news sites. Its diffusion has by no means remained restricted to the digital realm. Stills made their way back to the street, in graffiti and posters, even appearing as a cover image for print magazines both Egyptian and European. The established verification processes of editorial commissioning and selection barely function here. Instead, I argue, the scene acquires evidential character through repetition of use and a specific chain of images. Even if protest movements increasingly draw on media techniques to feed their dynamics, be these leaflets or wall newspapers, there is certainly no reason to parrot the talk of a Twitter or Facebook revolution, where social protest is handed over to social media corporations. But in view of the contemporary flood of digital images, the question remains how to conceive visual testimony.

---

1 | RT (Russia Today) is an international television news channel founded in 2005. For the video, cf. RT's "'Blue Bra Girl' Atrocity: Egyptian Military Police More Than Brutal," Isobel Coleman's article "'Blue Bra Girl' Rallies Egypt's Women vs. Oppression" on CNN, and "The Blue Bra Girl: The Shocking Video" on YouTube.

1. STREET POLITICS AND VULNERABILITY

If we consider the date of its publication, 18 December 2011, "The Woman in the Blue Bra" (or, belittling and eroticizing, the "Blue Bra Girl") tells us something about the political situation within the Egyptian protest movement at this specific point. In December 2011, parliamentary elections were in full swing, conducted by the Supreme Council of the Armed Forces. Since the uprising began in January that year with huge demonstrations, mass detentions, and the occupation of Tahrir Square, the protests had never ceased; not even after Mubarak's resignation. But they did flare up again massively that December in response to the electoral rules imposed by the generals. The video also says something about how the street can be the place of protest and resistance and the location of assertion and maintenance of state power at the very same time. I will pursue that relationship in the following (even if it initially leads away from my starting question).

Urban streets and squares are places where bodies gather, where they are always exposed to the dangers of an equally embodied state power: a state power and authority expressed in the video in practically untrammeled violence. Those who take the risk, who expose their vulnerability, are not arguing for their rights simply through slogans, but above all with their bodies. Judith Butler, who I follow here, emphasizes in a recent text on street politics that "for the body to exist politically, it has to assume a social dimension—it is comported outside itself and toward others in ways that cannot and do not ratify individualism" ("Bodies in Alliance"). That means that the demands raised, i.e., the right to mobility, political and social participation, and recognition as equals, are already articulated and staged within the act of protest itself. Of course, as Butler concedes (if only to dispel any suspicion of political romanticism), physical gathering and exposure is not the only possible or meaningful expression of dissent. But it is highly appropriate where the issue is to assert the demand for habitable streets and squares in a performative act. As in the case of the testing of "horizontal relations" (Butler, "Bodies in Alliance") during the occupation of Tahrir Square.

These ideas of Butler stand in connection with her thoughts on an elementary vulnerability that affects every subject equally, in the sense that we are fundamentally dependent on others. But asserting an elementary vulnerability does not mean that political and social norms, resource distribution, and center/periphery distinctions do not make people vulnerable in different ways; quite the contrary: Taken to extremes, particular lives do not fully count and are thus "ungrievable" (Butler, *Frames of War* 22). But Butler connects this specific vulnerability with an elementary form that applies to everybody, even the privileged, apparently invincible, to the extent that everyone stands in relationships and dependencies, is woven into a "set of relations" ("Bodily Vulnerability" 134). Dependency does not mean repression but constitutive relations to other people, life processes, and inorganic conditions of life.

In the context under consideration here, it is important, as Butler emphasizes in relation to street politics, that physical vulnerability and agency are not mutually exclusive. Bodies are not *either* vulnerable *or* viable. Instead they are always also vulnerable *in* their action, in their agency ("Bodily Vulnerability" 139). The opposition of strength versus weakness or vulnerability is just as irrelevant as the idea that resistance requires independence. In fact, the assertion of agency is intimately bound up with vulnerability, risking injury, as the "Woman in the Blue Bra" video makes abundantly clear: The violence strikes the woman in her act of demonstration, in her exposure, her assertion of the right to act. The violence, one could say, is directed at her assertion of agency. The assault she experiences cannot, of course, be explained solely in terms of elementary vulnerability, for female and gender-non-normative queer bodies have always been particularly subject to violence, especially when one considers that in many parts of the world—including Egypt—women's freedom of movement is just as restricted as their social and political participation. The female bodies visible on the street also expose structural and private violence against them. Gender power is exemplified in the female body. This does not only apply to women who wear an abaya over nothing but jeans and a bra—but it does apply to them in a specific manner, as is discernible in the video: The kicks are directed at the uncovered torso, the blue bra in its symbolism. "I don't believe this girl was veiled. You do not dress that way if you were veiled. She is a fake" (qtd. in Hafez 25) a woman tells an Egyptian television reporter, and a moderator comments: "Truthfully, what were you thinking wearing that abaya with nothing underneath" (qtd. in Hafez 25).[2] The woman associated with the

---

2 | Quotations originally from television programs Channel 1 and Nilesat, 18-21 December 2011.

blue bra is branded a *fake*. In a metonymic gesture she becomes the blue bra, and thus, under her Islamic veil, a fraud. Her manner of wearing hijab and abaya is interpreted as a false veiling or a veiling of the false, a false, non-normative femininity.

In relation to the nexus of vulnerability and agency Butler proposes, this interpretation by the television station is significant. Egypt's patriarchal order regards women as especially vulnerable, and protecting female vulnerability as integral to the male ethos (cf. Hafez 26). But in the moment when femininity is supposedly revealed as false, a question arises over which women deserve protection. A differentiation is drawn: On the one hand, the mood swings to the exclusion of the "Woman in the Blue Bra," making her injury ungrievable;[3] and on the other hand, abrogation of the male duty to female vulnerability engenders resistance. Ultimately, it is said, it was the recording of this incident and the dissemination of the video that created Egypt's largest women's movement to date (cf. El Shimi, "The Woman" 182).[4] Male marshals appeared to protect the women's protests, thus reinstating the normative gender order: female vulnerability under male protection. As Butler states, it is one and the same rationale of power that calls for protection of a supposedly especially vulnerable femininity—and pursues its exclusion (cf. "Bodily Vulnerability" 144). For paternalistic protection denies and undermines a capacity to take action that must by necessity risk vulnerability if it is not to be excluded in the protection of the domestic. Perhaps this is the point where it becomes unmistakably obvious that agency must go hand in hand with vulnerability if it is actually to represent resistance and not just decorum.

It has been criticized that the relationality in which Butler thinks relates solely to interdependencies between persons, but does not extend to dependencies on non-human actors (cf. Ott 52–54). However, her writings on protest movements and street politics certainly hint at an expansion of the concept of alliances to the non-human: simply because bodies are shaped and maintained in relation to infrastructural supports (or their defects), in relation to social and technological networks that are always economically and historically specific (Butler, "Bodily Vulnerability" 148).

---

3 | Hafez writes that the identity of the assaulted woman never became known (cf. 22).

4 | I would like to thank Florian Ebner for our discussions and the catalogue, without which this essay could not have been written.

The idea that bodies enter into connections with the street itself is a not uninspiring one, and one which leads away from assuming the exclusive dominance of the spoken to including forms of staging and performances on site. Urban architecture, city planning, and infrastructure enable and channel movements; here they are actants of uprising and carry levels of meaning into the protests: The historicity of squares and buildings grants occasions to speak, to assemble physically, and occupy them, to expose buried or denied meanings of these places (the square as a place of public gatherings, for example). But we can also go further and turn our attention to the digital media that are so significant in contemporary protest movements. Audio-visual recordings, whether analogue or digital, are essential to political impact, both in the local context and for global perception. This relation of global and local corresponds to a closeness of media technology and the human body. The popularity of digital gadgets worn close to the body, almost invisible but permanently transmitting and receiving, represents a danger to those who are recorded—and by implication also to those who carry them. Body and device enter a connection that far exceeds the character of instrumental media usage, an act of recording that integrates the body in its vulnerability. "It can be an effort to destroy the camera and its user, or it can be a spectacle of destruction for the camera, a media event produced as a warning or a threat," says Butler ("Bodies in Alliance"). The presence of a recording device alters the scene itself, triggers violent actions, precisely because anyone has the possibility to distribute the digital recording at any time. Recording devices thus not only report, but themselves become part of the scene and action to the extent that they (potentially) enable distribution beyond the local space. This is factored in by the actors and has already become one of the fundamental rights that are asserted.[5] In his "Pixelated Revolution" (2012), the artist Rahib Mroué addresses the connection of agency, vulnerability, and digital recording in a very existential manner. In a lecture performance, Mroué montages video footage from mobile phones from suspected regime opponents shot dead during the Syrian protests. The videos, which Mroué found on YouTube, function as visual remains

---

5 | "So the media not only reports on social and political movements that are laying claim to freedom and jusitce in various ways; the media is also exercising one of those freedoms for which the social movement struggles" (Butler, "Bodies in Alliance").

documenting the shooting of people discovered filming by soldiers; "they are recording their own death," as Mroué puts it with deliberate drama. We see blurred scenes such as could be recorded by a falling camera, from which Mroué, in a visual analysis of forensic dimensions, derives meaning and ultimately evidence.[6]

2. Follow the Video

Against the background of these thoughts, let us follow the video "The Woman in the Blue Bra": the possible circumstances of its origination and some of the channels by which it has been disseminated and modified. Let us look again more precisely. It was published on 18 December 2011 at 10:23 a.m. on *rt.com*. The recording dates from the previous day. The scene showing the woman's mistreatment lasts just a few seconds; the video also contains other material, including soldiers storming the tented camp on Tahrir Square. Authorship is not noted, aside from the station logo denoting ownership. Nor is it discernible whether the recordings originated from a single source (or even a single device) or whether this is a montage of material from different sources. The recordings could have been made by a Russia Today reporter, or they could more likely be amateur material, for example mobile phone clips made by bystanders and sent or sold to a news agency. The style of the footage, characterized by rapid panning and zooming, reflects above all the suddenness of the events; even a professional might never have found the opportunity for aesthetic composition. No longer is it exclusively professional reporters who are where the action is with a camera. Participants and bystanders have cameras and phones up and ready to record acts of violence and preserve the recordings as documentary evidence. Nor do distribution channels today require professional access to editorial structures with staff, equipment, and communications (historically that meant messengers and couriers, telegraph, telephone, fax, and computers). Publishing online, on YouTube, Facebook or blogs, has become a simple matter, although a distribution list of the kind available to news agencies is certainly helpful.

---

6 | Rahib Mroué's live lecture performance has been staged at various venues, including documenta13, where large-scale prints from the phone footage were also shown (cf. Krautkrämer).

No matter how spectacular the video, one can never fully depend on viral dissemination. So much can be said: In a digital age of social media, camera phones, and smartphones—in other words since the 2000s—the production and distribution of digital media have become 'democratized' or 'deprofessionalized,' depending on the point of view. Eyewitness reports by those involved (lauded as 'citizen journalists,' although if there is one thing they are not, it is journalists) are also highly regarded by commercial agencies. They substitute for the sense of 'being there' photojournalism has always sought but reporters can never fulfil properly when events occur so fast; ultimately, their local knowledge will always be inferior. During the protests in Egypt and other North African countries, Western journalists were content to observe and document the protests from places of safety: living in hotels, photographing from a distance (sometimes in fact from the hotel balcony),[7] and mainly interviewing English-speaking activists.

In the perspective of the English-speaking Egyptian filmmaker Philip Rizk, who has dissected this situation, Western journalists were seeking, above all, representations that confirm their concept of a non-violent liberation movement, in the sense of a democratization according to the Western model. "Only the fixation of certain images seen in daylight through the lens of a camera on Tahrir Square could appease you with that impression" (54), he writes in his "Open Letter to an Onlooker":

Other industries soon followed suit: hard on the heels of the journalists came academics, filmmakers, the world of art, and NGOs, all relying on us as the ideal interpreter of the extraordinary. They all eventually bought into and further fueled the hyper-glorification of the individual, the actor, the youth subject, the revolutionary artist, the woman, the non-violent protester, the Internet user. (54)

For Rizk that is an ignorance of both the violence and of the heterogeneity of the interests driving the protests. Rizk belongs to a group of artists and activists who ran the media collective Mosireen during the protests. Mosireen collected testimonies, audio-visual recordings in which eyewitnesses, the injured, and friends and relatives of the dead recorded their

---

[7] | Cf. the photo series by Peter von Agtmael of the renowned agency Magnum, in Ebner and Wicke, *Cairo*, 55, 56, and 129.

versions of events—and contradicted the official versions.⁸ According to Mosireen, documentations are not self-explanatory, but must be contextualized and interpreted. They need a framing that clarifies and corrects: Who is showing what to whom, and who or what is being left out. By contrast, the post-colonial historical discourse perceives only an emancipatory movement pursuing 'Western' values, striving against Islamism and dictatorship and for women's emancipation. Protests against capitalism, neo-liberalism, and economic imperatives—in other words against decidedly 'Western' norms—are simply not perceived or in fact not perceptible. Of course, equality for women and for gays and lesbians is by no means automatically given within Islamic communities, and those are values I regard as non-negotiable. But in view of the enthusiasm with which gender inequalities in Islamic countries are highlighted, despite gender equality having been achieved at best on paper in the West, Gabriele Dietze rightly speaks of an "Occidental dividend" ("Okzidentalismuskritik" 35; "Decolonizing" 263): That is to say, in contrast to the supposed other, we may regard ourselves as more 'progressive' than we actually are, while the other appears more 'backward' than they are.

On the very day of publication, various modifications of the "Blue Bra" video appeared on YouTube: One of these is backed with mournful singing and written commentary in Arabic (cf. "Brutal Egypt Security Force"), another has a trailer from FIN (Freedom Informant Network) and English-language text (cf. "Disturbing Video"). In both cases the video is given a moving, but also agitating framing. It is certainly probable that it may have circulated in e-mail and blogs before appearing on *rt.com* and then CNN, which might explain the simultaneous appearance of versions already provided with framing and commentary in diverse contexts. It is the explicit potential of digital images that they can be processed and modified by their users, which is not to say that there is always a fundamental question mark over their veracity. The quality of the technical image as a record of real events remains intact. What is added to the image are interpretations of events, reading instructions for an always negotiable truth. One user subjects the "Blue Bra" video to a virtually forensic reading

---

8 | Cf. *mosireen.org*. The videos are also available on a YouTube channel and on *Vimeo*. Mosireen also runs workshops where in particular rural citizens are equipped with media technology and shown how to use it.

using red frames to pick out details (cf. Creighton):[9] He shows that the woman was accompanied by at least two male demonstrators. One of the two manages to break free and flee, while the other is kicked and beaten, as are two passers-by who initially walk past the edge of the scene but seconds later are lying helpless on the ground. One member of the group of military police is identified as particularly brutal and unrestrained; this is a man wearing trainers rather than army boots and he is, it would appear, restrained by the others—not terribly firmly, rather hesitantly and unsuccessfully. Here, in the event itself, we witness the different ways of dealing with the violence against the "Woman in the Blue Bra" that re-emerge in the later discussion: the problem of paternalism versus the suspension of male protection, the ambivalence of risking one's skin or fleeing ...

Also on 18 December, the *Tahrir Newspaper* published a still from the "Blue Bra" video, freezing the moment when the woman's bare torso is kicked. This is plainly a manipulated frame or screenshot, as the original shows the event from a distance and quite blurred (noting that the designation "original" serves as a crutch here). The person who made the recording of the "Woman in the Blue Bra" first had to seek out the motif in and through the viewfinder or display of the recording device. The camera, whatever kind it was, picks out victim and perpetrators in the crowd, loses sight of them, then finds the scene again. The recordings are notably without sound. I imagine otherwise one would hear shouting and indications that helped to visually locate the thugs in the crowd. Alongside the acts of violence it documents, the video therefore also evidences something else, namely, the difficulty of focusing. As such it points to both the events and the circumstances of their recording. The motion of the searching camera, and consequently of its images, corresponds to the conditions under which the video was made. And it is precisely this contingency and spontaneity, the rapidity and confusion captured in the images, that confirm the authenticity of the events. They remind us that the event was by no means completely unexpected; in a certain sense *something* was expected to happen. But at the same time neither this concrete moment nor the specific person were foreseeable (cf. Derrida). So while here it is precisely the searching movement and blurring that

---

9 | A post in the rather obscure blog: willyloman.wordpress.com/2011/12/19/blue-bra-girl-video-a-remarkable-story-of-horror-and-heroism/.

confirm the authenticity of the recording, those indications of origin have little bearing on other registers. The idea that the more grainy or pixelated a photograph, film, or video recording, the more authentic, is nothing but ill-conceived formalism. Yet a blurred freeze-frame is unsuited as an iconic image for a front page. As well as enlarging the relevant detail, the still selected for the newspaper must at least have been subjected to later post-focusing, for neither analogue nor digital images gain in sharpness and precision when enlarged. Quite the opposite: Enlarge far enough and all that remains is grain or pixels, the technical materiality of the image, and certainly no gain in iconicity of the kind required in the text/image context of the newspaper page. The color must have been adjusted too, as the blue bra now contrasts dramatically with the soldiers' camouflage trousers. The iconic front page image fits the 'decisive moments' paradigm upon which photojournalism has based its impact since the 1950s.[10] So while the low resolution of the digital image—its overall 'poor' quality—is the precondition for endless uploading and forwarding, the image must be aesthetically and technically improved as soon as it comes to reproduction in a print medium, in other words in a 'classical' distribution medium. According to Hito Steyerl, 'poor images' are low-resolution digital images that circulate without reproduction rights (or whose copyright is ignored) and whose potential lies in forming political networks, new public spheres, and archives beyond established bodies and companies (cf. 32–33). Within the chain of "Blue Bra" images, such a 'poor' image is certainly a decisive trigger—but one that dovetails into the image strategies of established commercial agencies and their monetization strategies. After diffusing through various networks, the images bear marks and signatures that contradict both the division into public and counter public and the strict distinction between analogue and digital. The chain of reproductions and appropriations of the "Blue Bra Girl" video does not come to a halt even when the 'poor' video image is enriched to create a still. Instead it migrates back into the digital networks. Unlike a video, a still can be used on the street: In subsequent demonstrations the front page of *Tahrir News* was held aloft for the cameras.[11] Soon enlarged and cropped versions were

---

10 | The concept of the decisive moment originates from Henri Cartier-Bresson (cf. Peters).
11 | Cf. Rowan El Shimi's Flickr album "Kasr El Einy Street Street Battle Dec 18 …" and the references in Ebner and Wicke, *Cairo*.

appearing on protest marches, especially the Women's Protest March on 21 December, now in poster quality bearing the byline Reuters/Stringer.[12] "On the street, before the eyes and cameras of the media, the images were now fished out of the flood of digital images to become image objects, and immediately fed back into it," argues Tom Holert (61). "Image objects" can be held in the hand and displayed, not only in the local surroundings but also in subsequently circulated images showing the image objects together with the subjects carrying them. Hundreds of photographs of these demonstrations grouped by theme, motif, and event can be found on Flickr, complete with image objects and mobile phones held aloft by the crowd. Some of these photographs also appear on gallery walls outside Egypt, where some of the Egyptian photographers have attained fame (and wealth) (cf. "Cairo. Open City.").

Fig. 2: Aly Hazza'a, Women's Protest March to the Press Syndicate, Cairo, 20 Dec. 2011.

---

12 | Cf., for example, Kainaz Amaria's photo story "The 'Girl In The Blue Bra'" published on *npr.org*. "NPR is a mission-driven, multimedia news organization and radio program producer. [...] We are enthusiastically embracing digital media platforms and culture."

The adaptations and appropriations of the "Woman in the Blue Bra" appear in different places in different media with a range of genre references: A graffito appeared on Tahrir Square with the blue bra as an element of a Superwoman costume. The Brazilian caricaturist Carlos Latuff drew a blue bra scene imagining the woman's revenge. Murals echoed the style of martyr portraits; the blue bra turned up as a graffiti stencil. It has gelled into a symbol capable of encapsulating the entire situation. Whereas such adaptations of the image articulated a concept of female empowerment beyond and outside a supposedly vulnerable femininity and its paternalistic protectors, there were also collages showing the blue bra montaged onto the Egyptian flag, thus containing the women's movement within the nation (cf. El Shimi, "The Woman" 182).

Corporative, artistic, and more or less illegal appropriations of the images produced a mise-en-abyme, a sequence of images each related to the other; and not only a sequence of images, but also of persons who made them and in the process exposed themselves in different ways. The digital cameras and smartphones they carried with them were an essential part of this set of relations, this relationality. For these devices enable easy ad hoc distribution, or at least threaten that in the eyes of the regime. Thus, the protests are not only recorded and documented; the *recording* changes the protest movement, indeed becomes a part of it.

If it were possible to summarize this fragmenting proliferation of images, technical devices, and bodies, of architecture, slogans, and actions, it would be in two points with which I close this text.

1. Every reproduction of reality is subject to intentions to show and tell, which subject the recording to a process of selection and framing and place it in a specific context, which is already saturated with (ideally refutable) presuppositions. Accumulated evidence is the outcome of interaction between a wide range of elements, which cannot be reduced to any variety of determinism, whether technological, social, or political in nature, but instead places all these elements in relation to one another. With respect to digital media and the technologies for distributing, linking, and reproducing, we find that the possibilities of image manipulation, commentary, and circulation—the chain of images produced by digital retransmission—claim a decisive share in what is evidenced and how certainty is produced. Testimony has been shunted into an always controvertible space of negotiation where credibility is generated.

2. These testimonies and the technological means of capturing and recording are not mere tools providing images or recorded voices of a political event that would have been the same without these recordings. Following Judith Butler's theory of assembly, these technologies provide possibilities of appearance in the visual field (*Notes Toward* 19). Bodies gathering in social movements—what might include social networking in the virtual domain—are enacting by their appearance what they claim and are protesting for. Media technologies make part of this set of relations through which the protesting and resisting body appears and enacts. That does not mean that every gathering or assembly can be understood as a form of resistance. In the contrary, collectives orchestrated by states or groups claiming to be 'the people' already presume who is included and who is excluded. But it is crucial that "vulnerability and resistance can, and do, and even must happen at the same time" (Butler, *Notes Toward* 141).[13]

Translation: Meredith Dale

Images

Fig. 1: Screenshot of the CNN report, Dec. 2011. From: *Cairo: Open City: New Testimonies from an Ongoing Revolution*, edited by Florian Ebner and Constanze Wicke, p. 182.

Fig. 2: Aly Hazza'a, Women's Protest March to the Press Syndicate, Cairo, 20 Dec. 2011. From: *Cairo: Open City: New Testimonies from an Ongoing Revolution*, edited by Florian Ebner and Constanze Wicke, p. 183.

---

13 | Slightly modified translation of "Bilder des Protests: 'The Woman in the Blue Bra' und relationale Zeugenschaft." *Periphere Visionen: Wissen an den Rändern von Fotografie und Film*, edited by Heide Barrenechea, Marcel Finke, and Moritz Schumm, Courtesy of Wilhelm Fink Verlag, 2016.

WORKS CITED

Amaria, Kainaz. "The 'Girl In The Blue Bra.'" *NPR*, 21 Dec. 2011, www.npr.org/sections/pictureshow/2011/12/21/144098384/the-girl-in-the-blue-bra. Accessed 4 Aug. 2012.

"'Blue Bra Girl' Atrocity: Egyptian Military Police More Than Brutal." *RT*, 18 Dec. 2011, www.rt.com/news/egyptian-military-cruelty-beating-079/. Accessed 20 Feb. 2017.

"Brutal Egypt Security Force Beat Woman Unconscious." *YouTube*, uploaded by JusefElAbhar, 18 Dec. 2011, www.youtube.com/watch?v=oua2y11BMxw. Accessed 4 Aug. 2012.

Butler, Judith. "Bodies in Alliance and the Politics of the Street." *European Institute for Progressive Cultural Policies*, Sep. 2011, www.eipcp.net/transversal/1011/butler/en. Accessed 20 Feb. 2017. Expanded version in: *Notes Toward a Performative Theory of Assembly*. Harvard UP, 2015, pp. 66-98.

—. "Bodily Vulnerability, Coalitional Politics." *Notes Toward a Performative Theory of Assembly*, Harvard UP, 2015, pp. 123-53.

—. *Frames of War: When Is Life Grievable?* Verso Books, 2010.

—. *Notes Toward a Performative Theory of Assembly*. Harvard UP, 2015.

"Cairo. Open City. New Testimonies from an Ongoing Revolution: Ulrike Bergermann and Kathrin Peters in Conversation with Florian Ebner about the Exhibition." *ZfM*, 3 Apr. 2015, www.zfmedienwissenschaft.de/online/%C2%ABcairo-open-city-new-testimonies-ongoing-revolution%C2%BB. Accessed 20 Feb. 2017.

Coleman, Isobel. "'Blue Bra Girl' Rallies Egypt's Women vs. Oppression." *CNN*, 22 Dec. 2011, edition.cnn.com/2011/12/22/opinion/coleman-women-egypt-protest/. Accessed 20 Feb. 2017.

Creighton, Scott. "'Blue Bra Girl' Video: A Remarkable Story of Horror and Heroism." *American Everyman*, 19 Dec. 2011, willyloman.wordpress.com/2011/12/19/blue-bra-girl-video-a-remarkable-story-of-horror-and-heroism/. Accessed 4 Aug. 2012.

Derrida, Jacques. "A Certain Impossible Possibility of Saying the Event." *Critical Inquiry*, vol. 33, no. 2, 2007, pp. 441-61. *JSTOR*, doi:10.1086/511506.

Dietze, Gabriele. "Decolonizing Gender—Gendering Decolonial Theory: Cross-Currents and Archaeologies." *Decoloniality, Postcoloniality,*

Black Critique: Joints and Fissures, edited by Sabine Broeck and Carsten Junker, Campus Verlag, 2014, pp. 245-69.

—. "Okzidentalismuskritik: Möglichkeiten und Grenzen einer Forschungsperspektivierung." *Kritik des Okzidentalismus: Transdisziplinäre Beiträge zu (Neo-)Orientalismus und Geschlecht*, edited by Gabriele Dietze, Claudia Brunner, and Edith Wenzel, transcript, 2009, pp. 23-54.

"Disturbing Video: 'Blue Bra' Girl Brutally Beaten by Egypt Military. Sunday Dec. 18 2011." *YouTube*, uploaded by freedominfonetwork, 18 Dec. 2011, www.youtube.com/watch?v=1w7Co-NNPnE. Accessed 4 Aug. 2012.

Ebner, Florian, and Constanze Wicke, editors. *Cairo: Open City: New Testimonies from an Ongoing Revolution*, Ram Publications & Dist, 2013.

El Shimi, Rowan. "Kasr El Einy Street Street Battle Dec 18 ..." *Flickr*, www.flickr.com/photos/rouelshimi/sets/72157628474638813. Accessed 4 Aug. 2012.

—. "The Woman in the Blue Bra." *Cairo: Open City: New Testimonies from an Ongoing Revolution*, edited by Florian Ebner and Constanze Wicke, Ram Publications & Dist, 2013, pp. 182-83.

Hafez, Sherine. "Bodies That Protest: The Girl in the Blue Bra, Sexuality, and State Violence in Revolutionary Egypt." *Signs: Journal of Women in Culture and Society*, vol. 40, no. 1, 2014, pp. 20-28.

Holert, Tom. *Regieren im Bildraum*. b_books/Polypen, 2008.

Krautkrämer, Florian. "Revolution uploaded: Un/Sichtbares im Handy-Dokumentarfilm." *Zeitschrift für Medienwissenschaft*, vol. 11, no. 2, 2014, pp. 113-27.

Mozireen. mozireen.org. Accessed 20 Feb. 2017.

Ott, Michaela. *Dividuationen: Theorien der Teilhabe*. b-books, 2015, pp. 52-54.

Peters, Kathrin. "Entscheidende und andere zufällige Augenblicke: Momentaufnahmen bei Henri Cartier-Bresson und Rolf Dieter Brinkmann." *Portable Media: Schreibszenen in Bewegung zwischen Peripatetik und Mobiltelefon*, edited by Martin Stingelin and Matthias Thiele, Fink, Wilhelm, 2010, pp. 163-78.

Rizk, Philip. "2011 Is not 1968: An Open Letter to an Onlooker." *Cairo: Open City: New Testimonies from an Ongoing Revolution*, edited by Florian Ebner and Constanze Wicke, Ram Publications & Dist, 2013, pp. 53-67.

Steyerl, Hito. "In Defense of the Poor Image." *The Wretches of the Screen*, Sternberg Press, 2012, pp. 31–45.
"The Blue Bra Girl:The Shocking Video." *YouTube*, uploaded by BlueBraGirl2, 5 Jan. 2012, www.youtube.com/watch?v=SIFffdHWH-Y. Accessed 20 Feb. 2017.

Connecting Origin and Innocence
Myths of Resistance in European Memory Cultures after 1945

Stephanie Wodianka

My contribution aims at reflecting the characteristics that constitute European memory cultures of Resistance during the Second World War: What are the specific features of these memory cultures? Which modes of relating to a resistant past play the most important role in the process of making these memories? In order to approach these questions, I will pay particular attention to memory cultures in France and Italy, and especially to the time period after 1945. My concept of Resistance concentrates on both Resistance as a political, oppositional movement and individual acts against National Socialism and fascism: Résistance, Resistenza.

In order to focus systematically on this topic, I will give a short outlook on my main lines of argument and, at the same time, on what I consider to be the four particularities of remembering Resistance:

1. Remembering Resistance as history vs. remembering Resistance as myth; in this section, I will focus on the question of how different modes of memory, i.e., the different ways of relating to the past, can be distinguished.
2. Resistance as a national and transnational narrative of origin; here, I would like to discuss in how far and why Resistance can be understood as, on the one hand, a national, and, on the other hand, a transnational narrative of origin.
3. Stability and persistence: Networks of Resistance myths; in this section, my contribution explores the relationship between modern myths and their seeming 'inflation': What preserves myths of Resistance, what makes them durable and flexible enough to survive?

4. Evidence and ambivalence of Resistance; the last part of my contribution focuses on the aesthetical conditions and consequences of the mythical dimensions of Resistance in Italy and France. Which relationships between origin and innocence are constructed by memory cultures about Resistance, how do they try to reach their mythical 'evidence' and 'naturalization' (Barthes) of their impacts?

1. Remembering Resistance as History vs. Remembering Resistance as Myth

Individuals, groups, and institutions can be considered as agents of Resistance. Dealing with the mythical remembering of Resistance, I firstly would like to roughly define what I mean by this, and which alternative or competing modes of remembering there are. To be precise, apart from mythical memory, there is historical memory. What are the characteristics of myth on the one side and history on the other then?

Myth and history can be defined as two different modes of remembering/memory (cf. Wodianka, *Zwischen Mythos* 38-41), which, in turn, can be understood as a way of relating to the past that is characterized by three cognitive constituents: First, a specific relation of time the remembering subject establishes to the remembered object; second, a specific identification process within the group of remembering subjects and, third, a specific relation to the act of memory itself—as it is depicted in the model of closeness and distance of memory.

I would like to argue as follows (cf. Wodianka, "Closeness" 51-65): Myth and history—as illustrated by the model—are two different forms of memory, which imply different constellations of closeness or remoteness of memory: with regard to the subjects, to the objects, and to the process of remembering.

The *historical mode of memory* denotes a relation to the past that focuses on a specific relation of events that is described as history. Firstly, it is based on a static distance between remembering subject and remembered object, a historical time frame, for example, between a subject in present time and a remembered act of Resistance, e.g., the attempted assassination of Hitler in 1944. In this mode of memory, the objectively measurable distance in time ideally corresponds to the awareness of temporal distance. Secondly, the historical mode of memory is simultaneously marked by its self-reflexivity, i.e., by the actual doubt (of the remembering subject) whether or not this ideal is achieved: The question whether it is possible and necessary to establish an objective relation to the remembered object, pointed out by historical scholarship since Johan Gustav Droysen, Max Weber, and Marc Bloch, especially when discussing historicism, essentially refers to the awareness of time in the historical mode of memory (cf. Oexle 31, 34, and 39). Thus, thirdly, the historical mode of memory is characterized by a distinctly self-reflexive distance of the remembering subject to the very ways of establishing historical memory in the first place in that the mode of memory is constantly and explicitly being rendered conscious. For instance, remembering subjects relativize their representation of events by referring to or quoting other representations and justify why theirs is more accurate. Therefore, the historical mode of memory can be said to be marked by a modal distancing, reflecting itself regularly. This modal distance, then, implies consequences for the level of identification of the remembering subjects, as it results in an affirmative, relativizing, and critical, but not at all per se identificatory self-locating process in interaction with other historically remembering subjects—i.e., the remembering subjects do not necessarily identify themselves with other subjects only because they are 'working' on the same historical object.

The *mythical mode of memory* is a mode of reception which—following Barthes' understanding of myth (cf. 213-68)—can relate to different forms of narration and narrative objects, even in modernity. By myth, I understand a *subjective* mode of perception and memory with a *collective* impact. Firstly, it is marked by an apparent evidence: The signification of a myth is a subjective 'fact' which can even contradict other concurring subjective significations—that's what Claude Lévi-Strauss called the "ambivalent structure of myth" (242). Mythical memory transfers history into nature (cf. Barthes 213-68), it transforms history into a narrative which seemingly does not have an identifiable narrator, it is, in other words, quasi without narrator (cf. Ricœur 57). For the remembering subject, then, myths provide an individual and a collective potential of identification (cf. Nora). Knowledge of a mythically remembered event as, for instance, the Resistance during the Nazi regime, integrate the individual into a community constituted by a shared, identity-making memory. Myths function as frames for interpreting the world in order to convey norms and values (cf. Assmann 76). In this sense, then, mythical remembering creates a particular closeness of memory on the level of identification, i.e., between the different remembering subjects 'consuming' the myth. Furthermore, the mythical mode of memory creates a time level that undermines temporal distance.[1] On the one hand, mythical events are located on a cloudy and remote temporal horizon; on the other, by repeating and revising them, they are drawn into the present, into the proximity of memory, in order to transform their signification into experience. Finally, on a modal level, myths are also characterized by a relative lack of (self-reflexive) distance between the remembering subject and the process of remembering. In other words, the mythical in contrast to the historical mode of memory does not become conscious as such, it is a mere experience of evidence: Mythical figures and heroes seem to evidently represent certain norms and values (even if these norms and values contradict each other): A myth is not being subjectively remembered, a myth *is* (cf. Cassirer 125-26 and 130-31; Eliade 42).

Against this backdrop, I would like to argue that the memory culture of Resistance can draw upon two competing modes of memory: Resistance as history, and Resistance as myth. And it is my contention that the signification of Resistance in European memory cultures as well as its interpretation can be seen as a consequence of the two competing modes of memory. In the post-war period both modes mutually influenced each other. This is to be illustrated in the remaining part of my contribution.

2. Resistance as a National and as a Transnational Narrative of Origin

The precondition for the national and transnational conception of the Resistance against the Nazi-regime as a foundation myth was its predominantly collective dimension, the concentration on a 'heroic' collective rather than on the engagement of resistant individuals.

In 1945, France had already been dominated by narratives of Résistance in politics, literature, and film for more than ten years, which had created a mythological French people of partisans. Post-war France,

---

1 | Regarding this, Astrid Erll also differentiates between communicative and cultural memory by means of the time consciousness, not by means of the objectively measurable interval to the memory (cf. 48-49).

hence, became a remembering collective that, through memory, identified itself as a collective of Résistance. A similar development can be traced in Italy. Here, too, during the immediate post-war period, multiplying acts of memory that represented Italy as the nation of Resistenza, led to a downplay of Mussolini as a dilettante and gave way to the myth of the 'good Italian.'[2] This mythological mode of memory was disturbed by a historical one, the Paxtonian revolution, *la révolution paxtonienne*, when in 1972, the American historian Robert Paxton published his study *Vichy France: Old Guard and New Order* and caused—particularly after the English translation in 1973—a wave of memory narratives that also considers French collaboration and attentism and, as a consequence, focuses the memory of Résistance on individual agents of Résistance.[3]

Since 1945, Résistance and Resistenza have been at the core of both national and transnational narratives of origin in the collective memory. Already on 18 June 1940, Charles de Gaulle, when addressing the French people in his radio report from London, spoke about "the flame of French

---

2 | In post-war Germany, in contrast to France and Italy, a different memory culture is created: Contrary to the French nation of partisans, Germany, according to Hans Mommsen, seems to remember Resistance without a people. Whereas memory cultures of German Resistance seem to be impossible shortly after the war, the remembering gaze later turns to German Resistance fighters—not in order to downplay German fascism, but to contradict the legitimizing hegemonic narratives of the system, which were disabling German Resistance (cf. Danyel 227).

3 | "[...] La *France de Vichy* a proposé tout d'abord une interprétation globale du régime, de son idéologie et de son action concrète, qui a mis en lumière la profonde cohérence du projet vichyste. Celle-ci s'articule autour de l'idée centrale selon laquelle les élites dirigeantes du régime ont eu une assez claire conscience du lien qui existait entre les choix de 'politique extérieure' et de politique intérieure, entre la collaboration d'État—un concept mis en avant par Stanley Hoffmann et consacré désormais par l'usage—, qui croyait redonner à la France une part de souveraineté perdue dans la défaite, et la Révolution nationale, une idéologie et une pratique qui visaient à la constitution d'un régime en rupture avec l'héritage républicain. La grande originalité de ce livre est d'expliquer de manière concrète et argumentée en quoi la collaboration d'État constituait une condition nécessaire (mais non suffisante) à la réalisation de la Révolution nationale [...]" (Rousso).

Resistance must not and shall not die" ("The Flame"). He thus relates to the metaphor of light of the French Enlightenment period, the *siècle des lumières*. At the same time, he remembers the French Revolution and its tough struggle for values of liberty, equality, and fraternity, on which the national self-definition of France is based. Consequently, the Résistance becomes a prolonged French foundational narrative. This narrative is still alive and reaches to our times: In a speech on 31 March 2012, Nicolas Sarkozy did not only continue De Gaulles's metaphor of light, but also relocated the heritage of Résistance in a diffuse European context (Spain, Greece) as well as in contexts of globalization. He calls the French Résistance a 'generation' ("Cette génération-là, cette génération," "Pendant"), which fulfilled her duty and followed a quasi-natural necessity to resist: "ces jeunes Français qui en juin 1940 se retrouvèrent à Londres parce qu'ils ne supportaient pas de voir la France occupée et vaincues, ces jeunes Français de vingt ans" ("Pendant"). He implores his young public to follow their model and to fight for their (human?) rights ("parce que les droits, vos droits ne se reçoivent pas comme un dû, vos droits se meritent," "Pendant"), and a transnational, more abstract and generational level of interpretation of the Résistance is called into being.

Also in Italy, the Resistenza becomes a foundational narrative—here, it is especially the connection to the so-called Risorgimento of Italy in the 19th century which signifies the Resistenza as a national founding myth and gives it the historical depth: As Italy freed itself in the Risorgimento self-confidently from the bonds of particularism and the lack of sovereign self-determination, it freed itself also from the bonds of collaboration and fascism. Here, especially 25 April 1945, named as the *giorno della liberazione*, is of memory-cultural importance. On this day, the national committee called for the uprising of northern Italy against the German occupying forces, big northern Italian cities were freed, and "[t]hus, 25 April can be seen as a central Italian *lieu de mémoire* on which party political legitimation and identity constitutions infensify"[4] (Brandt 237; translation: Lea Brenningmeyer), as a national feast which, since 1949, has been, in the broadest sense, dedicated to a national "myth of dignity

---

4 | Original: "Der 25. April kann so als ein zentraler italienischer Erinnerungsort gesehen werden, an dem sich parteipolitische Legitimations- und Identitätskonstitutionen verdichten."

and decency"⁵ (Campani 174; translation: Lea Brenningmeyer) and to the democratic demarcation from fascism. Democracy and antifascism are equated, and accordingly, the Italian self-definition after 1945, as can be found in the constitution, follows the spirit of the Resistenza (cf. Petersen 5-17). Moreover, the equalization of 'democratic' and 'antifascist' is not only an Italian but a European phenomenon, which, consequently, serves as a basis for a transnational narrative of Resistance. Jennifer Roger gives the following summary of this 'European' process of mythification: "Resistance as a concrete movement is replaced by a moral self-understanding, the national construction by European meaning-making"⁶ (320; translation: Christoph Behrens).

3. Stability and Durability: Interconnection of Resistance Myths

The third section will deal with the stability and durability of the myth of Resistance: In how far do processes of inflation and canonization do interact with modern myths? What preserves Resistance myths as modern myths, what makes them persistent in European memory cultures? In the case of the Resistance against fascism, it is noticeable that it is strongly connected to other modern myths. One could even speak of a system of myth and sub-myths or a mythical cluster that gives evidence to the Resistance myth, stabilizes it, and anchors it within cultural memory. A first example from the Italian context was given in section two, concerning the interconnections between the Resistenza collectively and ritually remembered every 24 April as *giorno di liberazione* and the myth of the Italian 19th-century-Risorgimento as movement of national self-constitution, fighting for Italy as political and cultural unity. That this Italian 'myth-connection' is not a unique case, but reflects a tendency of modern mythology and its strategies in the struggle for stability, and that it is also observable in French memory cultures about Resistance will be shown in the following.

---

5 | Original: "Mythos von Würde und Anstand."
6 | Original: "Der Widerstand als konkrete Bewegung weicht damit einem moralischen Selbstverständnis, die nationale Auslegung einer europäischen Sinngebung."

Firstly, it is Charles de Gaulle as a political protagonist, who established the myth of French Resistance and in so doing, constituted the platform for various myth-connections. His speech that was broadcast by the BBC from London and directed to the French people on 18 June 1940 can be seen as a cultural text in its own right, the photograph, which shows him standing at the microphone, iconically creates the nucleus of the mythical narrative (cf. Flood 220-24).[7] A further dimension of its interconnectedness was laid out by Charles de Gaulle himself with his appeal: "Quoi qu'il arrive, la flamme de la résistance française ne doit pas s'éteindre et ne s'éteindra pas" ("Pendant"). The flame of Résistance relates to the light metaphor of the French Enlightenment, which found its socio-political expression in the French Revolution of 1789, which constituted a historical and foundational event in French national history as already outlined above. Hence, Résistance is not only a historical phenomenon but stands in close connection to the already established French national myth as a historical event. Following De Gaulle's words, the French people has the duty to carry on the spirit of revolution in their Résistance. Résistance and French Enlightenment or respectively the French Revolution are thus turned into parts of one and the same mythical network.

In 1942, the mythical cluster of Résistance is further connected to the expansion of the Matière de Bretagne, King Arthur and his Knights of the Round Table. In his poems of "Les Yeux d'Elsa," the French Résistance-poet and partisan, Louis Aragon, associates the situation of the Vichy regime collaboration with the forests in the threatened realm of King Arthur, the partisans with the virtuous knights. In retrospection, according to the poet himself, history does not seem to *repeat* the myths but to *confirm* them:

Even more than in 1941, in 1942 France resembled Brocéliande. In the forest, the witches of Vichy and the dragons of Germanie, gave to every word an enchanted and perverted value, nothing was called by its name anymore, and every grandeur was undermined, every virtue ridicules, and persecuted. Its way a time of enchanted ladies and imprisoned princesses. And when time went by, more and more knights without name took up arms, whose exploits, for all the armed

---

7 | https://en.wikipedia.org/wiki/Appeal_of_18_June. The picture shows a later, similar event, because no picture was taken during de Gaulle's 18 June speech on BBC radio—the icon has been created retrospectively.

men and hangmen, and the orgs and giants, spread from mouth to mouth in the French forest, even though, history confirmed the retold legend, it happened to me, Brocéliande written, to find in the poem a reality that I had never dreamed of, a precision in the painting that would have been impossible for me to consciously attain in July and August of 1942. (translation: Christoph Behrens)[8]

Significantly, the quotation was printed in a journal called *De l'exactitude historique en poésie* (*Of historical precision in poetry*) in 1945 (cf. Aragon 189-217). This is an example of the productive interplay between the historical mode of memory and the mythical mode of memory outlined above. The mythical mode of memory—which Aragon can be said to draw upon here—allows for an increase in historical precision. And the postulate of historically exact paintings authenticates the truth of the Résistance myth. In his works, Louis Aragon transforms Arthur's knights into partisans (or the other way around) in order to prevent them from being appropriated by Nazi Germany or the Vichy Régime. He confronts Wagner's Parsifal with the best of French knights: Chrétien de Troyes' Percéval and Lancelot.

Another myth connected to the French Résistance is Joan of Arc. She is said to be the icon of the *esprit de la résistance*, which she had to prove in the liberation of Orléans, and in the processes held against her. How complex these interconnection can be is best expressed in the 1999 film *Joan of Arc: The Messenger* by Luc Besson, a French-American co-production starring Mila Jovovich and Dustin Hoffmann, which became a French

---

8 | Original: "Plus encore qu'en 1941, en 1942 la France tout entière ressemblait à Brocéliande. Dans la forêt, les sorciers de Vichy et les dragons de Germanie avaient donné à toutes les paroles une valeur incantatoire pervertie, rien ne s'appelait plus de son nom, et toute grandeur *était* avilie, toute vertu bafouée, persécutée. Ah ! c'était un temps de dames enchantées et de princesses prisonnières [...]. Et plus il avançait, ce temps, plus nombreux s'armaient les chevaliers sans nom [...] dont les exploits, malgré les hommes d'armes et les bourreaux, et les ogres et les géants, se répétaient de bouche en bouche d'un bout à l'autre de la forêt de France ; [...] si bien que, l'histoire confirmant la légende reprise, il m'arriva, Brocéliande *écrit*, de trouver à ce poème une réalité que je n'avais pas rêvée, une exactitude dans la peinture qu'il m'eût *été* bien impossible de consciemment atteindre en juillet et août 1942."

and international blockbuster.⁹ In the film, Joan of Arc is represented as a partisan in many different ways: She frees Orléans from English occupiers, and simultaneously frees the myth from being appropriated by Anglo-American memory cultures: "L'histoire de France nous appartient!" (Gandillot and Grassin 6) ("French history belongs to us!"), the French director Besson expressed in an interview before the film's premiere. Jeanne d'Arc belonged to French history, and with the help of the film, Besson sets out to reclaim its French rootedness. So the Résistance myth, on the one hand, is connected to Joan of Arc, and connected to the fight for French cultural patriotism against the occupying Anglo-American film industry on the other (cf. Wodianka, *Zwischen Mythos* 411-15; Knabel 146). That this battle is fought out, of all things, in a French-American co-production with a Hollywood cast, is a paradox that only mythical reception is able to explain. It is striking that Besson does not identify Joan of Arc as a French national myth, but as French history—he tries to put the mythical dimension in the rear and instead favors the historical mode of memory. Joan of Arc is represented as a national myth only on a secondary level. As I have shown at the beginning of my contribution, any self-reflexive distance to the mythical mode of memory would destroy that mythical remembering he actually aimed at.

Last but not least, the French Resistance is connected to the myth of a small Gallic village, which, ever since 1961, has been fighting against the Romans through the medium of the Comic: *Asterix* de René Goscinny.¹⁰

In the year 50 BC Gaul is occupied by the romans—nearly. But one village full of unconquerable Galls still resists the intruders. And life is not the easiest for the Roman soldiers on the battles fields of *Babaorum, Aquarium, Laudanum et Petibonum...* (Goscinny and Uderzo 48; translation: Christoph Behrens)¹¹

---

9 | Cf. the French theatrical release poster: https://en.wikipedia.org/wiki/The_Messenger:_The_Story_of_Joan_of_Arc.

10 | The first volume has been published in 1961, two years before, in 1959, Goscinny had presented for the first time one page of Asterix-Comics in his journal "Pilote." For further information about the first volume, cf. http://www.asterix.com/la-collection/les-albums/asterix-le-gaulois.html.

11 | Original: "Nous sommes en 50 avant Jésus-Christ. Toute la Gaule est occupée par les Romains... Toute? Non! Un village peuplé d'irréductibles Gaulois résiste encore et toujours à l'envahisseur. Et la vie n'est pas facile pour les garnisons de

The Romans do not only remind us of the German occupiers because of their character and habitus (representatives of discipline and order), but they also wear the same khaki uniforms and perform the same salute. In France, the Résistance has always been center stage, only the media, the contexts, and the means have changed over time—this has been the message of Asterix and Obelix until today (cf. Hörner). Being famous on a global scale, translated into many different languages, the Résistance myth as rendered in the shape of the comic can thus also be conceived of as a transnational myth promoting a special habitus of Resistance, with the 'good' and appealing fighting against the not so clever and smart ones, i.e., those who only seem to be superior. This central position of the Résistance in French memory culture, as I have thus illustrated, is upheld by a mythological network that guarantees dynamic actuality, plurimedial distribution, and stability.

4. Evidence and Ambivalence of Resistance: The Dynamics of Origin and Innocence

The last section covers the afore mentioned self-mythification of a whole 'Nation of Partisans' in France and Italy, which dominated political discourses during the immediate post-war years, partly up until the 1950s, and which was functionalized as narration of origin to construct new national or transnational identities. This last argument is also inspired by the awareness of the discursive variety and the processes of transformation which characterize memory cultures about Resistance in France and Italy, and which therefore have to be considered here as well: Remembering Resistance is not a stable and uniform phenomenon, but it depends on various interests, modes and media of memory. In how far is even the very beginning of remembering Resistance in the years around 1945 characterized by the dynamics of constructing or deconstructing the possibility of collective 'innocence'? And—to link my interest in modes of memory to the special interest in the impact of the dynamics of origin and innocence—in how far is the mythical potential of transforming

---

légionnaires romains des camps retranchés de Babaorum, Aquarium, Laudanum et Petitbonum..."

ambivalence and complexity into apparent evidence also reflected in literary and filmographical fiction about Resistance?

If we only looked at one of the most known films of post-war-cinematography in France, our first impression of a dominant narrative of collective Resistance would be almost confirmed. The film *La Bataille du Rail* by René Clément, which won an award at the film festival in Cannes, 1946, makes the audience remember a French Résistance that metonymically represents the attitude of the whole nation. In the first part, the film shows various acts of Resistance and sabotage of railroaders as well as the brutal counteractions of German occupying forces. The second part tells the story of the successful sabotage of an armored train, which, under the name "Convoi Apfelkern," was supposed to bring supplies to the Norman front. The film ends up with the liberation of France: A train with cheering people, labeled with the slogan "Vive la France! Et la Résistance! Honneur aux Cheminots!" and accompanied with festive music, rides on the restored tracks toward a glorious future.[12] Technical and moral-patriotic competences are symbolically united in the closing scene, and the Resistance against the German occupation is inscribed in the French Enlightment's myth of progress. Superficially, limiting the Résistance to the railroaders seems to suppose a socially limited movement and to take the opportunity from the French people to identify, as a collective, with the Résistance against the German occupying forces. Taking a closer look, however, it becomes apparent that the focus on the group of railroaders virtually allows for the contrary: The involvement in the *Bataille du rail* ranges from the simple conductor and train driver to the technical engineer; the broad social embeddedness of the Résistance in all social classes of France is thus even emphasized. The film's striving for authenticity, historical factuality, and testimony[13] (cf. Langlois 67) increases the persuasiveness of this interpretation of the Résistance. The French appear as an absolutely positive counter-image to the fascist

---

12 | Cf. the screenshot which became an icon for the Résistance: http://www.cinema-francais.fr/images/affiches/affiches_c/affiches_clement_rene/photos/rail04.jpg.

13 | "La Bataille du Rail a répondu à l'ambition qu'a nourrie la critique envers le cinéma dans l'immédiat après-guerre, c'est-à-dire créer des témoignages qui pourraient s'apparenter à des sources historiques. [...] L'authenticité est ici un concept-clef" (Langlois 67).

German occupying forces, collaborationism is not mentioned as a topic. The failure of any intercultural communication underlines the distance between the non-fascist national-socialist Germans and the resisting French, who raise empathy by being portrayed as morally superior and through a range of close-ups. Christoph Vatter sums up, with reference to the film's underlying interest in memory

> Clément's film establishes the filmic myth of the *résistancialisme*, although still with rather communist than Gaullist imprint [...]. The time of the *Occupation* is represented as a merely German-French conflict whereas inner-French lines of conflict are largely ignored. [...] With the representation of the Résistance as a collective movement of France, Clément answers with 'La Bataille du Rail' to the needs for social integration of the French society after the end of the occupation.[14] (92; translation: Lea Brenningmeyer)

The myth of the collective and undivided Résistance of France is achieved and reinforced by the superficially historical mode of memory, which is already introduced in the opening credits of the film. It says in big letters which take up the whole screen: "Ce film qui retrace des scenes authentiques de la Résistance a éte réalisé avec la participation de la COMMISSION MILITAIRE DU CONSEIL NATIONAL DE LA RÉSISTANCE / et grâce à l'effort considérable de la SOCIÉTÉ NATIONALE DES CHEMINS DE FER FRANCAIS." Thus, the authenticity of the representation is claimed in a reception-guiding way, and, by the prominent acknowledgments of the 'French' railroad company in the film, the represented commitment of the railroaders is expanded from a regional to a national level. *La Bataille du Rail* not only celebrated success in the immediate postwar period—six of the numerous broadcastings of the film in France took place after 1982. The need to continue telling the Résistance as an origin myth and to free

---

14 | Original: "Cléments Film begründet den filmischen Mythos des résistancialisme, wenn auch noch ehre kommunistischer als gaullistischer Prägung [...]. Die Zeit der Occupation wird als rein deutsch-französische Auseinandersetzung dargestellt, wohingegen innerfranzösische Konfliktlinien weitestgehend ausgeblendet werden. [...] Mit der Darstellung der Résistance als kollektive Bewegung Frankreichs antwortet Clément mit 'La Bataille du Rail' auf die Bedürfnisse nach sozialer Binnenintegration der französischen Gesellschaft nach Ende der Besatzungszeit."

the entire French nation from the complicity in collaborationism persists well past the immediate postwar years.

In Roberto Rossellini's neo-realist classic *Roma: Città aperta* from 1945—award-winning at the film festival in Cannes, 1945—evidence is preferred over ambivalence, too. However, in comparison to *La Bataille du Rail*, here the stereotypical antagonism between the 'good Italians' and the 'bad Germans' is less pronounced: for example, a German officer criticizes the actions of the Germans, and there are also Italian traitors of the Resistenza—these ambivalences, however, exclusively refer to marginal characters. Rossellini's film puts the cruelty of the German fascists even more in the center of the representation than René Clément's *La Bataille du Rail* and, in face of the represented brutality and inhumanity, makes the actions of the Resistance seem all the more heroic. The partisan Luigi, despite being tortured to death, remains steadfast and does not reveal his fellow campaigners, and the partisan Pina follows the car deporting her fiancée until she dies, in sight of her little son, in the hail of bullets of the German officers—one of the most affecting scenes of the film,[15] which shows and, quite literally, makes visible the inhuman brutality of the members of the occupying forces in contrast to the very human but desperate commitment of the Resistenza figures—at least the protagonists in this film are evidently 'good' characters, martyr-like innocent heroes of Resistance.

Another kind of dynamics of origin and innocence was evoked by those narratives of Resistance which critically reflect on the self-proclaimed collective 'innocence' of France and Italy. In some texts and films of this kind, the idea of ambivalence is sometimes even metonymically incorporated in the shape of the fictional characters themselves. They represent a metonymy for the inhomogeneous and at times even contradictory attitudes towards holocaust and fascism, collaboration, and Resistance. In particular, when analyzing the fictional characters, who appear in texts and films which critically shed a light on Resistance, a tendency towards what I would like to call 'a medium hero' is observable. With 'medium hero,' I would like to characterize a protagonist

---

15 | A screenshot of the most famous scene of the film can be found at: https://it.wikipedia.org/wiki/Roma_citt%C3%A0_aperta#/media/File:Roma_citt%C3%A0_aperta_corsaPina.jpg.

of Resistance who, in a tragic sense, is neither morally good nor morally bad: but morally ambivalent.

In order to substantiate this claim, I would like to take a brief look at the ambivalence of Elio Vittorini's characters in the novel *Uomini e no* (1945). The title of the novel already indicates the ambivalence of human nature: There are no dichotomies of 'good humans' and 'bad humans.' Instead, human nature is characterized by its very ambivalence, its state of in-betweenness. The protagonist Enne 2 is a problematic character, who is rather characterized by reflection and doubt than by the determination to resist through action. 23 of the 136 chapters of the novel present metalepses, through which the author enters into a dialogue with the protagonist Enne 2 or comments on him as a character. Any unreflected-affirmative identification of the recipient with the protagonist thus becomes particularly difficult—any evidence of the Resistenza is impossible, both intra-diegetically and extra-diegetically. That Enne 2 (whose dualistic core is also expressed in the name), however, is no conventional hero in terms of the antique tragedy, becomes apparent in his romantic relationship with Berta: They do not die for each other, but witness fascist terror against old people and children. Even though both consider this experience as emblematic for their belonging together, Berta distances herself anew. In Vittorini's novel, there is thus no collectively shared memory, which could guarantee cohesion (not even between the two). *Uomini e no*, as the first Resistenza novel, becomes a narration of origin by means of a character who fails in the execution of an assassination attempt on German soldiers, because his gaze seems to him "troppo triste," and he recognizes himself in the soldier's eyes. The identification with the other 'as a human'—in his human inhumanity and inhuman humanity—is the origin myth which is told by this Resistenza novel and in which there is no room for innocence.

The last example discussed and analyzed here is the famous novella *Le Silence de la Mer* by Vercors (1942/1945), picturized in 1948 by Jean Pierre Melville.[16] The novella was initially published by the Geneva Clandestines "Éditions des Minuit" in 1942, before it could be 'officially' published by the Paris publishing company "Éditions des trois collines" immediately after the end of the war in 1945. At the same time, the author as well as Résistants associated with him already referred to the literary text

---

16 | About the film adaptation of the novella by Jean Pierre Melville (F 1949), cf. Langlois 139-47.

as "patrimoine de la France" (Nogueira 32), which had to be prevented from a film adaptation. Only after tough negotiations between Vercors and Melville and with the agreement of a committee of former Résistants selected by Vercors, Melville's film was released—a symbolic testimony of the novella as 'authentic' *Livre de Chevet* of the Resistance fighters, which, at the same time, attested and strengthened the novella's mythical potential (cf. Langlois 141; Vercors and Plazy 37). In the novella, the memory-cultural dynamic of Résistance as a narration of origin in its relationship to innocence becomes apparent in a special way: not only because it belongs to the earliest literary texts documenting and remembering the Résistance at the same time, whose 'innocence' and authenticity seemed to be endangered by the medial transition to the format of a feature film, but also, because the novella *Le silence de la mer*, in its ambivalences, deals with 'innocence due to silence' and 'guilt due to silence' at the very same time. Silence, in Vercors' stories, is no passive but an active act: Silence is even considered as an act and instrument of Resistance by both French protagonists. The German officer Ebrennac is accommodated as an occupying soldier in the house of the narrator and his niece—henceforth, without being asked, they are obligated to live together in a confined space. The German soldier ostentatiously strives toward a polite behavior, in no case utilizes his position as an occupier, and makes every effort to express his respect for the French culture.

The ritualized form of his behavior stands in a blatant contrast to the 'disorder' which rules occupied France. Every evening, he steps up to his two involuntary French hosts in the living room and, after his monologic reflections about the German-French relations, leaves with a 'Good night,' which remains unanswered. The French narrator and his niece never talk to their guest—a persistent silence defines their living together. Carried by the mythical-idealizing vision of a 'marriage' of Germany and France, which marks the beginning of an 'enlightened' Europe under their leadership ("le soleil va luire sur l'Europe" 12), Ebrennac reflects on French literature and German music, his love for France ("J'amai toujours la France" 10), and his trust that "de grandes choses" will emanate from the war (12). Until the end of the novella, he experiences a process of enlightenment himself—initiated by his disenchanting experience in Paris, when he had to realize that the true motive of the German occupying forces is the destruction and complete repression of France, which makes his world view collapse and drives him to the fatal decision to make himself available for a suicide mission.

The silence of the narrator and the niece, first, stands for the 'silent' opposition: Being exposed to living with the soldier, it is a form of protest, an everyday and constant 'act' of the Résistance. In doing so, especially the narrator's niece arrives at a hardness and strength that even surprises the narrator and also makes him doubt. Her 'innocence' is made explicit when the narrator talks about her "pur profil têtu et fermé" (14). Second, it becomes apparent that this persistent silence also connotes the 'guilty silence' of the French followers, as it also affects the communication between the narrator and his niece ("De cela je ne dis rien à ma niece" 23) and stands between them, and as it prevents the narrator from expressing his "absurd colère" and taking actions against "cette idiotie" (23). And third, the novella negotiates Vercors' question regarding the connection between innocence and silence: while the German occupying soldier Ebrennac is a rich source of storytelling, he is all the more embraced by the "gaz" (sic) of silence the French owners of the house persistently exude. The novella here draws connections to the gas chambers of the Holocaust in order to metonymically defy them. This henceforth pervasive silence lets the novella metafictionally emerge all the more as a narration that breaks the silence: The novella breaks the silence in the face of occupation and collaboration with a gaze to the sky, which, as expected, is not illuminated by the glistening light of the sun over Europe, which was predicted by Ebrennac in his National Socialist delusion. "Elle [ma nièce] me servit en silence. Nous bûmes en silence. Dehors luisait au travers de la brume un pâle soleil. Il me sembla qu'il faisait très froid." The cold silence of the French house inhabitants, which outlived the presence of the member of the occupying forces, is not capable of penetrating the mist. Vercors' novella, thus, ends with an appeal for a speech that opposes Ebrennac's visions: As a narration, the Résistance promises the expectation of and hope for that warming light which is withhold from the silence that believes to be innocent—Remembering Resistance means to break the silence.

This article has been translated from German by Lea Brenningmeyer and Christoph Behrens.

Works Cited

"Appeal of 18 June." *Wikipedia, The Free Encyclopedia*, 19 Feb. 2017, en.wikipedia.org/wiki/Appeal_of_18_June. Accessed 23 Mar. 2017.

Aragon, Louis. "De l'exactitude historique en poésie." *L'OEuvre poétique*, 2nd ed., vol. 4, no. 9, 1990, pp. 189-217.

Assmann, Jan. *Das kulturelle Gedächtnis: Schrift, Erinnerung und politische Identität in frühen Hochkulturen*. Beck, 1992.

Asterix: Le Site Officiel. Les Éditions Albert René / Goscinny-Uderzo, 2017, www.asterix.com/la-collection/les-albums/asterix-le-gaulois.html. Accessed 23 Mar. 2017.

Barthes, Roland. "Le Mythe, aujourd'hui." *Mythologies*, by Barthes, Seuil, 1957, pp. 213-68.

Brandt, Ina. "Memoria, Politica, Polemica." *Italien, Blicke: Neue Perspektiven der Geschichte des 19. und 20. Jahrhunderts*, edited by Petra Terhoeven, Vandenhoeck & Ruprecht, 2010, pp. 235-56.

Campani, Carlo. "Nationale Identität und Gedenken an den antifaschistischen Widerstand im republikanischen Italien." *Inszenierungen des Nationalstaats: Politische Feiern in Italien und Deutschland seit 1860/71*, edited by Sabine Behrenbeck and Alexander Nützenadel, SH-Verlag, 2000, pp. 171-90.

Cassirer, Ernst. "Das mythische Denken." *Ernst Cassirer Gesammelte Werke: Hamburger Ausgabe*, edited by Birgit Recki, vol. 1, Meiner, 2002.

Danyel, Jürgen. "Der 20. Juli." *Deutsche Erinnerungsorte*, edited by Etienne François and Hagen Schulze, vol. 2, Beck, 2001, pp. 220-37.

De Gaulle, Charles. "Pendant la guerre (1940-1946): Appel du 18 juin 1940—l'appel à la Résistance lancé par le général de Gaulle." *Charles-De-Gaulle*, www.charles-de-gaulle.org/pages/l-homme/accueil/discours/pendant-la-guerre-1940-1946/appel-du-18-juin-1940.php. Accessed 22 Feb. 2017.

—. "The Flame of French Resistance." *BBC*, 18 Jun. 1940, London. Speech. *The Guardian*, www.theguardian.com/theguardian/2007/apr/29/greatspeeches1. Accessed 22 Feb. 2017.

Eliade, Mircea. *Mythos und Wirklichkeit*. Insel, 1988.

Erll, Astrid. *Gedächtnisromane: Literatur über den ersten Weltkrieg als Medium englischer und deutscher Erinnerungskulturen in den 1920er Jahren*. WVT, 2003.

Flood, Christopher G. *Political Myth: A Theoretical Introduction*. Routledge, 2002.
Gandillot, Thierry, and Sophie Grassin. "Un fille ordinaire plongée dans l'exraordinaire: Entretien avec un réalisateur en quête de divin." *L'Express*, 28 Oct. 1999, pp. 59-61.
Goscinny, René, and Albert Uderzo. *Astérix chez les Belges*. Hachette Livre, 1979.
Hörner, Fernand. "Beflügelte Fantasie: Asterix, die unbeugsamen Gallier und der Widerstandsmythos." *Moderne Mythen: Inflation, Vernetzung, Kanon*, edited by Stephanie Wodianka and Juliane Ebert, transcript, 2016, pp. 163-94.
Joan of Arc: The Messenger. Directed by Luc Besson, performances by Mila Jovovich, Dustin Hoffmann et al., Gaumont, 1999.
Knabel, Claudia. "Ein Mythos im Prozeß: Von der Heiligen zur Superwoman: Jeanne dArc im Film." *Medienbilder: Dokumentation des 13. Film- und Fernsehwissenschaftlichen Kolloquiums an der Georg-August-Universität Göttingen*, edited by Jörg Türschmann and Annette Paatz, Dr. Kovac, 2001, pp. 143-56.
La Bataille du Rail. Directed by René Clément, Coopérative Générale du Cinéma Français, 1946.
Langlois, Suzanne. *La Résistance dans le Cinéma Francais: 1944-1994*. L'Harmattan, 2001.
Le Silence de la Mer. Directed by Jean Pierre Melville, performances by Howard Vernon, Nicole Stéphane, Jean-Marie Robain et al., Melville Productions, 1949.
Lévi-Strauss, Claude. "La structure des mythes." *Anthropologie structurale*, Plon, 1958, pp. 235-65.
Nogueira, Rui. "Le cinéma selon Jean-Pierre Melville." *Cahiers du Cinéma*, 1996, pp. 31-49.
Nora, Pierre. *Les lieux de mémoire*. 3 vols. Gallimard, 1984-1992.
Oexle, Gerhard. *Geschichtswissenschaft im Zeichen des Historismus*. Vandenhoeck & Ruprecht, 1996.
Paxton, Robert. *Vichy France: Old Guard and New Order, 1940-1944*. Seuil, 1973.
Petersen, Jan. "Mythos Resistenza." *Zibaldone: Zeitschrift für italienische Kultur der Gegenwart*, vol. 19, 1995, pp. 5-17.

René, Clément. "Rail04." *Le Cinema Francais*, 21 Sep. 2011, www.cinemafrancais.fr/images/affiches/affiches_c/affiches_clement_rene/photos/rail04.jpg. Accessed 23 Mar. 2017.

Ricœur, Paul. *Temps et récit*. Vol. 1, Seuil, 1983.

Roger, Jennifer. "Widerstand, Résistance, Resistenza." *Metzler Lexikon Moderner Mythen: Figuren, Konzepte, Ereignisse*, edited by Stephanie Wodianka and Juliane Ebert, Metzler, 2014, pp. 316-21.

Roma: Città Aperta. Directed by Roberto Rosselini, performances by Anna Magnani, Aldo Fabrizi, Marcello Pagliero, et al., Excelsa Film, 1945.

"Roma Città Aperta." *Wikipedia, The Free Encyclopedia*, 22 Mar. 2017, it.wikipedia.org/wiki/Roma_citt%C3%A0_aperta#/media/File:Roma_citt%C3%A0_aperta_corsaPina.jpg. Accessed 23 Mar. 2017.

Rousso, Henry. *Le syndrome de Vichy*. 2nd ed., Seuil, 1997.

Sarkozy, Nicolas. "Discours de Nicolas Sarkozy: rassemblement des jeunes pour la France forte." *YouTube*, uploaded by NicolasSarkozy, 31 Mar. 2012, www.youtube.com/watch?v=aqhKFDcsOBQ. Accessed 22 Feb. 2017.

"The Messenger: The Story of Joan of Arc." *Wikipedia, The Free Encyclopedia*, 15 Mar. 2017, en.wikipedia.org/wiki/The_Messenger:_The_Story_of_Joan_of_Arc. Accessed 23 Mar. 2017.

Vatter, Christoph. *Gedächtnismedium Film: Holocaust und Kollaboration in deutschen und französischen Spielfilmen seit 1945*. Königshausen u. Neumann, 2008.

Vercors and Gilles Plazy. *À dire vrai*. Bourin, 1991.

Vercors. *Le Silence de la Mer*. Trois Collines, 1945.

Vittorini, Elio. *Uomini e no*. Bompiani, 1945.

Wodianka, Stephanie. "Closeness and Distance of Memory to Joan of Arc: A National Myth in Transnational Imagined Communities." *Time Refigured: Myths, Foundation Texts & Imagined Communities*, edited by Martin Procházka and Ondreji Pilný, Litteraria Pragensia, 2005, pp. 51-65.

—. *Zwischen Mythos und Geschichte: Ästhetik, Medialität und Kulturspezifik der Mittelalterkonjunktur*. De Gruyter, 2009.

Into the Darkness: Revolutionary Critical Pedagogy for a Socialist Society
A Manifesto*

Peter McLaren

We are here, right now at this very precipitous moment, living in the fetid anti-Kingdom of Trumpland. We are armed with the counter-knowledge of the subaltern in our texts of counterinsurgency, languishing in some alternative rhetorical site where we are preoccupied with our catechrestic labeling of this or that aspect of imperial epistemic violence, pre-constituted by the limits of the ivory tower that has become our prison. So let's not be so smug. We cannot abstain from representation because they are also coming for us. Can't you hear the jackboots? So let's start at the end, as a series of beginnings. And so, to the final question, yes, the final question: where should critical pedagogy take us and where should we take critical pedagogy? We can only answer this with a response from our guts. To the plaintive and indignant voices of our establishment critics, we say this: We are inadaptable! We are maladaptable! We answer your charges of sedition with a burst of laughter. We will not be treated as overactive children with behavioral disorders. We will not swallow your pills. We do not live in treehouses but underground, in the sewers of Bogota, in the slums of Calcutta, in the Lacondan jungle of Chiapas, in *las calles* de Los Angeles, in *casas de carton* in the favelas of Rocinha, in Rio's South Zone, in classrooms without books, in restrooms without toilets, in board rooms without CEOs, in prisons without guards! We speak Chontal, Ch'ol, Tzltal, Tzotzil, Tojolab'al, Chicomuceltec, Mocho', and Akatek. We

---

* This paper is taken from a recent book and appears, with permission, from Peter McLaren, Pedagogy of Insurrection: From Resurrection to Revolution. New York: Peter Lang Publishers, 2015.

are the children of 1968 and of hip-hop, we will not accept bribes, we will not accept financial compensation, we refuse to let our subjectivities be cooked in the ovens of the state, we refuse to ask permission for anything, we refuse to be colonized or to colonize, we refuse to be exiled from our own flesh, we refuse to let our languages, our songs, our histories, and our dreams be expropriated by the mass media. We will not let capital disfigure us. We understand the hidden transcript of capitalist normality and we are making it manifest for the world to see. We are the Wikileaks of the seminar rooms and classrooms and we will expose the lies and corruption of all Ministries of Education. We will not burn our copies of Marx and genuflect at the altar of neoliberal capitalism. It's been a capricious ruse of corporate media to confuse capitalism with democracy. We know that we exist as intersubjective beings and will not let wage labor tear us from our friends, our families, our communities. We refuse to be decomposed by the social machinery of the state apparatuses. We will not be the subjects of your social experiments. We understand fully that there is no separation between the definition of justice and our obligation to do justice. We aren't proud to announce that The Forever Café has been closed, it just goes with the economic territory. We aren't embarrassed to wear vintage shirts from Pendelton Wollen Mills, turquoise jewelry, and 50's glass frames; so go ahead, be our guest, and criticize us as bourgeois, we don't care. If we want to stuff gloves in our hip pocket and go barefoot like Billy Jack or choose to dress like a NASA scientist, then so be it. You follow YouTube instructions on how to look like a hipster so by definition you can't call yourself one. We're freeskiers and do backflips off fluffies and shart on impact. We read Hegel and Marx in an abandoned portapotty near our favorite road house, so don't expect us to be impressed when you read your Wittgenstein under a table in Ralph Lauren's new Polo Bar. Give our best to Ralph, will you? Tell him that he looks most elegant in fitted Scottish wool suits. We lost our front teeth playing hockey in the minor Canadian leagues and we aren't interested that you drove your Holland & Holland Range Rover with a custom gun box to your field level seat for game 6 of the World Series at Fenway Park. We say, good for you! We were just as content to drive to the nearest bar on our Harleys and watch the game on the big screen. If we appear overburdened by a rash of obloquies and excoriating invectives directed against the transnationalist capitalist class, please know that it is not because we are especially prone to rage but because we are morally exhausted in our refusal to accept their constant barrage of lies and deceptions. If this paragraph sounds like I miss the 60s, you're right, but you're wrong if you think my critique is fueled by nostalgia alone.

We read the following quotation by Noam Chomsky and not only do we agree with it, we see it as an understatement:

> Europe has a very bloody history, an extremely savage and bloody history, with constant massive wars that was all part of an effort to establish the nation-state system. It has virtually no relation to the way people live, or to their associations, or anything else particularly, so it had to be established by force—centuries of bloody warfare. That warfare (in Europe) ended in 1945—and the only reason it ended is because the next war was going to destroy *everything*. So it ended in 1945—we hope; if it didn't, it *will* destroy everything. The nation-state system was exported to the rest of the world through European colonization. Europeans were barbarians basically, savages: very advanced technologically, and advanced in methods of warfare, but not culturally or anything else particularly. And when they spread over the rest of the world, it was like a plague—they just destroyed everything in front of them. [...] They fought differently, they fought much more brutally, they had better technology—and they essentially wiped everything else out. The American continent is a good example. How come everyone around here has a white face and not a red face? Well, it's because the people with the white faces were savages, and they killed the people with red faces. (314)

And hasn't the US exceeded Europe in its brutality? Do we need to go through all of the US invasions since 1945? And the horror it has reigned down on Southeast Asia and Latin America?

And do you think the history of Christianity will protect you? Did not religious leaders in Spain justify the war against indigenous peoples in Las Americas on the grounds that they be converted to Christianity? Did anybody utter a peep about this in your holy Council of Trent? Didn't Bishop Moscos of Cuzco condemn the rebellion by Tupac Amaru against indigenous slave labor and didn't he describe Tupac Amaru as a "rebel against God, religion, and the law"? Didn't the Vatican's Holy Office officially deny on 20 June 1886 that slavery was contrary to natural law? Before the Spanish executed him by decapitation, did not Tupac Amaru cry out, "Ccollanan Pachacamac ricuy auccacunac yahuarniy hichascancuta!" ("Mother Earth, witness how my enemies shed my blood!")?

We don't care if you live in a converted granary with handmade clay tiles. Take your make-believe ruralism and shove it up the copper pipes of your neo-vernacular estate! We proudly sing "Rejoice, O Virgin" from Rachmaninoff's Vespers, wearing denim overalls from the Dust Bowl and if Putin wants to put us into prison, we say, let him try! We appear every 200 years like Brigadoon, with Cyd Charisse playing my sister. Capitalism has made us feel alone together and homesick at home and we won't allow you into our community unless you can enrich the debate about the future of humanity! We want to engage in acts of self-creation, you have forced us to act in self-preservation because you compel us into acts of self-alienation for our survival. We want to be self-motivated, you want to coerce us! You want ownership in severalty, we want collective ownership! You want to create our needs, we want to create our future! You want to manufacture our consent, when we are unable to consent to having a life! We will not be cast into your world; we will not let your despotic capitalist mind lead us to suffocate in the urban sprawl of an extractive economy. You can fly the fish you catch on the US coast to Japan for processing and then send it back here to fancy seafood restaurants at Pier 39 in Fisherman's Wharf, but we are not impressed. We don't care how many frequent flyer miles your fish have accumulated. We would rather eat corn grown in an urban garden than be part of this insanity! You are interested in science for preserving your hair and teeth until you die. We are interested in fathoming the mysteries of the universe. Don't try to send us into a brick cell with a whiteboard and then have us read a book about nature. We prefer to live *in* nature than read *about* nature in a classroom that supports the expropriation of the means of production. Every time one of you Republicans talks about abolishing social security because it's socialist you are sentencing Americans to death. Every time one of you Democrats runs away from the word socialism you are sentencing the entire world to death! Your corporations pretend to be one-worlders but they always turn to their national government when they are in crisis and need to be bailed out. We are not interested in *The Expendables* or *Independence Day*, or Adam Sandler films, so decry us as elitist post-universal cosmopolitanists or post-national liberals, we don't care. We prefer to stay at home and watch Pier Paolo Pasolini's *The Gospel According to St. Matthew*. By the way, your nerd couture doesn't impress us, although if you gifted us your Nintendo bow-tie and muted red jacket, we wouldn't turn you down. Please try to understand us: We don't want to break with the history of the last century, we want to break with the history of the past two thousand years! Now do you get it? You can gawk at Miley Cyrus's boyish buttocks all you want and whip up sentiment about her 'freeing the nipple' but we are more interested in freeing workers from necessity. We know that you know that you have created a mass society of dopamine deprived, stressed-out citizens and that you need to modulate our brain/body chemistry—deliver to our brains enough dopamine, serotonin, spinephrine, and all the neurotramsitters and hormones and all the other systems of comfort needed to prevent us from keeping us from storming the barricades that you have constructed and seizing our freedom. You can addict us to reality television shows, expand the sports channels, disorient us in your shopping malls so that we can only relieve our anxiety with a purchase. Yes, you can do all of these things. Go ahead and hijack our neurotransmitters, make us feel our submission, pump up our stress hormones and then, like missionary heroes, offer us a means of relieving our stress by patting us on the back and calling us good consumers who are helping to strengthen the economy. And then literally take over our working-class youth by offering them a free education in the military so that they can go and beat up little countries every so often—intermittent reinforcement, catch them unawares—and let the world know that we mean business. And of course, we are talking about business, so you had better give our corporations free reign. You have predisposed us to acting like your serfs, but we know that we are predisposed to violating our own predispositions and the hard-wiring that has gone into our brains, courtesy of your schoolmasters and clergy, can be overruled (cf. Smail). We hereby overrule you!

You have ripped Marx's ideas out of their revolutionary soil by decades of toxic bombardment by the corporate media and repotted them in greenhouse megastores where, under hydrofarm compact fluorescent fixtures, so that they can be deracinated, debarked, and made safe for university seminars and condominium living alike for highly committed twentysomethings who like to whistle to ballpark tunes in their faux-Victorian bathtubs. Shame on you! And shame on you for disturbing my slumber. Now, when I dream, I discover myself squatting atop a Gothic cathedral, whose gargoyles perched below my feet are spouting the blood of history's time-enduring saints to quell the maelstrom of angry crowds below—crowds made up of the powerless, the forgotten, the excluded, victims caught in the crossfire of capitalism (the result of watching too many of your Zombie or vampire films, no doubt). I peer down at the collarless, blood-covered, and spindle-shanked figures below, shafts of brilliant light slicing through the clouds that hover hesitatingly over the entangled gloom, and then the noxious exhalation and clouds of putrid effluvia wafting upwards from the dank and pungent sewer mist rises to meet the light, and suddenly everyone is playing and celebrating in the city streets, like neighborhood kids who have yanked open a fire hydrant during a heat wave. But what are they celebrating? Their new credit card advance?

You are the heirs of the Magna Carta, that 800 year-old document signed at Runnymede on the banks of the Thames between Windsor and Staines. Congratulations on that! I'm glad that King John was finally subjected to some oversight by a panel of wealthy barons! I'm glad that world historical document resulted in some limitation on taxation without representation; that certainly helped out a lot of important aristocrats. That's just great! And I'm gratified that my ancestral homeland, Scotland, was able to survive as an independent state and the King was prevented from turning it into his own feudal stomping ground. No king (or queen) is above the law these days, so thank you for that, heirs of the Magna Carta.

Excuse our bad breath, but are not the poor and the powerless also heirs to the Magna Carta, and what about them? Now taxes are no longer extracted in an arbitrary way by an acquisitive king, but systematically by the state, advantaging the rich, white property owners, as always. Free men are no longer arbitrarily imprisoned, except for African American men caught 'being black' and warehoused in our penitentiaries as part of the school-to-prison pipeline. I suppose they are the modern day equivalents to feudal serfs. Well, we have the US Constitution, you tell us. But that mainly protects the rich, white property owners, courtesy of the extermination of most of the indigenous population. Damn any concentration of power—be it church or state—that dares to mess with white male property owners! And so the rich have always presented themselves as the oppressed each time the law prevents them from buying up everything, including us!

And what about your hero, Samuel Adams, one of the so-called Founding Fathers of the United States, whose namesake beer you quaff down in buckets and whose praises you used to sing during your internship at the Cato Institute? And whose name (along with James Madison) you sometimes mixed into your witty retorts and bon mots at Vauclus, on

Sunset Boulevard in West Hollywood, or the Algonquin Hotel in New York City, both of which were happy to serve you a 10,000 dollar diamond martini (thanks to your calling in advance to pre-order the diamond). Did you know Samuel Adams drafted the Riot Act that suspended habeas corpus so that debtors and protesters could be kept in jail without trial? That didn't sit well with a group called the Regulators, who wanted to shut down the courts and turn debtors out of jail. Adams believed that while all men were equal under the law and in the eyes of God, they would always be unequal in beauty, talents, and fortunes. James Madison argued that the abolition of debt and the institution of an equal division of labor was absolutely wicked. Sorry, but I'm with Shays' rebellion, led by revolutionary war veteran Daniel Shays, the spirit of which I hope is reflected here. We also take our inspiration from the communism of the early Christian Church, the Gospel message of the Kingdom of God and the rich homiletic material made available in the parables of Jesus. You take the parable of the "talents" (Matthew 25.14-30; Luke 19.12-27) to argue that Jesus preached the glories of capitalism and usury, but we see it as a warning to the rich not to exploit their workers! You bring your own desire to the interpretation, we try to understand it from the worldview of a first-century Palestinian.

The human logos will not suffice to explain the mystery which is inexpressible, impenetrable, and wholly other, unable to be represented by our eyes that lust for the visible, or any of our other senses. We can only reply to your theologians that we know God through our admission that God is unknowable. And for that matter, ours is a suffering God—the scourged Christ—who suffers along with the poor and the oppressed and yours is the triumphant Christ ruling all from His heavenly throne!

We struggle with the texts of scripture in community while you sit in your suburban church pews. You see the Bible as some kind of aperture through which you can know how God worked in the days of old; we see the Bible as a reflection of our lives as we suffer the daily indignities of life.

But all this talk is about ancient history, you tell me. Okay, let me talk about something closer to home. Ok, squint hard, will you?

How about Los Angeles? Can't you see in the distance the Sheriff of Skidberry, patrolling San Pedro and San Julian streets, tipping his bald plate to The Hurricane, Bow Leg, Slow Bucket, and Thick 'n' Juicy? Can't you see him handing out a donated hygiene kit to a woman shooting heroin between her toes, while nearby a beer baron sells 2 dollar bottles outside of

AA meetings (cf. O'Neil)? You can't? Well, have you ever been to downtown Los Angeles, not far from City Hall? Have you ever gone 'sliding down The Nickel,' you know, made the trek to Skid Row, where the city warehouses its homeless population from Third Street on the north, Seventh Street on the south, Alameda Street to the east, and Main Street to the west? Do you know that the 2000 down-on-their-luck men, women, and children who live under tarps strewn across shopping carts in this one-square mile are now at risk of losing their squalid surroundings to gentrification, since urban development—residential lofts, trendy bistros, influx of yuppies, etc.—has brought 50,000 people next door and developers are lining up, salivating to grab more territory for their urban hipsters clients? Have you ever wondered what happened to low-income housing? Have you ever been on the mean streets of L.A., this city of angels, and watched thousands of hardscrabble members of Marx's always unpopular reserve army of unemployed and their blank-faced children line up uncomfortably outside of the Los Angeles Sports Arena to get their yellow wristbands, their once-in-a-million ticket to see in the flesh a doctor, a dentist, a healthcare volunteer? When thousands line up all night, in the desert climate chill, to see a dentist, what does that portend for their future, aching molars aside? Even the health care aides of the sick wait patiently beside their own brittle-boned patients, who wait beside undocumented day laborers, who wait beside Orange County housewives abandoned by their gambling husbands, who wait beside teachers seeking mammograms and treatment for their diabetes. What will it take for you to be outraged? Do you have to be pushed into the ranks of the living dead to fight back?

I have stood on the banks of the Yangtze River, which flows 3,200 miles across central China to the sea, waters in which Mao liked to swim. Like Mao, we will swim against the current and arrive on the opposite bank and show the goddess of the mountain a new world!

Will this population be the first to be shipped off to a labor camp somewhere should fascism consolidate its legal, economic, criminal justice and affective regime in the United States? Will we muster a fight or be compelled to join them? Will we all end up singing "Tomorrow Belongs to Me" from the film, *Cabaret*? And does a *'volkisch'* community have to be fascist? Can't an effect precede its cause? Can't our 'American' tradition be led not be some jerry-rigged assemblage of backward-looking times, some broken remnants of the past, but by a dream of the future—by a feeling of contemporaneity, of sharing the present time collectively, whose arc is wide enough to harness our collective, generalized affect for the liberation of humanity from capital, even in this prevailing apotheosis of despair? The present, after all, is no longer mostly the past. Well, at least for those who are wired to the World Wide Web.

Our struggle is eschatological, the possibility of making a dialectical leap into a new aeon where the Gospels and education can create synergistically a transitional functionality for building a world free from necessity and needless suffering. The notion of free clinics for the poor has stoked the ire of those who think this is 'socialism,' helping all those 'freeloaders,' and especially the scraggly immigrants south of the border, while those responsible for the overexploitation of *las Americas* sit in their mahogany offices, wet their kerosene lips on shipwrecked 1907 Heidsieck champagne (which, at $275,000 a bottle could subsidize all those diagnosed for root canals and then some) and watch the fascism of the nation unfold, as Hannity, Beck, and O'Reilly call for liberal heads to roll. Francisco Franco, beloved fascist dictator of Spain, allegedly slept beside the incorruptible arm of Saint Teresa de Avila (can't you see him using it to scratch the hairs on his back), clutching it like a crucifix to fend of the dark prince. Perhaps George Bush Jr. has hidden some religious relic under his bed, perhaps even the skull of Geronimo, while Barack Obama, needing no protective relic, sleeps soundly, unperturbed by terrorists, or Marx's reserve army snaking around the block in the city of angels, as his own angels of steel hover overhead, their tactical control systems humming Yankee Doodle Dandy. Instead of calling upon Michael, Gabriel, Uriel, or Raphael, our beloved leader feels safe enough under the watchful eyes of Predator, Global Hawk, Fire Scout, and Hunter as he called for the birth of new nations under god, liberated by the mighty F-16. May God bless America. And nobody else. Our new leader, the soul-eating Leviathan that has emerged from the cultivated swamp of history, who lives inside his own brainpan lined with mirrors so he can admire himself even in his dreams, readies himself to squeeze the planet like a petulant child with a piece of clay. Long after your bones and our excrement have been fossilized and studied in a spaceship circling a space station where earth's survivors were first sequestered after experiments in engineered algae and synthetic biology failed, your ancestors will look back at you in disgrace and it won't be with heroic recrimination but just plain, measured disgust.

We therefore proclaim that we will treat our fellow human beings as ends in themselves and not as a means for something else. As far as entering your normal universe is concerned, we are on permanent strike. And this is but a short prelude to a path for social change. We stand firm for a multitendency revolutionary democracy that advocates direct forms of mass self-rule.

Today during the worst economic crisis since the Great Depression, we know that corporations are reaping huge profits but they are not spending their profits to hire workers or build factories but to enhance their own share prices. In contrast to this reality, we all live with a certain image that is constantly being embellished: that we live in a meritocracy where we are rewarded fairly for our hard work and perseverance. Hagiographers of American life surely will describe the first decade of the twenty first century as a decade of disaster piled upon disaster. The misery of everyday life in capitalist society comes for many in the form of a pink slip or a home foreclosure notice. As critical educators, we search for a reprieve. We know from the alienation and suffering that has afflicted humanity for centuries that history can never be trusted to bend one particular way or another. Our purpose as revolutionary educators has never been to trust history, or whatever prophetic insights we believe we have pertaining to the future of humankind, but to understand history's movement and give it direction and momentum in the interests of social justice. Viewed from any point within the socio-historical panorama of despair that now confronts us, such a task seems more daunting than ever. Besotted by ideological belligerence, capitalism relies to a greater extent today than ever before on ideological rationalizations and obfuscation to defuse and deflect criticism of its recent developments.

Yet even against logo-swathed backdrops and image-based commentaries of daunting corporate grandeur, we keep ransacking Marx's tomb, especially when an economic crisis hits that demands some kind of explanation not afforded by the pundits of the *Wall Street Journal*. Everywhere it seems—perhaps especially in education—you find Marxism being derided with a leering flippancy or galvanized indifference. You can't escape it, even in coffee shops for the urban literati, as a recent visit to a popular Los Angeles establishment taught me. There, among the hard-nosed expresso drinkers, a stranger approached me waving heavy hands. Bobbing over a thin nose and pair of succulent roasted lips were a set of lobster eyes, as if they were clumsily plopped onto plump, fleshy stumps that sprung out ominously from deep within his sockets. With wobbling eyes and an oversized tongue straining to escape his overly caffeinated oral cavity, he remarked with a theatrical intensity: "Oh, you're McLaren, the one that writes that Marxist shit." After conveying his sentiments, an unpleasant patina of decay descended upon his flapping jowls as if he had suddenly aged a generation. I responded with a simple retort, as quickly as if I had rehearsed it in advance: "I assume you're already so full of capitalist shit that I wonder how you noticed mine."

When we look around us at the age in which we live, we see a ruling class with an unimaginably dense accumulation of wealth undertaking innumerable efforts to establish new organizations to reproduce the same social practices. Those who control capital control the government, forcing governments to become part of a corporate superstructure, overseeing capital's base. And there has been an accompanying corporate colonization of civil society as well, effectively stifling any ameliorative function that might be offered by many new educational movements, those very pragmatic organizations that have become a more capital-friendly substitute for revolutionary manifestos of groups bent on overthrowing the regime of capital.

Those of us who have to sell our labor-power for a wage remain ensepulchured by the realities of the global meltdown and the militarization of the country. The poor are left to face the organized burden of being American in the paradise created by the rich and for the rich.

The attempt by the Right to exorcise the insinuation of too much diversity into the US Anglosphere, and the mass media's long-imposed separation between dialectical thought and everyday life have united to bring about a terrifying calcification of the public mind that has turned politics into a circus of pantomime, and has helped to secure both political parties as organs of interest for the corporations, which have become the servo-mechanisms of the corporate state.

It is the daily taunt of many on the Right that socialism leads to mindless conformity. But what could be gloomier than the politics that has arisen out of the ashes of bourgeois capitalist democracy? The word socialism is disparaged in the United States, and rather than socialism being an unsettled question, it is used as an unsettling noun, intended to frighten and to create panic among the popular majorities. The Left has yet to overcome this obstacle.

The cataclysmic social and political changes of this present historical moment have unleashed the most unholy aspirations among the modern Manicheans of the Christian Right. The Tea Party, the prehensile tail of libertarianism, has made a vertiginous descent into the bowels of the American Armageddon psyche, resurrecting itself in the gratuitous sepulchral cant of Christian dominionism and reconstructionism. Armed with a message that is an eerie amalgam of generalized resentment, a nympholepsy of self-hatred, and nativism sutured together by theocratic aspirations, these activists are clawing their way towards the New Jerusalem with their rabble rousing war-cry of dismantling the federal government. Television personality and Republican necromancer, Glenn Beck, makes a messianic overture to masses of Tea Party supporters gathered at the Lincoln Memorial in Washington, DC, while at the same time immolating the historical memory of the civil rights movement, by claiming Martin Luther King, Jr. as his forebear. In an atmosphere of big tent religious revivalism dripping with a fascist miasma of national rebirth, a furor of white backlash zealotry, political demagoguery, fear-engendering, and resentment-mongering, he grandly asserts that the civil rights movement was not really about black people, but rather about white conservatives under assault from evil liberals.

As advocates of revolutionary critical pedagogy, we stand at the turning point in this process. Critical pedagogy is an approach that we have chosen as a necessary (albeit insufficient) vehicle for transforming the world. The work that we do has been adapted from the pathfinding contributions of the late Brazilian educator, Paulo Freire, whose development of pedagogies of the oppressed helped to lay the foundations for approaches (feminist, post-structuralist, Marxist) to teaching and learning that utilizes the life experience of students in and outside of traditional classrooms to build spaces of dialogue and dialectical thinking. We have renamed our pedagogy, revolutionary critical pedagogy. We have done so because we believe that dialogical approaches to teaching can help to create a critical citizenry capable of analyzing and transforming capitalist societies worldwide. In doing so, we denounce the domesticated versions of critical pedagogy that are insufficiently critical of capitalism and even hostile to a socialist alternative.

Critical pedagogy has been discredited by the Right as administering propaganda for a communist insurrection, or it has been domesticated by those on the Left who do not want directly to challenge capital and state power. But critical pedagogy as a revolutionary praxis has never been extinguished. Like a burning ember, it can be stamped out by the jackboots of fascism, as is happening today, or rekindled to serve as a funeral pyre for the colonialist regime we are bound to serve as citizens of capital.

We are so reverentially preoccupied with what others have to say about the struggle for socialism that we fear to trust our own understanding and consequently we have no eyesight left to look upon these historical events themselves. Marx's writings that tell us untraditional truths about the social and economic order tap a world-weary longing that stretches back through the centuries. Here the term "world-weary longing" is not meant to refer to the existential despair often experienced by intellectuals as fathomless as the abysms of the earth. We are talking about the anguish that accompanies what have been for the majority of humanity the failures of attempting to overcome necessity. Current struggles to overcome oppression anchored to liberal appeals to fairness and equality and built upon the crusted-over sediments of past choice—seven those made with considerable autonomy—are no longer relevant to the present day.

Critical pedagogy teaches us that we have the collective power to overcome the inimical forces of capital. The Promised Land can promise only to be a place of struggle, springing up where hope is conjugated with the movements of the people toward an anti-capitalist future. We are all merely seeds in the moist soil of the counter-world. It is up to us to decide what that world is to look like and how to get there. We need to extend the ambit of critical pedagogy from persons with 'authority,' to whom, by convention and precept education has hitherto been confined, to those who are 'least' among us, not in numbers, surely, but in social legitimacy—the poor and the dispossessed. We are not talking about the dispossessed as dispossessed, but as a revolutionary force for socialism. They are carrying a much larger freight than their single selves. It is in their name that we begin to fathom that which we have been formed to be, and begin the arduous and painful process of remaking ourselves in a deliberately new way that often takes us on a collision course with the systems of intelligibility, ways of knowing, and received terms that we have inherited to create habitual and resigned agents.

The fact is, surely, that we are faced with two choices about how to live our humanity—the liberal model of pleading with corporations to temper their cruelty and greed, and the reactionary model that has declared war on social and economic equality. And on the evidence that each of these models is fiercely and hopelessly entangled in each other's conflictual embrace, we can accept neither.

Critical pedagogy is more than throaty bursts of teacherly impropriety, more than enumerating in ironic detail the problems faced by the youth of today, more than hurling invective at government policies, but a sustained march toward a revolutionary consciousness and practice.

We must become more like the unknown sailor who tried to smash the statue of Napoleon's head with a brick during the days of the Paris Commune, or like the Iraqi journalist who threw his shoe at the head of President George W. Bush while Bush was standing tall before cameras of the transnational corporate media like a Texas version of the Vendome Column wrapped in a jock strap.

Revolutionary critical pedagogy questions the official, hegemonic view of ahistorical educational change, isolated from the capitalist social and productive relationships. As revolutionary critical educators, we need to understand how the dynamics of the capitalist system—its movement from global capitalism to transnational capital, for instance—has guided the meaning and purpose of educational reform and has impacted institutions and approaches with respect to what counts as educational change.

We follow Che's dialectical conception of education which is formed internally through analyzing the continuous contradictions of external influences on the life of individuals. We agree with Paulo Freire that dialogical pedagogy can achieve the kind of class consciousness necessary for a powerful social transformation. It also suggests that as we participate in an analysis of the objective social totality that we simultaneously struggle for a social universe outside the commodity form of labor. If we are to educate at all, we must educate for this! Statist socialism has collapsed and weighs heavier on the minds of the living with its inevitable decay into the oblivion of historical time. Libertarian socialism as well lies rotting on its deathbed, as capitalism continues to wreak its revenge, despite its present state of unprecedented crisis. Anti-systemic movements of all shapes and stripes are still around, but have for the most part, become domesticated into reformist shadows of their previous revolutionary selves, forming enfeebled and enfeebling popular fronts that fall like spent cartridges on the heels of any real challenge to capitalism.

Critical educators must take a stand, working for political or direct democracy, for the direct control of the political system by citizens, for economic democracy, for the ownership and direct control of economic resources by the citizen body, for democracy in the social realm by means of self-management of educational institutions and workplaces, and for the ecological justice that will enable us to reintegrate society into nature. The struggle for a new historic bloc built up by the working class will not be easy. If critical educational studies is to avoid being corralled into accepting the dominant ideology, or annexed to pro-capitalist forces among the some on the Left, or transformed into a recruiting ground for liberal reform efforts, or even worse, turned into an outpost for reactionary populism, it will largely be due to our efforts as revolutionary critical educators.

We need to awaken from our dream into another dream, but one dreamt with open eyes, a collective dream that will take us out of the homogeneous, monumental, and chronological time of capital and beyond the consolatory pretensions of the bourgeoisie to create the 'time of now' discussed so poignantly by Walter Benjamin—the time of the revolutionary. We need to capture the revolutionary fervor of the communards, whose battle-tested hearts managed, if only for a brief time, to dump the muck of ages into the sewers of history. It is precisely the socialist partisanship of critical pedagogy—not to the point of dogmatism or inflexibility—that reveals its power of critique. We need to reclaim the power of critique as the sword arm of social justice and not relinquish it. For in doing so we reclaim our humanity and the world.

We cannot be evasive in our search for justice, tranquilized by self-deception, led to political hibernation by our own topor, or unwarrantably adventitious in our actions. We must recognize those whom Jesus reproofed with 'fierce censure' for not bearing fruit (i.e., for not loving one's neighbor) and for not recognizing that the end of history has already arrived in history (cf. Miranda 168-71) with the coming of Jesus as the Messiah. For those of us who call ourselves Christians, we must challenge those in our communities of faith who prevent the Messiah from being truly recognized (i.e., prevent love and justice from being seen as one and the same), those who relegate Jesus to an indefinitely postponable future, keeping him 'eternally pre-existent' or 'eternally future' but never existing in the 'now,' that is, in the 'supra-individual reality' that is the Kingdom of God (cf. Miranda 196-201). The Kingdom of God is where faith and justice determine our being as we confront history in its totality and as we bring forth through faith and class struggle those fruits of love, *communalidad*, and peaceful intercultural existence that have been annulled by the forces of capital.

Tell your teachers to become attentive to their self-transforming potential, to stop loitering around the trash cans of tradition and to stop resisting the prospect of a possible future. Please tell them to leave the shepherd's crook and the winnowing whip in a stone reliquary for old school hand-me-downs; they don't need them anymore. Instruct your teachers that they have become endowed with the capacity to become more aware of their mission. Ask them to remove the cover from the straw basked at their feet. In it they will find a serpent coiled in three and a half turns. Tell them to place the serpent in an empty baptismal font or a crystal aspersorium and anoint themselves. Insist that the teachers take up the ladle of public service and drink from the elixir of immortality. Invite them to partake of its grace. For if you are committed to serve the people you are serving all of eternity. For time was brought into existence out of nothing to give us an opportunity to share an infinite compassion and active receptivity to the anguished cries of our people and a graced realization that we are one with all those who suffer and are heavily burdened. The sound of Einstein's equation, $E=MC^2$ is OM. Aristotle freed us from the bondage of the gods but we cannot transform reality through the waking consciousness of rationality alone. Advise your teachers to abandon their altars of capital and the slaughter bench of imperial war. It's time to put aside such childish myths about America's providential mission to civilize the world; our rulers cling to this myth, even if it means bombing that world back into the Stone Age. It is time to put aside such childish things. The abyss-like presence of alienation from nature both inwardly and outwardly, and from our divine nature, can be defeated and the divine destination of our lives can be realized. Be one with the people—not only meditatively but through praxis—through acting on and in and even alongside the world with them. You are not them, but you are not other to them. Accustom yourself to wonder. Abide in the miracle of life. As Saint Francis de Sales put it, the only measure of love is to love without measure. I beckon you to go forth and teach, acting lovingly. For it is only by teaching that you can learn, and only by learning that you are fit to teach. And it is only through love that we can transform this world.

When we contemplate our state of spiritual infinitude, we are confronted with a myriad of choices. We can imagine the putrid stench of flesh decaying from regret; ambition lying fallow from an over-tilled darkness; voices rasping, hollowed out by unwelcomed perseverance; hope rattling like a dust-choked dream coughing in your brainpan. We can let death jeer at us, its chilling rictus pulled tight over our fears like a Canadian winter cap or we can use the past not as the deathbed of our last remorseful slumber but transformed into a bow forged from our weary heartstrings, sending us spinning, a delirious flame shot into the temple of fate. Let us always be fearless teachers, even unto our last breath, and hope that such fearlessness will lead to wisdom. And such wisdom will lead to a transformation of this world to another world where love and justice prevail.

Perhaps one day, while decamping from your conference on the common core, or value added instruction, you'll find time to ponder this choice. After your continental breakfast at Motel 6, you might consider glancing across the street at the empty lot of jimsonweed, concrete shards, gasoline soaked soil, and mercury vapors. There you will find a man in seamless twill-woven pants, clutching his rake handle with a long iron ridged nail driven into the tip colorfully festooned with collapsed styrofoam cups and Chuck E. Cheese and Happy meal coupons. He's the one spearing paper wrappers along the spongy gutters. Look to the right and you will notice a communion chalice and a bagel crust sitting on a collapsed lawn chair. Are you telling me that it's a coke can? Then focus your spirit. In the distance someone will play a trumpet. And a glint of sunlight will catch a swarm of windborn mustards seeds redounding from the future that will circle your head and you will cry out with indescribable joy.

WORKS CITED

Chomsky, Noam. *Understanding Power: The Indispensable Chomsky*. Edited by Peter R. Mitchell and John Schoeffel, The New Press, 2002.
Miranda, Jose Porfirio. *Being and the Messiah: The Message of St. John*. Translated by John Eagleson, Orbis Books, 1977.
O'Neil, Ann. "On Patrol with Skid Row's 'Angel Cop.'" *CNN*, 3 Jan. 2015, www.cnn.com/2015/01/02/us/skid-row-cop/. Accessed 23 Jan. 2017.
Smail, Daniel. *On Deep History and the Brain*. University of California Press, 2008.
The Bible. English Standard Version, Crossway Bibles, 2001.

List of Contributors

Lea Brenningmeyer is a PhD student in American Studies, associate member of the PhD program "Cultures of Participation," and coordinator of the international study program "European Studies in Global Perspectives" at the University of Oldenburg, Germany. Her research focuses on contemporary US-American literature and (popular) culture, disability studies, and questions of participation and subjectivization; she is currently writing her PhD thesis on representations of the diagnosis Asperger's Syndrome in US-American TV series with a focus on degrees of and conditions for participation of the diagnosed.

Micha Brumlik is Emeritus Professor at the Department of Educational Sciences at Goethe-University, Frankfurt/Main, Germany. He was head of the Fritz Bauer Institute, Study and Documentation Center on the History and Impact of the Holocaust in Frankfurt/Main, from 2000 to 2005; city councilor of the Green Party in Frankfurt/Main from 1989 to 2001; since 2013, Senior Professor at the Center for Jewish Studies Berlin-Brandenburg; co-editor of "Blätter für deutsche und internationale Politik"; author and regular columnist for the German newspaper *taz*: "Gott und die Welt." Recent book publications: *Innerlich beschnittene Juden* (Konkret Literatur Verlag, 2012); *Messianisches Licht und menschliche Würde: Politische Theorie aus den Quellen des Judentums* (Nomos, 2013). More information at michabrumlik.de.

Martin Butler is Professor of American Literature and Culture at the University of Oldenburg, Germany. His research focuses on popular culture, including the history of political music, forms and figures of cultural mobility, as well as cultures of participation in Web 2.0 environments. Apart from a broad range of articles in these fields, he published a monograph on Woody Guthrie (*Voices of the Down and Out*, Winter, 2007) and co-edited a number of essay collections, including *Sound Fabrics: Studies on the Intermedial and Institutional Dimensions of Popular Music* (WVT, 2009, with Patrick Burger and Arvi Sepp), *Precarious Alliances: Cultures of Participation in Print and Other Media* (transcript, 2016, with Albrecht Hausmann and Anton Kirchhofer), as well as a special issue of *Popular Music and Society* on musical autobiographies (Routledge, 2015, with Daniel Stein).

Alex Demirović is Apl. Professor at the Goethe-University Frankfurt/ Main and Senior Fellow at the Rosa-Luxemburg-Stiftung. His research interests include critical social theory, theory of democracy, and discourse analysis. Recent publications: Alex Demirovic, ed.: *Transformation der Demokratie—demokratische Transformation* (Westfälisches Dampfboot, 2016); "Die Selbstreflexion des Marxismus. Fünfzig Jahre Negative Dialektik," (*Prokla*, 184.3, 2016).

Sabine Hess has been professor at the Institute for Cultural Anthropology/ European Ethnology, Göttingen since 2011. Her main areas of research and teaching are migration and border regime studies, anthropology of globalization and transnationalism, anthropology of policy with a focus on EU integration and processes of Europeanisation, gender studies and anthropological methodologies.

Ulaş Başar Gezgin is Associate Professor of Applied Communication, a journalist, a social science researcher, and an academic with 17 years of teaching experience in various institutions in Turkey, Vietnam, Thailand, and Malaysia, and research experience in New Zealand (PhD work), Australia (joint project), and Latin America (journalism). He holds degrees in education, psychology, cognitive science, and urban planning. As of 2017, he has published 14 books, 16 e-books, and a high number of book chapters and journal articles in various fields. A novel, an opera libretto, edited collections, poetry, a compilation of his stories, textbooks and translations, etc. are among his works. He works in Hanoi and lives in Hoi An, Vietnam.

Jens Martin Gurr, born 1974, has been Chair of British and Anglophone Literature and Culture at the University of Duisburg-Essen since April

2007. His research interests include urban studies (urban literature and culture, theories and methods of interdisciplinary urban research, narrative models of urban complexity), contemporary Anglophone fiction, contemporary US literature and culture, 17th- and 18th-century British literature, and British Romanticism. He is director of the University of Duisburg-Essen's Joint Center "Urban Systems." Co-edited volumes include *Understanding Complex Urban Systems: Multidisciplinary Approaches to Modeling* (Springer, 2014), *Romantic Cityscapes (WVT, 2013)*, *Cityscapes in the Americas and Beyond: Representations of Urban Complexity in Literature and Film* (WVT, 2011), and *EthniCities: Metropolitan Cultures and Ethnic Identities in the Americas* (WVT, 2011).

Kemal İnal was Associate Professor of Sociology at the Faculty of Communication at Gazi University (Ankara), where he was dismissed by a governmental decree after the failed coup in July 2017 in Turkey. His research focuses on the educational policy and socio-cultural problems of Turkey. He has published a high number of academic books in Turkish and English as well as many articles on different subjects, and has translated many books from English and French into Turkish. He is the deputy Middle East editor for *Journal for Critical Education Policy Studies* and the co-founder (with Ulaş Başar Gezgin) of the *Revolutionary Critical Education Initiative*. He co-edited the book *Neoliberal Transformation of Education in Turkey: Political and Ideological Analysis of Educational Reforms in the Age of the AKP* (Palgrave Macmillan, 2012, with Guliz Akkaymak). With Ulaş Başar Gezgin and Dave Hill, he co-edited the book *The Gezi Revolt: People's Revolutionary Resistance Against Neoliberal Capitalism in Turkey* (Institute for Education Policy Studies in Brighton, England, 2014). He would be a faculty member at Helmut Schmidt University for a year since August 2017 if he is given the right to get a new passport and to leave Turkey.

Kaspar Maase, born in 1946, studied German Literature, Sociology, Arts, and Cultural Studies in Munich and Berlin. He earned his PhD at Humboldt-University in Berlin (GDR) in 1971. In 1992, he received his Habilitation in European Ethnology at Bremen University with a thesis on "The Americanization of Youths: A Study on the Westernization of the Federal Republic in the 1950s." From 1995 to 2011, he has been teaching at the Ludwig-Uhland-Institut für Empirische Kulturwissenschaft at the

University of Tübingen as an adjunct professor. His main research focus is on the history and theory of popular culture and entertainment from the 19th century.

Peter McLaren is Distinguished Professor in Critical Studies, College of Educational Studies, where he serves as Co-Director of the Paulo Freire Democratic Project and International Ambassador of Global Ethics and Social Justice. Professor McLaren is the author and editor of over 50 books, and his writings have been translated into 30 languages. He received the Lifetime Achievement Award from Division B of the American Education Research Association in 2017 and in 2013 was named Outstanding Educator in America by The Association of Educators of Latin America and the Caribbean. His most recent book is *Pedagogy of Insurrection: From Resurrection to Revolution* (Peter Lang Publishers, 2015).

Paul Mecheril is Professor for Migration and Education at the Carl von Ossietzky University of Oldenburg, Department for Pedagogy, and head of the Center for Migration, Education and Cultural Studies. His main research interests include: Migration and Pedagogy, Racism, Cultural Studies. He is the (co-)author of nine and (co-)editor of 26 books. Recently he edited *Handbuch Migrationspädagogik* (Beltz, 2016) and co-edited *Dämonisierung der Anderen: Rassismuskritik der Gegenwart* (transcript, 2016, with María do Mar Castro Varela).

Kathrin Peters is Professor for Visual Culture Studies at the University of the Arts Berlin. She received her PhD in Cultural Studies from Humboldt University Berlin and is the author of *Rätselbilder des Geschlechts: Körperwissen und Medialität um 1900* (diaphanes, 2010) on images of the body in sexology. Recently, she co-edited *Gender & Medien Reader* (diaphanes, 2016, with Andrea Seier). She is member of the editorial board of the journal of media studies (*Zeitschrift für Medienwissenschaft*).

Rainer Winter is Professor and Chair of Media and Cultural Theory and Head of the Institute of Media and Communications at Klagenfurt University in Austria. Since 2013, he has been Honorary Adjunct Professor at Charles Sturt University in Sydney, Australia. He was Visiting Professor at Capital Normal University Beijing, at Shanghai International Studies

University and Southwest University Chongqing. He is the (co-)author of eight and (co-)editor of more than twenty books.

Stephanie Wodianka has been Professor of Romance Literature at Rostock University, Germany, since 2010. Her research interests include representations, practices, and theories of collective memory (literature, films, *chanson française*), the European meditative literature of the 17th century, the relations between aesthetics and the construction of (trans) cultural identities, and concepts and poetics of modern myth. Among her publications are *Zwischen Mythos und Geschichte* (De Gruyter, 2009); *Metzler Lexikon Moderner Mythen* (J.B. Metzler, 2014), *Inflation der Mythen?* (transcript, 2016). Since 2013, she has been chairing the interdisciplinary doctoral program on *Cultural Encounters and the Discourses of Scholarship*. Since 2014, she has been a member of the graduate school *Deutungsmacht: Religion und Belief Systems in Deutungsmachtkonflikten* (both Rostock University). She is currently working on a project on cultural semiotics of the cardinal directions (i.e., *Localisations de l'Europe: sémiotiques culturelles des points cardinaux,* eds. Stephanie Wodianka and Sebastian Neumeister, 2016).